Pelican Books
Marx before Marxism

David McLellan is Senior Lecturer in Politics
and Government, University of Kent at
Canterbury. He is the author of *Karl Marx:
The Early Texts, The Young Hegelians and
Karl Marx, Marx's Grundrisse* and
The Thought of Karl Marx. He is currently
working on a major biography of
Karl Marx.

DAVID McLELLAN

Marx before Marxism

PENGUIN BOOKS

Penguin Books Ltd, Harmondsworth,
Middlesex, England
Penguin Books Australia Ltd, Ringwood,
Victoria, Australia

First published by Macmillan & Co. 1970
Revised edition published in Pelican Books 1972

Made and printed in Great Britain by
Richard Clay (The Chaucer Press) Ltd,
Bungay, Suffolk
Set in Linotype Baskerville

Contents

To Annie and Gabrielle

Preface

Marx's early writings have suffered, in the few detailed studies devoted to them in English, from being discussed in books concerned to argue a particular interpretation. The aim of this book is to present Marx's early writings, as neutrally as possible, in their historical context.

If there is any merit in the style of this book, this is due in large part to Graham Thomas, whose help has been invaluable and unstinting.

Littlecroft　　　　　　　　　　　　　　　　　D. M.
Chilham
Kent.
December 1968

Preface to the Penguin Edition

For the Penguin edition I have made minor alterations and additions to the text and have tried to bring the bibliography up to date. I am grateful to all those who offered me their comments on the first edition.

Littlecroft　　　　　　　　　　　　　　　　　D. M.
Chilham
Kent.
May 1971

GERMANY
1815—1848

Königsberg

Danzig

HOLSTE

MECKLENBURG

HANOVER

Berlin

PRUSSIA

NETHERLANDS

WESTPHALIA

PRUSSIA

Halle
Leipzig

SILESIA

Cologne
Bonn

THURINGIAN
STATES

Jena

RHINELAND

HESSE

SAXONY

Dresden

Trier

Frankfurt

R. Main

Paris

Kreuznach

Nuremberg

Metz

Hambach

BAVARIA

Toul

BADEN

Strasbourg

WURTTEM-
BERG

Augsburg

FRANCE

Münich

Zürich

AUSTRIAN
EMPIRE

SWITZERLAND

VENETIA

0   50   100   150 MILES

CHAPTER ONE

Germany before 1848

1. ECONOMIC

Germany immediately after the French Revolution was an underdeveloped country. The German 'destitution' – a common expression at the time – was evident when compared with France, whose economy was passing from agriculture to manufacture, and even more so when compared with England, which was already entering the industrial stage. Germany – at this time merely a geographical expression commonly used to denote a group of states sharing a common language and a common past membership of the Holy Roman Empire – was still essentially a rural country with three quarters of her 23 million population gaining their living from the land. What characterized the German economy in the thirty or so years between the defeat of Napoleon and the revolution of 1848 was a rapid development towards the status of an industrial power, a development achieved by the imposition from above of a market economy on a rural society.[1]

1. For accounts of the socio-economic background of the period which are fuller than can be given here, see A. Ramm, *Germany: A Political History* (Methuen, London, 1967) pp. 103 ff.; G. Mann, *The History of Germany since 1789* (Chatto & Windus, London, 1968) pp. 15 ff. A wealth of detail and sound interpretation is given in J. Droz and P. Ayçoberry, 'Structures sociales et courants idéologiques en Allemagne prérévolutionnaire', *Annali*, VI), (Feltrinelli, Milan, 1964), pp. 164 ff. For the working classes, see W. Conze, 'Vom Pöbel zum Proletariat', *Vierteljahrsschrift für Sozial- und Wirtschaftsgeschichte*, XLIV (Wiesbaden, 1954); J. Kuczynski, *Die Lage der*

In Prussia the old feudal land structure was destroyed by three reforms: in October 1807, Baron von Stein, Frederick William III's Minister of Internal Affairs, abolished the prohibitions on the buying and selling of land and also suppressed the status of the serf, though the peasants still owed dues and services to their landlords; in 1811 the Prussian Minister Hardenberg introduced a further reform by which peasants ceded part of their land to landlords in order to become complete owners; finally, in 1821, an Act enabled all peasants to buy off any dues still remaining, but at the average price of twenty-five times their annual value. The result of these reforms was far-reaching: Prussian agriculture was rationalized and estates became much larger, the area of small and middle-sized holdings decreasing by 40 per cent between 1815 and 1848, and one million hectares passing into the hands of the big landowners. These latter began to exploit their estates economically, which had never been done before, and increasingly shared the views of the bourgeoisie on economic development. The former serfs, having acquired liberty of marriage and domicile, either stayed on as day labourers on the large estates or moved to the towns to form the growing proletariat.

At the beginning of the nineteenth century, textiles were the only manufacture that existed on a large scale. This was favoured by the blockade of the Continent during the Napoleonic wars, but the lifting of the blockade flooded Germany with cheap English goods and almost ruined what industries there were. These were forced to modernize or go out of business and took the next fifteen years to recover. There was a certain imbalance in the

Arbeiter unter dem Kapitalismus, 1. (Akademie Verlag, Berlin, 1961) A reliable background book is F. Schnabel, *Deutsche Geschichte*, 5th edn (Herder, Freiburg, 1959).

economic development of the German states caused by the Napoleonic occupation and the different laws that that entailed. Undoubtedly the leader in industrial development was Rhineland-Westphalia, the province where Marx was born, which had been annexed by France from 1795 to 1814 and had thus had the benefit of economic, administrative and political reforms. What had before been 108 small states were divided into four districts, feudal organization was abolished, and political, juridical and fiscal equality was established. The corporations and customs barriers were done away with, much could be exported to France and producers were protected against competition from England. Expansion was so great that in 1810 the Prefect of the Ruhr could plausibly claim that it was the most industrial region in Europe. Textiles took the lead in this expansion. They did not need much capital investment and a ready supply of manual labour was available. After the lifting of the continental blockade and enforced modernization, linen was abandoned for the more easily mechanizable cotton. One further result of the occupation was a profound sympathy for France and French ideas among the population of the Rhineland, who did not welcome the decision in 1815 of the Congress of Vienna to reattach them to Prussia, which was at that time a poor country ruined by war. This antipathy was only gradually overcome by the economic recovery of Prussia in about 1830.

In Germany as a whole, industrial production was still small compared with France and England but was increasing fast. The output of the mines went up by 50 per cent between 1800 and 1830 and doubled between 1830 and 1842. Metallurgical output tripled between 1800 and 1830 and the production of consumption goods was eight times as great in the decade 1830–40 as in the decade 1800–1810. But it was not until eighteen states entered the *Zollverein*

(Customs Union) in 1834 that very rapid expansion began. The development of steam-machine production was slow until the mid thirties, being still fifty years behind England in 1831. The steel firm of Krupp did not begin its expansion until about 1835. Typical of this expansion was the boom in railways: the first track in Germany was laid in 1835 and by 1847 there were 2,500 kilometres. Iron production moved from 134,000 tons in 1834 to 170,000 in 1841, the importation of cotton increased from 187,000 tons in 1836 to 446,000 tons in 1845 and the number of steam machines trebled between 1837 and 1848.

This expansion of industry went hand in hand with a huge demographic increase, which was in the region of 50 per cent between 1815 and 1855, and which also profoundly affected the economic and social structure of the country. This increase was generally higher in the rural areas of the east than in the west, partly owing to the relaxation of restrictions on the age of marriage, partly owing to increased cultivation of potatoes, which could feed larger families. There was also a sharp rise in the population of the industrial areas of Rhineland-Westphalia, the valley of the Main, and Saxony, owing to the impossibility of limiting the families of industrial workers and also, though later, to the influx from the surrounding countryside; the chronic underemployment in Germany began in agricultural areas which could not support the increase in population, and this surplus was only later transferred to the towns. There was also an immense emigration to other European countries and to America – 750,000 in the thirty years before 1848.

Thus the fact that there was a huge expansion of industry at just this time was partly due to previous agricultural reforms, the demographic explosion and the amount of cheap labour available; partly too, those German industries which had survived the shock of foreign competition were now in a position to expand; partly, the reform of the customs system greatly facilitated trade; and finally, among the younger generation that started on business careers in the mid thirties, there was a new attitude: this was the first generation to have had the benefit of a technical education and the opportunity to travel widely in their own country and abroad. Emancipated from traditional beliefs, they were in a position to realize the potentialities of the demographic explosion.

2. SOCIAL

This industrial development, encouraged by the rural crisis and the rapid increase in population and bringing with it the factory as the unit of production, necessarily brought about many changes in the social structure. The large landowners who exploited their estates according to the laws of the market still kept certain feudal privileges: they were exempt from property tax, had their own police and courts for petty justice, enjoyed ecclesiastical patronage and dominated provincial parliaments. Though not all nobles, they combined fortunes usually built up by speculation with the prestige accruing from tradition. Although they tended to lose control over the administration of towns, they still retained their hold on the highest public offices and on the Army.

The middle classes were the real beneficiaries of the industrial expansion; favoured by the Napoleonic legislation, they transformed themselves from large-scale merchants into industrialists and entrepreneurs. There were hard times – particularly after the wars of liberation – and the necessity of concentrating on their economic interest partly explains their very slow development of a political consciousness. Also, unlike the French bourgeoisie before the revolution of 1789, the German middle classes were strongly pietistic, a typical area being the valley of the Wupper where Engels was brought up. Here the Calvinist spirit maintained a rigid sense of hierarchy and of the duty of increasing God-given wealth for His greater glory. The exception was the Rhenish bourgeoisie who, owing to their advanced industry and French influence, began to ask for greater representation in the provincial Parliament, more freedom of expression and stronger legal guarantees.

Much more numerous than the bourgeoisie were the artisans, and their social position was the one most threatened by economic developments. The strict meaning of the word 'artisan' was a master craftsman who worked in his own home and employed 'companions'. In the original organization of the work the merchant entrusted the whole process of production to each of his artisans. Then came the stage of manufacture, that is, division of labour. Sometimes the tools belonged to the owner of the business and thus the independence of the artisans was further diminished. The third stage was the introduction of a factory, that is, centralization and mechanization of production. In this process the artisans were gradually squeezed out of business by industry and lost their independence, some becoming dependent on wholesalers and others being forced into factories. Previously the artisans had been protected by restrictive corporations, by innumerable customs barriers throughout Germany and by the different currencies in most states: Prussia had sixty-seven customs barriers and there were seventy-one different currencies in the Western Provinces. During the 1830s those artisans working in building, mechanics and luxury goods were quite prosperous, as the beginning of the industrial expansion gave them a market, but soon afterwards its immense progress removed the economic viability of one trade after another. The number of companions was de-creasing and there was a lot of movement, either abroad or into the factories. Those left were opposed to the effects of capitalism and in favour of the restoration of corporations. The master artisans were in the same position as their com-panions and were often even more conservative, as they had further to fall socially if deprived of their position. Thus throughout most of the period the artisans were in an ambivalent position; the suppression of the corpora-tions and the growth of the towns had given many of them a temporary prosperity, but the advent of industry made them dependent on the bourgeoisie.

It was, of course, among industrial workers that there was the most rapid expansion of numbers – a sevenfold in-crease between 1800 and 1848. This was the age of the lengthening of the number of hours in the working day and the employment of women and children. Although it is true that it at least gave an opportunity to work to land-less peasants and unemployed artisans, yet the life of a factory worker did not offer much compensation. Wages continued to sink: if an index of 100 is taken for 1800, by 1830 this was 86 and by 1848 it was 74, with a minimum of 57 in the crisis year of 1847. And case studies show that most industrial workers lived at well below subsistence level. Yet these workers did not yet amount to a class-conscious proletariat. For firstly there were not very many of them: in the mid 1840s there were still more artisans than industrial workers in Prussia; secondly, each type of worker tended still to cling to his professional title, cus-toms and way of working. 'Social questions' were first brought to the fore by worried sections of the bourgeoisie, and though *Bildungsvereine* (study circles) began to form among the workers, it was the Germans working abroad who were the most class-conscious.

Although it is true that the real industrial expansion did

not take place in Germany until after 1850, that the country was still predominantly rural and that the corporations and *Junkers* still retained considerable control over society, yet the agricultural reform, the rapid increase of population, the urban societies dislocated by the new rich and the jobless artisans, the rapid mobility and growing class oppositions afforded a rich field for the development and propagation of political ideas.

3. POLITICAL

The political ideas in Germany before 1848 did not, of course, correspond with any exactness to the socioeconomic groups described above. Moreover, there were no political parties and some states, notably Prussia, did not even have a constitution. Nevertheless, it is possible to group political attitudes into five main streams: conservatism, political Catholicism, liberalism, radicalism and nascent socialism.[2]

a. Conservatism

German conservatism was no mere negative reaction to the growing forces of liberalism and democracy, and thus no movement simply to restore old powers. It aimed at giving society some sort of immanent order. Whereas in England the nobility maintained their influence through controlling Parliament and in France they were a more or less clerical remnant, having lost power in 1789, in Germany the conservative nobility were powerful but not

2. Two excellent accounts of the German political thought of this period are to be found in E. R. Huber, *Deutsche Verfassungsgeschichte* II, (Kohlhammer, Stuttgart, 1960) 324 ff., and in the second half of the article by Droz and Ayçoberry cited above.

organized. They formed no political party and their only formal groupings were in certain pietist movements.

The leaders of the main stream of conservative thought were the brothers Gerlach, the political philosopher Stahl, the theologian Hengstenberg and the historian Leo. They were uniformly hostile to any sort of rationalism and thus not merely anti-liberal and anti-democratic, but also opposed to the sort of absolutism practised by Frederick William III or Joseph of Austria on the grounds that it was a rationalist conception of power. They believed that the whole was definitely superior to its parts, looked back with admiration to the Empire of the Middle Ages and gave their support to the supra-national Holy Alliance. They laid emphasis on tradition and legitimacy and thus were strong royalists, integrating these conceptions into a hierarchical and organic outlook stemming from the romantic political philosophers like Müller and Friedrich Schlegel.[3] They were thus firm supporters of the 'Christian state' and, when in favour of a constitution, wished to see it based on the old estates.

Certain conservatives had a strongly developed social conscience and were among the first to draw attention to social problems and the misery of the poorest classes.[4] Some inherited this from the sense of responsibility for

3. On this aspect, see H. Reiss, *The Political Thought of the German Romantics* (Blackwell, Oxford, 1955).

4. It was a romantic philosopher, Franz Baader, who, with reference to his native Bavaria in 1835, seems first to have used the word 'proletariat', and pointed out its significance for society. In an essay entitled *Über das dermalige Missverhältnis der Vermögslosen oder Proletairs zu den Vermögen besitzenden Klassen* (1835), he described the law of the accumulation of capital in a few hands and claimed that neither charity nor police measures nor a constitutional state with citizenship limited to property-holders could help the working classes, who should be given the right to defend their own interests, under the guidance of the Church, by forming associations.

those under their protection that their feudal predecessors had possessed. These were men such as Victor Aimé Huber and Lorenz von Stein, who advocated a 'social monarchy' and called on the king to aid the property-less classes against the property-owners. Frederick William IV was profoundly affected by this attitude and worked hard to found charitable relief organizations. There was also a distinct group of such liberal conservatives as Ranke and Radovitz, whose chief concern was German unity and a certain amount of representative government.

b. Political Catholicism

Up to 1837 the political views of Protestants and Catholics were not distinguishable on confessional grounds. 1837 was the year of the 'Cologne affair', which awakened the political consciousness of Catholics throughout Germany. The new Archbishop of Cologne decided to enforce the hitherto neglected papal edict on mixed marriages requiring promises from both parents that the children would be brought up as Catholics. Since this was contrary to the Royal Edict of 1825, the king had no alternative but to arrest the archbishop, who was thus able to appear as a martyr. This focused Catholic opposition to the Government until he was released in 1840 when Frederick William IV succeeded to the throne. That the Prussian Government had, in the end, been forced to give in, gave Catholics a sense of triumph and made for a renewal of ultra-montane spirit. This Catholic revival was not, as in France and Belgium, a liberal one, for its supporters were anti-democratic and romantic. Believing that the Church was founded by God as an instrument of eternal salvation, they held that in no circumstances should it be subordinate to the state. Thus they appeared to share the liberal thesis of the separation of Church and state and to be in favour of liberty of expression, information and assembly as means of achieving this.

Most politically-minded Catholics were, however, profoundly conservative and wished to see a Christian monarchy in which the Church, free in discipline and teaching, imbued the state with its moral precepts. They did not aim for the restoration of the old secular power of the Church, but wanted public recognition and guarantee of the position of the Church with a view to her spiritual effectiveness. This involved an official acceptance of Christian marriage as a fundamental state institution and a condemnation of mixed marriages. Education, too, was held to be the province of the Church, and state education was viewed with suspicion. There was not much unity among Catholics on purely political questions, though most of their active members came from the nobility of south and west Germany and Silesia. To any conception of individual freedom their philosophers Baader and Jarcke opposed an organic philosophy of the state. They were in favour of representation by estates, and the idea of the restoration of the old empire and its constitution exercised a very strong influence on them.

The leading group of political Catholics formed around Josef Görres, who, though in his youth a follower of Kant and an enthusiast for the principles of the French Revolution, became in the thirties chief spokesman for the Catholic party. He exercised a wide influence through his pamphlets, of which the most widely read was his *Athanasius* supporting the Church's position on the 'Cologne affair'. Other members of his group included Baader, Jarcke and Döllinger, who later became famous for his opposition to the decrees of the Vatican Council. In the Rhineland there also arose among the bourgeoisie a Catholicism that was politically liberal and did not exclude the principles of the French Revolution. There was, too, a group around Buss and Bishop von Ketteler, who were interested in social questions and advocated a form of 'social state'. Both these two latter groups were, however, relatively small.

c. Liberalism

The desires of the commercial bourgeoisie to have a greater say in the decision-making process gave strength to the various currents of liberal thought.

Two main parties can be discerned.

The ideas of the first, and more conservative, whose chief thinker was Dahlmann, had close affinities with those of the conservative, organic state. For them, the individual was no isolated atom without any necessary connection with his fellow men. He had the position and function of a free and responsible member of a society. The state was a juridical person, and it was in the state as such that sovereignty resided. These liberals rejected equally the idea that sovereignty resided in the king and the idea that it resided in the people. Indeed, they maintained that only if the state were sovereign could the freedom of the individual be guaranteed, a freedom that would be endangered, if not destroyed, by the sovereignty of either king or people. The power of the state was not, of course, limitless, as it was bounded by a balance of powers and a written constitution. Moreover, each person had a double status: his rights and duties as an individual could not contravene the inborn rights he possessed as a citizen. The liberalism of England was more of a model here than that of France, for the English development seemed organic, less artificial, and thus appealed to men with a historical and evolutionary view of politics. The more conservative German liberals were against a system based on a parliament and advocated a constitutional monarchy where power would be divided equally between a hereditary monarch and elected representatives of the people. Executive power would be vested in ministers appointed by the king and responsible to, though not dependent on, parliament. These ideas were strongest in the north of Germany, being championed by liberal Hegelians like Strauss and Rosenkranz, and particularly so in the Rhineland, where there was a continuous and successful struggle, led by businessmen like Camphausen and Mevissen, to safeguard the 'Code Civil' and the principle of the equality of all citizens before the law. This struggle kept alive in the Rhineland a spirit of autonomy and dislike of Prussia's religious policies and semi-feudal absolutism. In East Prussia a section of the aristocracy, impelled by the incapacity of the state bureaucracy to deal with the problems of decreasing markets for agricultural products and increasing rural misery, gave their support to a liberal movement centred on the town of Königsberg, where Kant had lived and taught. The President of East Prussia, von Schön, published a pamphlet emphasizing that an Estates-General belonged to the fundamental rights of every country, and Dr Johann Jacoby was arraigned on a charge of high treason for publishing a demand that the king grant the constitution he had promised.

The other major current of liberal thought laid much more emphasis on the freedom of the individual, and was influenced by the French liberals like Benjamin Constant, who had opposed the Bourbon restoration and gained a victory in the July Revolution. This current was orientated towards France and the principles of 1789. The Baden politician Rotteck was typical of these liberals, who were most numerous in the west, in states (like Baden) where there was a parliament and open discussion of political issues. They held Rousseau and Montesquieu in high esteem, laid great emphasis on the sovereignty of parliament, and advocated a parliamentary monarchy on the model of the 'bourgeois monarchies' of France and Belgium.[5]

d. Radicalism

Whereas liberalism was a movement with much support (at least tacit) among large sections of the population, aiming at something practical and limited – a say in the government of the country – radical ideas were confined to groups of intellectuals, of which the most prominent was that of the Young Hegelians. These ideas had little popular influence apart from the poems of Hoffmann von Fallersleben, Freiligrath and Herwegh, and such opposition movements within the Churches as the Protestant *Lichtfreunde* and the Catholic *Deutschkatholizismus*. The liberals had no attitude of systematič opposition to government proposals and set great store by legality. Their aim was to adapt, not to destroy, the monarchic system, and they emphasized the importance of uniformity and a lack of sectarianism: Rotteck and the Baden liberals were opposed to voting in their Parliament and wished all decisions to be taken by consensus. The radicals, on the other hand, were *a priori* revolutionary and accepted very little compromise in their advocacy of popular sovereignty, universal suffrage and even republicanism.

The central idea of the radicals was that of popular sovereignty, their interpretation of which was obviously inspired by Rousseau's doctrine that the general will was omnipresent and omnipotent. For they held that all state power – executive and judicial as well as legislative – had

5. Further on the liberalism of this period, and particularly the part played by the academics, see R. H. Thomas, *Liberalism, Nationalism and the German Intellectuals, 1821–1847* (Heffer, Cambridge, 1951).

its origin in the people. Having none of the historical and evolutionary considerations of the liberals, they were also in favour of a national democracy in a single, indivisible state. This carried with it the idea of a republic, and radicals opposed unconditionally any idea of monarchy. Like the liberals, they demanded elections to a national parliament, but insisted on there being only one chamber, as the people had only one will. The government would be an executive committee of this parliament and entirely dependent on it. Radicalism rejected any idea of balances and checks, since it considered the only guarantee of freedom to be participation of all citizens in the government of the country. Underlying these ideas was a conception of equality fundamentally different from that of the liberals. Liberals, when they talked of the 'people', did not mean all the individuals in the state, and Rotteck declared himself in no way opposed to 'the natural and real inequality of political influence according to a man's different talents, moral weight and wealth'.[6] The radicals, on the other hand, denied that class inequality could ever be either natural or rational. On the contrary, they considered that inequality of class position should be compensated by equality of political rights and that universal suffrage was fundamental to any just and rational constitution.

This radicalism, which only gradually separated itself from liberalism and did not achieve a complete break until the early 1840s, first appeared as a force in the manifestations in Germany that followed the July Revolution in France. In 1831 there was a short-lived *coup* engineered by radical elements in Göttingen; in 1832, at a political rally to condemn the suppression of Johann With's association for the support of a free press in Hambach in the Palatinate, 30,000 people assembled, many sporting the

6. *Staatslexikon*, ed. Rotteck and Welcker (Altona, 1837) IV, p. 252 f.

black, red and gold of the banned *Burschenschaften* (radical student organizations); and in 1833 there was even an attack on the city of Frankfurt.

These manifestations led Metternich, the Austrian Chancellor, to introduce into the federal Diet in 1832 the six articles reaffirming that all power was in the hands of the princes and that parliaments had no power to impede the princes' government. These articles reaffirmed the censorship, and further laws forbade political societies and the holding of public meetings except under close observation. The failure of the radicals' haphazard political demonstrations meant that thereafter opposition inside Germany had to confine itself to literary and religious fields. In literature, the tone was set by the 'Young Germany' movement; they were strongly influenced by Saint-Simonian ideas, their leader was Karl Gutzkov and their most famous writer Heinrich Heine.[7] In religion, the radical disciples of Hegel, Karl Marx among them, developed an attack on their master's synthesis of religion and philosophy. The movement quickly became political and some of its members left Germany and joined the radical associations of German emigrants that had begun to form in France, Belgium and Switzerland and soon after Metternich's repressive measures. Here socialist ideas were already beginning to spread.

e. Socialism

It was not the working classes in Germany who were at the origin of socialist ideas. Germany was only in the process of becoming an industrialized country, and industrial workers were nowhere near the majority of the population. They did not have sufficient organization and were nostal-

7. On the movement, see E. Butler, *The Saint-Simonian Religion in Germany* (Cambridge University Press, 1926).

gic for the past rather than revolutionary. Socialist ideas were spread by a party of the intellectual élite, who saw the proletarian masses as a possible instrument of social renewal.

French utopian socialism began to have an influence inside Germany during the 1830s.[8] In Trier itself (where Marx was born), Ludwig Gall spread Fourierist ideas; but in Berlin the poems of Heine and the lectures of Gans gained a wider audience. The first book by a native German communist was *Die heilige Geschichte der Menschheit* ('The Sacred History of Mankind'), written by Moses Hess, who had picked up communist ideas after running away to Paris from his father's factory in Cologne.[9] The book was mystical and meandering, but contained quite clearly the idea of the polarization of classes and the imminence of a proletarian revolution. A year later a tailor, Wilhelm Weitling, active in the expatriate German workers' association in Paris and Switzerland, published a booklet entitled *Die Menschheit wie sie ist und wie sie sein sollte* ('Mankind as it is and as it ought to be').[10] It was a messianic work which defended, against the rich and powerful of the earth who caused all inequality and injustice, the right of all to education and happiness by means of social equality and justice. But the book which most helped to spread knowledge of socialism was Lorenz von Stein's inquiry, *Der Socialismus und Kommunismus des heutigen Frankreichs* ('The Socialism and Commun-

8. ibid.

9. On Hess, see the definitive biography by E. Silberner, *Moses Hess* (E. J. Brill, Leiden, 1966). On 'The Sacred History', see ibid, pp. 31 ff.; D. McLellan, *The Young Hegelians and Karl Marx* (Macmillan, London, 1969) pp. 137 ff. Hess's book is reprinted in *Moses Hess. Philosophische und socialistische Aufsätze*, ed. A. Cornu and W. Mönke (Akademie Verlag, Berlin, 1961), pp. 1–74.

10. On Weitling, see C. Wittke, *The Utopian Communist* (Louisiana State University Press, Baton Rouge, 1950).

ism of Present-Day France').[11] Early in the 1840s some of
the radical disciples of Hegel, following Feuerbach's
humanist interpretation of Hegel's philosophy, evolved a
socialism based on the idea of man as a 'species-being'.[12]

4. INTELLECTUAL

a. The Principles of 1789

Both liberals like Rotteck and also socialists owed a large
debt to the thinkers of eighteenth-century France – Voltaire, Diderot, Condillac, Helvétius and Rousseau.[13] They
were essentially rationalists and had a limitless faith in the
power of reason to explain and improve the world. In this
belief they tempered the dogmatic rationalism of the classical metaphysicians like Leibniz with the British empiricism of Locke and Hume. They believed that they were
capable of showing that men were by nature good and all
equally rational; the cause of human misery was simply
ignorance, which resulted partly from unfortunate
material circumstances, and partly from a deliberate suppression or distortion of the truth by those in authority,
whether civil or religious, in whose obvious interest it was
to perpetuate the deceptions under which mankind

11. For a fuller account of Stein's ideas, see below, p. 125

12. A more detailed account of the origins of German socialism
can be found in A. Cornu, *Karl Marx et Friedrich Engels* (Presses
Universitaires de France, Paris, 1955) I, 33 ff.; G. D. H. Cole, *A
History of Socialist Thought* (Macmillan, London, 1953) I, 219 ff.,
and G. Lichtheim, *The Origins of Socialism* (London, 1969).

13. See Marx's own account of these thinkers in *Die heilige
Familie* ('The Holy Family'), reprinted in K. Marx and F. Engels,
Historisch-kritische Gesamtausgabe, ed. D. Rjazanov and V. Adorat-
skij (Berlin, 1927 ff.) I, iii, 173 ff. (hereafter referred to as MEGA)
and translated in *The Essential Writings of Karl Marx*, (Mac-
Gibbon & Kee, London, 1967) pp. 25 ff.

laboured. One of the chief means of destroying this state of affairs was education; another was change in man's environment. Most of the editors of the *Encyclopedia* shared to some extent the determinist views of the materialist La Mettrie in his notorious book *L'Homme machine*. Yet the French materialists put most emphasis on reason, self-consciousness and the power to shape the future as the characteristics that distinguished human beings from animals. They intended to do for social life what men like Kepler and Newton had done for the physical sciences. Most prominent in this crusade for free and rational inquiry into personal and social issues was Voltaire, whose talents as a propagandist spread the new ideas far and wide. Rousseau, although his ideas were fundamentally different from those of his contemporary radicals, made common cause with them when it was a question of opposition to the *ancien régime*. His language was altogether more emotional and gave to will a place equal to, if not higher than, reason; often the mystical vagueness of his language added to its attraction, and Rousseau was quoted as a support for incompatible theories: Kant drew from Rousseau an individualistic approach to politics, whereas Hegel's disciples quoted him in favour of a transcendental state.[14]

b. Hegel

Meanwhile in Germany, where the French Revolution was greeted with enthusiasm, it was Kant above all who gave these principles their philosophical foundation and car-

14. For the views of the eighteenth-century materialists and their expression in the French Revolution, see Kingsley Martin, *French Liberal Thought in the Eighteenth Century*, 3rd ed. (Phoenix House, London, 1962); J. L. Talmon, *The Origins of Totalitarian Democracy* (Secker & Warburg, London, 1952).

ried further the struggle against dogmatic religion and
the emphasis on the value of human reason already expressed by literary writers such as Lessing. Kant considered
that human reason was limited to the world of phenomena
and that things in themselves were outside its scope. But
reason was free to discover the world of experience and its
laws. The moral philosophy of Kant was based on the
autonomy of the individual conscience as the source of
obligations, and thus, although he reintroduced God, freedom and immortality as legitimate hypotheses, his emphasis on the centrality of human reason was the same
as that of the French materialists.

The discussion of the problems of knowledge raised
by Kant was continued by Fichte and Schelling. Fichte
found the fundamental unity of being, after which all
idealists hankered, in the creativity of the human mind, a
creativity that included the whole of the objective world.
Schelling also laid emphasis on the primacy of spirit and
described the progress from nature to spirit which then in
its turn penetrated nature to such an extent that, in a work
of art for example, they were both one. In addition to this
search for a single principle from which to explain all
being, the German idealists were also concerned to reject
any transcendence and believed that the regulative principle of the world was immanent to it. Thirdly, they
considered that the ideas of development and change were
fundamental to an understanding of the world; and finally, they saw contradiction and opposition as the source
of all change.

Hegel's major contribution was to take up these dis-
parate themes and unite them into a comprehensive system.[15] Hegel was a Swabian, born in Stuttgart in 1770,

15. It is obviously impossible to give an adequate account of the
ideas of so complex a thinker in so short a space. What is aimed at
here is a very brief conspectus; the more detailed aspects of Hegel's

the year that Kant took up his professorship at Königsberg. He studied theology at the University of Tübingen for five years, and then became a private tutor while evolving his ideas in several long articles, most of which were only published in 1907. A legacy enabled him to join Schelling, a friend from his student days, at the University of Jena, though he soon began to part company with Schelling's ideas, which he considered vague and romantic. This break came into the open with the appearance in 1807 of Hegel's first major published work and his most influential, *Phänomenologie des Geistes* ('The Phenomenology of Spirit'). The victory of Napoleon at Jena the same year deprived Hegel of his living and he became headmaster of a grammar school in Nuremberg, during which period he wrote his second major work, *Wissenschaft der Logik* ('Science of Logic'). In 1816 he obtained a chair of philosophy at Heidelberg, and then in 1818 he accepted the chair in Berlin, where he remained until his death in 1831. While in Berlin, Hegel published his major political work, *Grundlinien der Philosophie des Rechts* ('Outlines of the Philosophy of Right'). The notes of his various lectures taken by his students were published after his death.

The great merit of Hegel's philosophy, wrote Engels, was that 'for the first time the totality of the natural, historical and spiritual aspects of the world were conceived and represented as a process of constant transformation

---

doctrines will be dealt with as they affect the development of Marx's thought. Two good recent books in English dealing with Hegel's philosophy in general are J. N. Findlay, *Hegel: A Re-examination* (Allen & Unwin, London, 1958), and W. Kaufmann, *Hegel* (Doubleday, New York, 1965). See also H. Marcuse, *Reason and Revolution* (Oxford University Press, New York, 1941) and the more analytic approach in J. Plamenatz, *Man and Society* (Longmans, London, 1963) II, 129 ff.

and development and an effort was made to show the organic character of this process'.[16] Hegel started from the belief that, as he said of the French Revolution, 'man's existence has its centre in his head, i.e. in Reason, under whose inspiration he builds up the world of reality'.[17] In his greatest work, the *Phänomenologie*, Hegel traces the development of mind or spirit, reintroducing historical movement into philosophy and asserting that the human mind can attain to absolute knowledge.[18] He analyses the development of human consciousness, from its immediate perception of the here and now, to the stage of self-consciousness, the understanding that allows man to analyse the world and order his own actions accordingly. Following this is the stage of reason itself, understanding of the real, after which spirit, by means of religion and art, attains to absolute knowledge, the level at which man recognizes in the world the stages of his own reason. These stages Hegel calls 'alienations', in so far as they are creations of the human mind yet thought of as independent and superior to the human mind. This absolute knowledge is at the same time a sort of recapitulation of the human spirit, for each successive stage retains elements of the previous ones at the same time as it goes beyond them. This movement that suppresses and yet conserves Hegel called

16. F. Engels, 'Socialism, Utopian and Scientific', reprinted in K. Marx and F. Engels, *Selected Works* (Moscow, 1962) II, 162.

17. G. W. F. Hegel, *Werke* (Berlin, 1832 ff.) IX, 441.

18. On this work, see the translation by Sir James Baillie, 2nd edn. (Allen & Unwin, London, 1949); also J. Loewenberg, *Hegel's Phenomenology* (Open Court Publishing Co., La Salle, Ill., 1965). The classical commentary is J. Hyppolite, *Genèse et structure de la phénoménologie de l'esprit de Hegel*, 2 vols. (Aubier, Paris, 1946). For a brilliant Marxist-Existentialist interpretation, less true to Hegel, see A. Kojève, *Introduction à la lecture de Hegel* (Gallimard, Paris, 1947).

Aufhebung, a word that has this double sense in German. Hegel also talked of 'the power of the negative', thinking that there was always a tension between any present state of affairs and what it was becoming. For any present state of affairs was in the process of being negated, changed into something else. This process was what Hegel meant by dialectic.

It is worth while looking more closely at Hegel's ideas on the state and on religion, as these were the fields where he was most strongly criticized by his disciples. According to Hegel's political philosophy, which was part of his general effort to reconcile philosophy with reality, human consciousness manifests itself objectively in man's juridical, moral, social and political institutions. These institutions permit spirit to attain to a full liberty, and the attainment of this liberty is made possible by the social morality present in the successive groups of the family, civil society and the state. The family educates a man to moral autonomy, whereas civil society organizes the economic, professional and cultural life. Only the highest level of social organization – the state, which Hegel calls 'the reality of concrete liberty' – is capable of synthesizing particular rights and universal reason into the final stage of the evolution of objective spirit. Thus Hegel rejects the view that man is free by nature and that the state curtails this natural freedom. For him the state is the only means of making man's freedom real. And because Hegel believed that no philosopher could move outside his own times and thus rejected theorising about abstract ideals, he considered that the state he described was to some extent already present in Prussia. Hegel's political philosophy was undoubtedly rather ambivalent: on the one hand he described the French Revolution as a 'glorious dawn' and throughout his life drank a toast on the day that the Bastille fell; on the other hand many of his pronouncements, particularly later in life, tended to a more conservative, not to say reactionary, position.[19]

Hegel's view on religion, which played a central role in the formation of his thought, were also open to more than one interpretation. Religion, together with philosophy, was for him the highest form of man's spiritual life. Religion – and by this Hegel, who remained a practising Lutheran all his life, meant Protestant Christianity, which he considered the highest and final form of religion – was the return of the Absolute Idea to itself. The content of religion was the same as that of philosophy, though its method of apprehending was different. For whereas philosophy employed concepts, religion used imagination. These unsatisfactory imaginings afforded only a fragmentary and imprecise knowledge of what philosophy comprehended rationally. But religion could be linked to philosophy by means of a philosophy of religion, and Hegel considered that the particular dogmatic contents of the religious imagination were necessary stages in the development of Absolute Spirit. The philosophy of religion interpreted at a higher level both naïve faith and critical reason. Thus Hegel rejected the view of the eighteenth-century rationalists that religion did inadequately what only science was competent to do; in his eyes, religion (or his philosophical interpretation of it) fulfilled man's con-

19. On the question of how liberal in politics Hegel really was, see Z. A. Pelczynski's introduction to *Hegel's Political Writings* (Clarendon Press, Oxford, 1964) and criticism of Pelczynski by Sidney Hook in his articles 'Hegel Re-habilitated', *Encounter* (Jan 1965), and 'Hegel and his Apologists', *Encounter* (May 1966), together with the replies by S. Avineri and Pelczynski, *Encounter* (Nov. 1965 and Mar. 1966). These articles are collected in : W. Kaufmann (ed.), *Hegel's Political Philosophy* (New York, 1970).

stant psychological need to have an image of himself and of the world by which he could orientate himself.[20]

c. The Hegelian School

In the years immediately following Hegel's death, his school was united and supreme in the German universities. Its influence spreading out from Berlin, where Hegel had had his chair, it had outposts in every university in Germany, its own philosophical club and its own periodical. The Prussian Minister of Culture, Altenstein, was favourable to Hegelianism and had helped to advance the academic careers of Hegelians. A complete edition of the master's works was prepared by seven of his pupils. These considered that the philosophical achievement of Hegel was, as a whole, exhaustive. His followers thus did not seek to innovate in philosophy. They were content to defend and elaborate the principles of the master in fields that he had only touched on. 'Hegel', said Gans, one of the seven, 'has left behind a host of gifted people, but no successor.'[21]

In time, however, the inevitable differences of opinion began to occur within the Hegelian school that were to lead eventually to a split between Right and Left Hegelians.[22] These terms, though they had a political origin in the French Convention, were used exclusively to designate religious attitudes, and indeed sometimes were quite in-

20. For Hegel's views on religion, see K. Barth, *From Rousseau to Ritschl* (S.C.M. Press, London, 1959) pp. 268 ff.; P. Asveld, *La Pensée religieuse du jeune Hegel* (Desclée de Brouwer, Paris, 1953); A. Chappelle, *Hegel et la Religion*, 2 vols (Paris, 1964); K. Löwith, 'Hegel and the Christian Religion', in *Nature, History and Existentialism* (Northwestern U.P., Evanston, Ill., 1966) pp. 162 ff.

21. E. Gans, *Vermischte Schriften* (Berlin, 1834) p. 251.

22. The first person to use these terms of the Hegelian school was D. F. Strauss in his *Streitschriften* (Tübingen, 1837) III, 93.

appropriate politically: Gans, for example, who was certainly regarded as an Old Hegelian, was Left politically.

The orthodox Hegelian Michelet described the differences between the two sides thus: [23] the Right of the school held to the slogan that 'the real is the rational', and saw nothing irrational in the traditional representation of religion. They considered that the major representation of religion, the transcendental personality of God, the uniqueness of Christ, the individual immortality of the soul, were part of its essential content. Thus they upheld the Hegelian doctrine of the unity of philosophy and religion. The Left Hegelians could not admit this unity; they began to ask (and here they were joined by many orthodox Lutherans to whom any type of Hegelianism was abhorrent) whether Hegel was not really a pantheist. Questions began to be asked about the personality of God and the immortality of the soul. Hegel's teaching on these points was not clear, and the verbal tradition of his lectures often varied. The principle that the Left Hegelians held to was that 'the rational is the real'. Thus the Left side of the school opposed the Right's optimism with a pessimism that set out to destroy the dogmas enshrined in religious representations that were now outdated. These representations all had to be judged by a progressive reason, not one which, as Hegel had said, only 'paints grey with grey' and thus merely recognized what already existed. For the master had also said that an age comprehended in thought was already in advance of its time, and the Left side drew the conclusion that the comprehension of religion already modified even its content, while its form became a pure myth.

This argument came right out into the open with the publication in 1835 of David Strauss's *Das Leben Jesu*

23. Cf. C. Michelet, *Entwicklungsgeschichte der neuesten deutschen Philosophie* (Berlin, 1843) pp. 316 ff.

('The Life of Jesus'). Strauss had studied theology at Tübingen, where he was taught by the radical Old Testament critic F. C. Baur, and had come to Berlin in time to attend the last few of Hegel's lectures. Whereas Hegel had considered the historicity of the Gospels to be comparatively unimportant and concentrated on interpreting their symbolic content, Strauss considered that the essence of the Christian religion was to be found in the Gospel narratives, and he treated them not as symbols but as myths translating the profound desires of the people. Strauss thus opposed the Hegelian reconciliation of philosophy and religion by maintaining that dogma could not be reduced to philosophical concepts without profoundly altering the content of religion. Having failed to extract a picture of the historical Jesus from the Gospel narratives Strauss considered that these narratives were expressions of the Messianic idea present in the primitive Christian communities, myths never intended to be taken as real historical narratives. In the conclusion to his book,[24] Strauss maintained that the idea of Christianity was unaffected by his researches; the only difference was that this idea was no longer revealed in a single individual, but in the whole species. What the evangelists had said about the person of Christ applied to the whole of humanity: 'it is not the way of the Idea to realize itself by spending its whole richness on a single exemplar and refuse it to all others, to express itself fully in that single individual, and incompletely in all others. No, it likes to spread its riches in a multitude of exemplars that complement each other....'[25]

The publication of Strauss's book caused the Hegelians to take sides for or against it, with Bruno Bauer, lecturer

24. D. F. Strauss, *Das Leben Jesu* (Tübingen, 1835–6) II, 691 ff. There is a translation by Marian Evans (George Eliot) (London, 1854).
25. ibid.

in theology at Berlin and soon to become the most out-spoken of the radicals, leading the attack from the Right. The different interpretations to which Hegel's system was open were well put by Engels:

As we have seen, the doctrine of Hegel, taken as a whole, left plenty of room for giving shelter to the most diverse practical party views. And in the theoretical Germany of that time, two things above all were practical: religion and politics. Whoever placed the chief emphasis on the Hegelian *system* could be fairly conservative in both spheres: whoever regarded the dialectical *method* as the main thing could belong to the most extreme opposition, both in politics and religion. Hegel himself, despite the fairly frequent outbursts of revolutionary wrath in his works, seemed on the whole to be more inclined to the conservative side. Indeed, his system had cost him much more 'hard mental plugging' than his method. Towards the end of the thirties, the cleavage in the school became more and more apparent. The left-wing, the so-called Young Hegelians, in their fight with the pietist orthodox and the feudal reactionaries, abandoned bit by bit that philosophical-genteel reserve in regard to the burning questions of the day which up to that time had secured state toleration and even protection for their teachings.[26]

It was quite natural that the discussion should at first be a theological one, as most members of the Hegelian school were interested in religion above all and, as Engels remarked in the article cited above, at that time 'politics was a very thorny field'. Yet granted the Establishment of the Church in Germany and the close connection between religion and politics, it was inevitable that a movement of religious criticism would swiftly become secularized into one of political opposition. It was as a member of this rapidly changing movement that Karl Marx first began to work out his views on philosophy and society.

26. Marx and Engels, *Selected Works*, II, 366.

CHAPTER TWO

Childhood and Adolescence

1. TRIER

Karl Marx was born on 5 May 1818 in Trier, a town of 12,000 inhabitants on the banks of the river Moselle and the administrative centre of the Moselle region. Trier was in the southern, agricultural part of the Rhineland, a province which had only recently been reattached to Prussia. It had a peaceful, rural setting and an impressive array of buildings indicating past splendour. Under the Romans the town had borne the name of Augusta Treverorum and had been the northern capital of the Empire. There were numerous buildings dating from those times, including the famous Porta Nigra, in whose shadow the Marx family lived, and Trier claimed to have more churches than any other town of comparable size. The Prince-Archbishop of Trier, whose feudal régime had been swept away by the French invasion in 1794, had exercised jurisdiction over Metz, Toul and Verdun, and had adorned the town with numerous convents, abbeys and monasteries. The citizens of Trier were easy-going people, open and tolerant. The French were welcomed with enthusiasm and, as elsewhere, a liberty tree was planted and a Jacobin club was founded, but the enthusiasm turned to indifference and hostility as the demands made by the Napoleonic wars increased. Prussia, however, soon dissipated the initial goodwill of the Rhinelanders by the reactionary measures of the Holy Alliance and an inability to deal with the crises in wine production, upon which the Moselle region principally depended. For Trier had very little industry and its inhabitants were mainly officials, traders and artisans, whose activities were largely bound up with the vineyards.

This hostility to Prussia increased greatly after the revolution of 1830, which marked the end of the Holy Alliance. The July Revolution also awakened in the Rhineland a wave of liberalism and sympathy for French principles. Pamphlets began to appear demanding autonomy for the Rhineland, and the Moselle wine-growers sent a large delegation to the Hambach demonstration.[1] The Rhenish liberals, like the other German liberals, were against economic restrictions and privilege, and in favour of constitutional government and freedom of the Press. This liberal opposition was seconded by the growing poverty of the Moselle wine-growers: the price of agricultural produce was constantly decreasing, and the situation was made worse by the customs union in 1828 of Prussia and Hesse, which virtually closed the former as a market for the Moselle peasants.

This weak economic situation provided a ready ground for the spread of socialist ideas. The doctrines of Saint-Simon gained disciples at Trier, as in the rest of Germany, so much so that the archbishop was led to issue an official condemnation of them from the pulpit. More significant still, the teachings of Fourier were actively propagated in Trier itself by Ludwig Gall, who has been called the first German socialist. Born in 1791 of a peasant family, he studied law at Cologne and became secretary to the city council in Trier in 1816, and in 1818 founded there a 'Union to provide all Germans in poverty with work, wages and sufficient lodging and property'. A year later he emigrated to America, founded at Harrisburg in Pennsylvania a community modelled on Fourier's phalansteries, and after its rapid failure returned to Trier to publish his

1. See above, pp. 25 ff.

experiences. In the late 1820s Gall continued his propaganda by highlighting the increasing social problems and pointing out that bourgeois society could not satisfy human needs to the full because work was the slave of money and exploited by it. Class opposition was only accentuated by the growing division in wealth between the haves and the have-nots. 'Those whose privileges depend on wealth and the working classes are fundamentally opposed to each other and have contrary interests; the circumstances of the former improve in precisely the proportion by which those of the latter get worse and become more precarious and miserable.'[2]

Gall's solution, again inspired by Fourier, was for the state to set up factories of its own as a step towards a collectivized economy. Since there would be no exploitation here, the wages would be higher and social ills remedied. From this analysis, Gall did not draw revolutionary ideas any more than Fourier; he simply wished, inside the framework of bourgeois society, to create a new and fairer organization of labour.

Not surprisingly, these ideas met with the disapproval of the authorities, and in 1832 Gall again left Trier; he went to Paris, where he met Fourier, and thence to Hungary to experiment with new methods of distillation. But in 1835 he was back in Trier and continued to publish his proposals for a reform of society. Although the socialist ideas gained very little hold in Trier, liberal ideas had quite a large following.

2. L. Gall, *Beleuchtung der Försterschen sogenannten Kritik der gerühmtesten Distilleriegeräte* (Trier, 1835) p. 37.

2. GENEALOGY

It would be difficult to find anyone who had a more Jewish ancestry than Karl Marx.[3] The name Marx is a shortened form of Mordechai, later changed to Markus. His father, Heinrich Marx, was born in 1782, the third son of Meier Halevi Marx, who became rabbi in Trier on the death of his father-in-law and was followed in this office by his eldest son Samuel, Karl Marx's uncle, who died in 1827. Meier Halevi Marx numbered many rabbis among his ancestors, who came originally from Bohemia, and his wife, Chage, had an even more illustrious ancestry: she was the daughter of Moses Lwow, rabbi in Trier, whose father and grandfather were also Trier rabbis. His father, Joshue Heschel Lwow, was chosen rabbi of Trier in 1723, corresponded with the leading Jewish personalities of his time, and was widely known as a fearless fighter in the cause of truth. It was said of him that no important decision was taken in the Jewish world without his having first been consulted. His father, Aron Lwow, was also rabbi in Trier and then moved to Westhofen in Alsace, where he held the rabbinate for twenty years. Aron Lwow's father, Moses Lwow, came from Lemberg (the German name for Lwów) in Poland, and numbered among his ancestors Meir Katzenellenbogen, head of the Talmudic high school in Padua during the sixteenth century, and Abraham Ha-Levi Minz, rabbi in Padua, whose father had left Germany in the middle of the fifteenth century owing to persecutions there.

3. For detailed research on Marx's genealogy, see B. Wachstein, 'Die Abstammung von Marx', in *Festskrift i anledning af Professor David Simonsens 70-aaroge födseldag* (Copenhagen, 1923) pp. 277 ff.; E. Lewin-Dorsch, 'Familie und Stammbaum von Karl Marx', *Die Glocke* (Berlin, 1924) IX 309 ff., 340 ff.; H. Horowitz, 'Die Familie Lwow', *Monatsschrift für Geschichte und Wissenschaft des Judentums* (Frankfurt, 1928) LXXII, 487 ff.

Not so much is known of the ancestry of Karl Marx's mother, but she seems to have been no less steeped in the rabbinic tradition than her husband. She was Dutch, the daughter of Isaac Pressburg, rabbi in Nijmegen. According to Eleanor Marx, in her grandmother's family 'the sons had for centuries been rabbis'.[4] In a letter to the Dutch socialist Polak, Eleanor wrote: 'It is strange that my father's semi-Dutch parentage should be so little known ... my grandmother's family name was Pressburg and she belonged by descent to an old Hungarian Jewish family. This family, driven by persecution to Holland, settled down in that country and became known, as I have said, by the name Pressburg – really the town from which they came.'[5]

It would be quite mistaken to dismiss the influence of this immense tradition on Karl Marx. To assert that 'it is impossible to say that his Jewish origin had any influence on any part of his life'[6] betrays a facile disregard for both Marx's heredity and his environment that even the enlightened atmosphere of Marx's home and his father's very loose attachment to Judaism should not conceal. For Jewishness, above all at that time, was not something that it was easy to slough off. Heine and Hess, both intimate friends of Marx, the one a convert to Protestantism for cultural reasons, the other an avowed atheist, both retained their Jewish self-consciousness until the end of their lives. Even Marx's youngest daughter Eleanor, though only half Jewish, proclaimed constantly and with a certain

4. W. Liebknecht, *Karl Marx zum Gedächtnis* (Nuremberg, 1896) p. 92.

5. Letter of Eleanor Marx to Henri Polak, 31 Oct 1893, quoted in W. Blumenberg, 'Ein unbekanntes Kapitel aus Marx' Leben', *International Review of Social History* I (1956).

6. H. P. Adams, *Karl Marx in his Earlier Writings*, 2nd edn. (Frank Cass, London, 1965) p. 11.

defiant pride at workers' meetings in the East End of
London: 'I am a Jewess.'[7] The position of Jews in the
Rhineland, where they were often scapegoats for the
farmers' increasing poverty, was calculated to increase this
self-consciousness. Although civil equality had been
achieved under the Napoleonic laws, the inauguration of
the Holy Alliance and its policy of the 'Christian state'
inevitably involved an anti-semitism on the double count
that the Jews professed an alien faith and an alien citizenship – that of the people of Israel.

3. MARX'S PARENTS

Heinrich Marx must have had considerable influence on
his son's development both because of the strong patri-
archal tradition in Jewish families and also because of the
high esteem in which Karl Marx always held his father. In
Heinrich Marx the Jewish inheritance appears in a very
secularized and enfeebled form. He had broken early with
his family, from whom he claimed to have received nothing, and often mentioned to his son the great difficulties
he had had to go through to obtain his eventual position
of lawyer to the high court of appeal in Trier. He had
adopted the ideas of the Enlightenment and was, according to his granddaughter Eleanor, a 'true eighteenth-century Frenchman. He knew his Voltaire and Rousseau by
heart.'[8] Heinrich Marx's religion was a shallow and
moralizing deism: Edgar von Westphalen, Karl Marx's
future brother-in-law, described Heinrich Marx as a
'Protestant *à la* Lessing'.[9] His outlook on life is well

7. Cf. E. Bernstein, *Die neue Zeit*, (1898) XVI, p. 122.

8. Eleanor Marx, ibid. (1898) p. 5.

9. Quoted in O. Maenchen-Helfen and B. Nicolaievsky, *Karl Marx*,
2nd edn. (Europäische Verlagsanstalt, Frankfurt-am-Main, 1963) p. 5.

summed up in the advice he gave to his son: 'A good support for morality is a simple faith in God. You know that I am the last person to be a fanatic. But sooner or later a man has a real need of this faith, and there are moments in life when even the man who denies God is compelled against his will to pray to the Almighty ... everyone should submit to what was the faith of Newton, Locke and Leibniz.'[10]

Yet Heinrich Marx was far from abandoning his Jewishness completely. It has been maintained that he had himself baptized out of conviction, as a logical consequence of his deistic beliefs, which were quite widespread in the German Protestant Church of his time.[11] But researches have shown that this view is completely mistaken and that he was compelled to choose between his religion and his job.[12] Until 1815, the principal law applying to the Jews in the Rhineland was the Napoleonic law of 1808, which went back to some extent on the decree of the French National Assembly of 1791 which gave Jews complete equality. The content of the Napoleonic law was solely economic and did not directly affect Heinrich Marx: a system of licences for engaging in trade had been instituted and special authority was required before taking up mortgages. The question was what would happen to the Jews when the Rhineland was reattached to the Prussian crown in 1815. On the occasion of the annexation, Heinrich Marx addressed a memorandum to von Sack, the Governor-General, entitled 'Some Remarks on the Napoleonic De-

10. *MEGA* I, i (2) 186.

11. See, for example, F. Mehring, *Karl Marx* (Allen & Unwin, London, 1936) p. 3; W. Sens, *Karl Marx. Seine irreligiöse Entwicklung* (Halle, 1935) p. 12.

12. See A. Kober, 'Karl Marx' Vater und das Napoleonische Ausnahmegesetz gegen die Juden, 1808', *Jahrbuch des kölnischen Geschichtsvereins*, XIV, 111 ff.

13. Reprinted ibid., pp. 120 ff.

cree of 17 March 1808',[13] in which he very respectfully asked
that the laws applying exclusively to the Jews be annulled.
Here he speaks of his 'fellow believers' and fully identifies
himself with the Jewish community. The Governor-
General seems not to have replied.

In any case, the Jews got the worst of both worlds: in
1818 a decree was issued keeping the Napoleonic laws in
force for an unlimited period. Two years earlier the Prussian Government had decided that the Rhineland too
should be subject to the laws that had been in force in
Prussia since 1812 and which, while granting Jews rights
equal to those of Christians, nevertheless made their holding of positions in the service of the state dependent on
the king's granting a special exception. The President of
the Provincial Supreme Court, von Sethe, went on a
journey through the Rhineland in April 1816 and inter-
viewed Heinrich Marx, who impressed him as someone
'of wide knowledge, very industrious, articulate and
thoroughly honest'. As a result he recommended that
Heinrich Marx and two other Jewish officials be retained
in their posts. But the Prussian Minister of Justice, Kir-
cheisen, was against exceptions and Heinrich Marx was
forced to change his religion to avoid becoming, as von
Sethe put it, 'breadless'. He was baptized some time before
August 1817[14] and changed his name from Heschel to
Heinrich.

It is not surprising that Heinrich Marx, who admired
Voltaire so much, was connected with the Rhenish liberal
movement, though this connection was rendered ambivalent by his constant attachment to Prussia and its

14. At the registration of his children's baptism in 1824, Heinrich
Marx described the clergyman who had baptized him, Pastor Müh-
lendorf, as merely a 'district preacher'. So his baptism must have
occurred before the Protestant parish of Trier was set up on 17 Aug
1817.

Government. He was a member of the Trier Casino Club, a literary society founded during the French occupation and so called from its meeting place, the Casino in Trier, a large building containing the municipal library and concert hall. The liberal movement gained force after the July Revolution in France, and the Club held a banquet in honour of the liberal deputies from Trier who sat in the Rhenish Parliament. This banquet, unique in Prussia, was one of a series held above all in southern Germany as part of a campaign for more representative constitutions. Heinrich Marx was one of the organizers of the Trier banquet, and gave a speech which was nevertheless of an extremely moderate and deferential tone. The nearest he got to the demands of the liberals was effusively thanking Frederick William III, to whose 'magnanimity we owe the first institutions of popular representation'.[15] He ended: 'Let us confidently envisage a happy future, for it rests in the hands of a benevolent father, an equitable king. His noble heart will always afford a favourable reception to the justifiable and reasonable wishes of his people.'[16] Several revolutionary songs were then sung and a police report informed the Government that Heinrich Marx had joined in the singing. The banquet caused anger in government circles, and this anger was increased by a more radical manifestation two weeks later, on the anniversary of the founding of the Casino Club, when the 'Marseillaise' was sung and the Tricolour brandished. The Prussian Government severely reprimanded the provincial governor and put the Casino Club under police surveillance. Heinrich Marx was not present at this second manifestation: he was no francophile and hated Napoleon and what he termed his 'mad ideology'.[17] His profound ad-

15. Quoted in Maenchen-Helfen and Nicolaievsky, *Karl Marx*, p. 10.

16. ibid.

17. *MEGA* 1, i (2) 205.

miration for Prussia is evident in his letter to von Sack and also in the surviving portion of an essay written on the 'Cologne affair', in which he defended the right of an absolute monarch to transgress natural laws in order to safeguard the state.[18] Knowing that his son Karl was writing poetry, he even encouraged him to attempt an ode which 'should glorify Prussia and afford an opportunity of praising the genius of the monarch ... patriotic, emotional and composed in a Germanic manner'.[19]

Of Karl Marx's mother comparatively little is known; there survive several letters written in a very ungrammatical German and without any punctuation at all. The fact that her letters to her Dutch relations were also in German indicates that she probably spoke Yiddish in her parents' home. Being very closely attached to her own family, she always felt somewhat of a stranger in Trier. The few indications that survive portray her as a simple, uneducated, hard-working woman, whose horizon was almost totally limited to her family and home, rather over-anxious and given to laments and humourless moralizing. She was the last person in the Marx family to be baptised. All the children were baptized together at home at a ceremony to which a large number of friends were invited. This took place in August 1824, some six or seven years after the father's baptism, at a time when the eldest children were of an age to start school. At the children's baptism, the mother's religion was entered as Jewish, with the rider that she consented to the baptism of her children, but wished to defer her own baptism on account of her parents. Her father died in 1825 and she was baptized the same year. The delay in her baptism and her attachment to Jewish tradition lead one to suppose that this tradition must have had some influence on Karl Marx as a young child. He

18. Reprinted in *MEGA* I, i (2) 231 ff.
19. *MEGA* I, i (2) 204.

must have learnt a lot from his mother about his ancestors and their religion, and in spite of the (reluctant) conversion many Jewish customs and attitudes must have survived in the Marx household.

Little is known of Karl Marx's attitude to his mother, apart from his references to her, when writing to his father, as an 'angel of a mother'. She lived until 1863, but there was a certain bitterness caused by financial disputes, though Marx kept on intimate terms with his maternal relatives in Holland. With his father, on the other hand (who died in 1838), Marx was on very intimate terms. For his fifty-fifth birthday, his son presented him with a volume of his own poems 'as a feeble sign of eternal love', and his sole surviving letter to his father is full of endearments. According to Eleanor Marx, Karl Marx always carried with his a photograph of his father. 'The face seemed very beautiful to me. The eyes and the forehead were like those of his son, but the lower part of his face around the mouth and chin were more tender. The whole was of a markedly Jewish type, though handsomely Jewish.'[20]

There were nine children in the Marx family, of whom Karl was the eldest, an elder brother, Moritz-David, having died soon after birth. Four others died young from tuberculosis. Heinrich Marx's income was quite considerable, and the year after Karl Marx's birth the family moved into their own house in the Simeonstrasse in the fashionable part of the town, right by the Porta Nigra. His daughter Eleanor said that Marx's aunts had often told her that as a child he was a fearful tyrant vis-à-vis his sisters; he drove them like his own horses up and down St Mark's hill in Trier and, what was worse, insisted that they ate the 'cakes' that he himself prepared with dirty hands from yet dirtier dough. Yet they did not protest at this

20. Eleanor Marx, *Die neue Zeit* (May 1883) p. 441.

treatment, for 'Karl would pay them back by relating such marvellous stories'.[21]

4. SCHOOL DAYS

For the five years 1830–35 Karl Marx attended the High School in Trier.[22] It had formerly been a Jesuit school and then bore the name Frederick William High School. The liberal spirit of the Enlightenment had been introduced into the school by the late Prince-Elector of Trier, Clement Wenceslas, who had adopted the principles of his famous predecessor Febronius and tried to reconcile faith and reason from a Kantian standpoint. In order to combat the ignorance of the clergy he turned the school into a sort of minor seminary. It sank to a very low level under the French occupation, but was reorganized after the annexation of the Rhineland and contained several very gifted teachers.[23] The chief influence in the school was its headmaster, Hugo Wyttenbach, Karl's history teacher and a friend of the Marx family. He had made a favourable impression on Goethe as 'an adept of the Kantian philosophy',[24] and took part in the founding of the Casino Club. After the Hambach demonstration, Wyttenbach was put under police observation and the school was searched: copies of the Hambach speeches and anti-government satire were found in the pupils' possession. As a result of the Casino affair in 1834, Karl Marx's fourth year at the

21 Eleanor Marx, *Erinnerungen an Karl Marx* (Züurich, 1934) p. 223.

22. For more detail than can be given here, see Cornu, *Karl Marx et Friedrich Engels*, 1, 61 ff.

23. Cf. C. Gruenberg, *Archiv für die Geschichte des Sozialismus und der Arbeiterbewegung* (1926) pp. 239 ff.

24. J. Goethe, *Die Campagne des Frankreichs*, 25 Oct 1792.

school, the mathematics teacher was accused of materialism and atheism, and the Hebrew teacher of having joined
in the revolutionary songs. Wyttenbach himself was
threatened with dismissal, but in the end a reactionary
co-headmaster, Loehrs, was appointed to counteract the
prevalent liberalism. Karl Marx's attitude here can be
gauged by the complaint addressed to him by his father
that Karl and another pupil had made themselves con-
spicuous by deliberately omitting to say good-bye to
Loehrs when they left the school.[25]

Among Karl Marx's fellow pupils, four-fifths were
Catholic, and most were of lower middle-class origin, the
sons of farmers and artisans. Karl is said to have been
feared by his fellow pupils 'for the ease with which he composed satirical verses and lampoons against his enemies'.[26]
In a letter to Engels much later, he spoke disparagingly of
the 'denseness and age' of the 'country bumpkins who
were preparing themselves for the Catholic seminary and
for the most part lived on *stipendia*'.[27] Marx made no
lasting friendships among his fellow pupils, though among
them was his future brother-in-law, Edgar von Westphalen, whom Edgar's sister Jenny described as 'the idol
of my childhood and youth'. He later proved an unstable
character with vaguely communist ideas and emigrated
twice to Texas, though Marx always retained an affection
for him.

The academic level of the pupils was not high and half
of them failed their final examination. Intellectually, Karl
Marx was a good average; he was one of the youngest in
his class, whose average age, when they left school, was
around twenty. The school put most emphasis on lan-

25. Cf. *MEGA* I, i (2) 186.

26. Eleanor Marx in D. Rjazanov, *Karl Marx als Denker usw.*
(Moscow, 1927) p. 27.

27. Letter of 17 Sep 1878, *MEGA* III, iv, 478.

guages, and Marx's Latin and Greek verse were good, his Religion satisfactory, his French and Mathematics weak and his History, strangely, weakest of all.[28] The earliest surviving documents in Marx's hand are the three essays he wrote for his *Abitur*, the German school-leaving examination. The essay in Latin on the Emperor Augustus is of no importance. The one on Religion, however, and the one for German composition show more individuality. Both are filled with idealism and an enthusiasm for the development of one's personaliy to the full by avoiding exterior power and glory and working with self-sacrifice for the good of humanity as a whole. The theme of the religious essay was 'a demonstration, according to St John's Gospel, chapter 15, verses 1–14, of the reason, nature, necessity and effects of the union of believers with Christ'.[29] Marx begins by saying that history, 'the great teacher of mankind', shows us that, from antiquity onwards, human nature has always tried to raise itself to a higher morality. 'Thus the history of mankind teaches us the necessity of union with Christ. Also when we consider the history of individuals, and the nature of man, we immediately see a spark of the divine in his breast, and enthusiasm for the good, a striving after knowledge, a desire for truth.'[30] Although these natural instincts are countered by sinful desires, the union of believers with Christ can overcome these and afford a 'happiness which the Epicurean in his simple philosophy and the more profound thinker in the furthest depths of knowledge seek in vain, which only one bound unconditionally and childlike to Christ, and

28. See C. Gruenberg, 'Marx als Abiturient', *Archiv für die Geschichte des Sozialismus und der Arbeiterbewegung,* (1925) XI, 424 ff.

29. First published in *MEGA* I, i (2) 171 ff.; reprinted in *Karl Marx: Texte zu Methode und Praxis,* ed. G. Hillmann (Rowohlt, Hamburg, 1966) pp. 11 ff.

30. *MEGA* I, i (2) 171.

through him to God, can know, and which makes for a finer and more elevated life.'[31] The essay is written with considerable pathos and rather sugary piety, but has a basically rational structure, explaining how the advent of Christianity is necessary for the full moral development of humanity. Marx has a very distant and colourless deistic conception of God, akin to that of his father, and that of the Pastor Josef Küpper who gave religious instruction at the school. Küpper was also in charge of the small Protestant parish in Trier and a friend of Heinrich Marx. He was particularly interested in ethical questions, and his approach to religion, strongly influenced by Kant, held that it was the best means of educating men to a 'true humanity'. Küpper based his teaching on the person of Jesus and on the Bible, and avoided any sectarianism, being strongly influenced by rationalist elements.[32] Marx's essay is very much in the style of his teacher, who praised it, though he also commented, with justification, that 'the essence of the union in question is not dealt with and the reason for it only dealth with from one aspect'.[33]

The German composition, entitled 'Reflections of a Young Man on the Choice of a Career', shows more originality.[34] Marx's theme was that, though man's choice of a career could not be completely arbitrary, yet it was this freedom that distinguished him from animals. One should not be carried away by ambition or quick enthusiasm:

31. *MEGA* I, i (2) 174.

32. Further on Küpper, see Sens, *Karl Marx. Seine irreligiöse Entwicklung*, pp. 13 f.

33. *MEGA* I, (2) 174.

34. First published in *MEGA* I, i (2) 164 ff. Reprinted in Karl Marx, *Frühe Schriften*, ed. H.-J. Lieber and P. Furth (Cotta, Stuttgart, 1962) I, 1 ff.; *Text zu Methode und Praxis*, pp. 7 ff. Translated in *Writings of the Young Marx on Philosophy and Society*, ed. L. Easton and K. Guddat (Doubleday, New York, 1967) pp. 35 ff. (hereafter referred to as Easton and Guddat).

what was important was to take the opportunity offered of working in the service of humanity while avoiding being carried away by abstract truths. The essay ended with an impassioned profession of faith in the value of a life sacrificed for the good of mankind.

In theme and structure, the essay is much the same as those of Marx's fellow pupils. Its underlying ideas are those of the humanist ideal of the German Enlightenment and classical period – the full development of the individual and the full development of the community of mankind being interdependent.[35] There is no trace in Marx's essay of a transcendental God: the words God, nature and creation are interchangeable and the process of history is an immanent one. Marx begins his essay:

Nature has assigned to the animal the sphere of its activity, and the animal acts calmly within it, not striving beyond, not even surmising that there is another. To man, too, the deity gave a general goal, to improve mankind and himself, but left it to him to seek the means by which he must attain this goal, left it to him to choose the position in society which is most appropriate and from which he can best elevate both himself and society.

This choice is a great privilege over other creatures but at the same time an act which can destroy man's entire life, defeat all his plans, and make him unhappy.[36]

To every person there had been allotted his own purpose in life, a purpose indicated by the 'soft but true' interior voice of the heart. It was easy to be deluded by ambition and a desire for glory, so close attention was necessary to see what one was really fitted for. Once all

35. For striking parallels between Marx's essay and Rousseau's *Émile*, see the detailed commentary in G. Hillmann, *Marx und Hegel* (Europäische Verlagsanstalt, Frankfurt-am-Main, 1966) pp. 33 ff.

36. *MEGA* 1, i (2) 164; Easton and Guddat, pp. 35 f.

factors had been coolly considered, then the chosen career should be eagerly pursued. 'But we cannot always choose the vocation to which we believe we are called. Our social relations, to some extent, have already begun to form before we are in a position to determine them.'[37] This sentence has been hailed as the first germ of Marx's later theory of historical materialism.[38] Lewin-Dorsch goes as far as to say that 'It is nothing less than historical materialism that wakes in that short sentence and opens its eyes for the first time. It is a light whose brightness grew from year to year until finally it shone with a blinding brightness.'[39] However, that human activity is continually limited by the prestructured environment is an idea at least as old as the Enlightenment and the Encyclopedists. It would indeed be surprising if even the germ of historical materialism had already been present in the mind of a seventeen-year-old schoolboy. It would be a mistake – to be avoided here as also later – to think that, in his early writings, Marx was raising questions to which he would later produce answers. To consider the young Marx's development as a progress towards a definite goal is to misunderstand its various stages by viewing them solely in terms of what they led up to: Marx is 'not yet' this and only shows 'anticipations' of that. In any case, the subsequent sentences, with their mention of physical or mental deficiencies, show that Marx here merely means that when choosing a career one should consider one's circumstances.

Marx then goes on to recommend that a career be chosen that confers as much worth as possible on a man by permitting him to attain a position that is 'based on

37. *MEGA* I, i (2) 165; Easton and Guddat, p. 37.

38. See, for example, Mehring, *Karl Marx*, p. 5; Cornu, *Karl Marx et Friedrich Engels*, I, 64.

39. E. Lewin-Dorsch, 'Der junge Marx', *Die Glocke*, (Berlin, 1924) XII, 1502.

ideas of whose truth we are completely convinced, which offers the largest field to work for mankind and approach the universal goal for which every position is only a means: perfection'.[40]

This idea of perfectibility is what should above all decide the choice of a career, always bearing in mind that

The vocations which do not take hold of life but deal, rather, with abstract truths are the most dangerous for the youth whose principles are not yet crystallized, whose conviction is not yet firm and unshakeable, though at the same time they seem to be the most lofty ones when they have taken root deep in the breast and when we can sacrifice life and all striving for the ideas which hold sway in them.[41]

Here, too, commentators have tried to discover a forerunner of Marx's later idea of the 'unity of theory and practice'.[42] Once again, this is to read into Marx's essay much more than is there. All that Marx says is that the sort of profession that deals with abstract ideas should be approached with special circumspection, for 'they can make happy who is called to them; but they destroy him who takes them overhurriedly, without reflection, obeying the moment'.[43] The problem is above all a practical one and not at all posed in terms of theories. What is noteworthy here is Marx's habit of thinking in opposites which he pursues to their furthest consequences, while at the same time trying to comprehend them as different facets of a totality.

40. *MEGA* I, i (2) 166; Easton and Guddat, p. 38.

41. *MEGA* I, i (2) 166 f.; Easton and Guddat, pp. 38 f.

42. Cf. Cornu, *Karl Marx et Friedrich Engels*, I, 65; G. Mende, *Karl Marx' Entwicklung vom revolutionären Demokraten zum Kommunisten*, 3rd ed. (Berlin, 1960) p. 26.

43. *MEGA* I, i (2) 167; Easton and Guddat, p. 39.

The essay ends with a purple passage revealing a pure, youthful idealism:

> History calls those the greatest men who ennoble themselves by working for the universal. Experience praises as the most happy the one who made the most people happy. Religion itself teaches that the ideal for which we are all striving sacrificed itself for humanity, and who would dare to destroy such a statement?
>
> When we have chosen the vocation in which we can contribute most to humanity, burdens cannot bend us because they are only sacrifices for all. Then we experience no meagre, limited, egotistic joy, but our happiness belongs to millions, our deeds live on quietly but eternally effective, and glowing tears of noble men will fall on our ashes.[44]

The essay was marked by Wyttenbach, who qualified it as 'fairly good' and praised Marx for being rich in ideas and well organized, though he criticized with justification Marx's 'exaggerated desire for rare and imaginative expressions'.[45] This love of excessive imagery and the penchant for poetry that Marx displayed in the following years are due in large part to the influence of Baron von Westphalen, a friend of the Marx family and Karl Marx's future father-in-law. He was twelve years older than Heinrich Marx. Born in 1770 of an aristocratic family, his father, Philip von Westphalen, had been Chief of Staff to the Duke of Brunswick during the Seven Years War and rendered so great a service to the cause of Prussia and England that he was ennobled by George III of England. He had married an aristocratic Scotswoman, Jeanie Wishart, who was the niece of the general commanding the British troops and a descendant of the Dukes of Argyll. Thus their son, Louis von Westphalen, had an origin very

44. ibid.
45. *MEGA* I, i (2) 167.

different from that of most Prussian officials. He welcomed
the Napoleonic reforms in his native Brunswick, and was
sent to Trier in 1816 by the Prussian Minister Hardenberg as government adviser with special reference to
judicial matters. Here he came into contact with Heinrich
Marx, who in 1819 bought the house next door to the von
Westphalens. Baron von Westphalen had four children by
a first marriage, of whom the eldest, Ferdinand, made a
rapid career and was Prussian Minister of the Interior
from 1850 to 1855 in Manteuffel's reactionary Cabinet. Of
the three children by his second marriage, Jenny was the
intimate friend of Sophie Marx and became engaged to
Karl in the summer of 1836, and Edgar was in the same
class as Karl at the High School.[46]

Baron von Westphalen was an extremely cultivated
man, spoke English as well as he spoke German, read
Latin and Greek without any difficulty and particularly
liked romantic poetry. Eleanor Marx wrote that Baron
von Wesphalen 'filled Karl Marx with enthusiasm for the
romantic school and, while his father read Voltaire and
Racine with him, the Baron read him Homer and Shakespeare, who remained his favourite authors all his life'.[47]
The Baron devoted much of his time to the young Marx,
and the two went for intellectual walks through the 'won-
derfully picturesque hills and woods' of the neighbour-
hood. As well as being a man of culture, the Baron was
keen on progressive political ideas and interested Marx
in the personality and work of Saint-Simon. Marx continued to be so grateful for the friendship of the Baron
that in 1841 he dedicated his doctoral thesis to him in a
most effusive manner:

46. On the family in general, see F. Mehring, 'Die von Westphalen', *Die neue Zeit* (1891–2) x, 481 ff.

47. E. Marx, quoted in 'Karl Marx', *Die neue Zeit* (May 1883)
p. 441.

Forgive me, my dear fatherly friend, for prefacing an unimportant brochure with a name so beloved as yours: but I am too impatient to await another opportunity of giving you a small proof of my love. May all who have doubts of the power of the spirit have, like myself, the good fortune to admire an old man who has kept his youthful impulses and who, with wise enthusiasm for the truth, welcomes all progress. Far from retreating before the reactionary ghosts and the often dark sky of our time, you have always been able, inspired by a profound and burning idealism, to perceive, behind the veils that hide it, the shrine that burns at the heart of this world. You, my fatherly friend, have always been for me the living proof that idealism is no illusion, but the true reality.[48]

48. *MEGA* I, i (2) 7; *Texte zu Methode und Praxis*, I, 128.

CHAPTER THREE

Marx the Student

1. POETRY IN BONN AND BERLIN

This interest and enthusiasm for romanticism that Baron von Westphalen had aroused in Marx was increased by the year that he spent at the University of Bonn. In October 1835 Marx left Trier and sailed down the Moselle to begin his studies in law at Bonn, the intellectual centre of the Rhineland. The town itself was small, scarcely larger than Trier, but the university was an important one with more than 700 students. Marx carried with him the high hopes of his father, who expected great things from the most promising of his children. 'I want you to become', he wrote soon after his son's arrival, 'what I might perhaps have become had I been born under such favourable auspices. You can either fulfil or destroy my greatest hopes.'[1] Thus encouraged, Marx began by working very hard and put his name down for nine lectures (which he subsequently reduced to six on his father's advice) and, according to his end-of-term report, attended them all with enthusiasm and keen attention. By the beginning of 1836 he was ill from overwork and in the summer term reduced his lecture commitment to four, which he followed with much less enthusiasm. At the same time he took a more active part in the social life of the university, became President of the Association of Students from Trier and was even imprisoned for a day by the university authorities for 'disturbing the peace of the night with

1. *MEGA* I, i (2) 186.

drunken noise'.[2] In August 1836 he was slightly wounded above the left eye in a duel with a young Prussian aristocrat. Marx was also once denounced to the police for carrying forbidden weapons, but the subsequent investigation petered out, and when he left Bonn at the end of the year his certificate said he was not connected with any suspect political organization.

What occupied most of Marx's intellectual energy during this year at Bonn was poetry. He joined a poets' club where members' compositions were read aloud and criticized. This club probably had political undertones: among its members were Karl Grün, who collaborated with Moses Hess and was one of the founders of True Socialism, and F. C. Bernays, who later edited *Vorwärts* ('Forwards'), the radical newspaper of the German workers in Paris. Half the lectures that Marx attended were on artistic subjects; the intellectual climate at Bonn was romantic, being dominated by Schelling and Schlegel, whose lectures on Homer and Propertius were among Marx's favourite six.

Heinrich Marx at first approved of his son's interest in poetry which, he said, pleased him better than the tavern. But on being asked to bear the cost of the publication of some of the poems, he advised him to wait a little: 'A poet must these days know that he has something sound to offer if he wants to appear in public.... I would be very sorry to see you appear in public as a minor poet.'[3] In general, the letters of Heinrich Marx welcome the bewildering variety of his son's propositions: he approved of a plan to edit a review and even for his son to busy himself with dramatic criticism. At the same time, however, the letters of both his parents are full of bitter complaints

2. ibid. p. 194.
3. *MEGA* I, i (2) 180.

of their son's lack of affection for his family and his extremely disordered style of living.

In any case, Heinrich Marx was so little satisfied with his son's progress in Bonn that he decided to transfer him to the University of Berlin. Here, though he gave up the 'wild rampaging' of Bonn, he continued to write poetry, all the more ardently as he had become secretly engaged to Jenny von Westphalen shortly before his departure for Bonn in 1836.

When I left you [he wrote a year later to his father] a new world had just opened for me, the world of love, at first a love that was frenzied with yearning and void of hope. Even the journey to Berlin, which otherwise would have extremely delighted me, would have incited me to contemplate nature, would have inflamed me with the joy of living, left me cold. It even depressed me profoundly, for the rocks I saw were no rougher, no harsher, than the feelings of my soul; the big cities were not more lively than my blood; the tables in the inns were not more overladen, the food not more indigestible than were the contents of my imagination; and, to conclude, art was not so beautiful as Jenny.[4]

As soon as he got to Berlin he reluctantly made a few necessary visits and then completely isolated himself in order to immerse himself in science and art. Lyric poetry was his first concern; at least, as he himself put it, it was 'the most agreeable and most obvious'.[5] The poems that Marx wrote while he was in Bonn and those written during the autumn of 1836 in Berlin have not survived. These latter comprised three volumes entitled 'Book of Love, Parts 1 and 2' and 'Book of Songs', all three being dedicated to Jenny von Westphalen. According to Mehring, these poems, with one exception, were all love lyrics and

---

4. *MEGA* I, i (2) 214; Easton and Guddat, p. 41.
5. ibid.

romantic ballads. He had had the opportunity of reading them before they were finally lost and judged them 'formless in every sense of the word'.[6] They were full of gnomes, sirens, songs to stars and bold knights, 'romantic in tone without the magic proper to romanticism'.[7] They were, said Marx,

in accordance with my position and whole previous development, purely idealistic. A remote beyond, such as my love, became my heaven, my art. Everything grew vague, and all that is vague lacks boundaries. Onslaughts against the present, broad and shapeless expressions of unnatural feeling, constructed purely out of the blue, the complete opposition of what is and what ought to be, rhetorical reflections instead of poetic thoughts but perhaps also a certain warmth of sentiment and a struggle for movement characterize all the poems in the first three volumes I sent to Jenny. The whole horizon of a longing which sees no frontiers assumed many forms and frustrated my effort to write with poetic conciseness.[8]

The only poems that survive are those written during the first half of 1837, together with fragments of a dramatic fantasy and a comic novel. Marx tried to publish some of these poems and sent them to Adelbert von Chamisso, editor of the annual *Deutscher Musenalmanach*, but the issue had already gone to press. The only two poems ever to appear in print in Marx's lifetime were published in the Berlin *Athenaeum*, a small Young Hegelian journal, in January 1841. The general tone of all these poems reflected the prevailing climate in Bonn and also the lectures Marx attended during his first term in Berlin, where he heard Savigny and Steffens give a romantic interpretation

6. F. Mehring, introduction to *Aus dem literarischen Nachlass von Karl Marx, Friedrich Engels und Ferdinand Lassalle* (Stuttgart, 1902) I, 26.

7. ibid.

8. *MEGA* I, i (2) 214 f.; Easton and Guddat, pp. 41 f.

of the philosophy of law. His models are Heine, Goethe and Schiller, and they contain all the well-known themes of German romanticism, with the exception of political reaction and nationalism. Hans Kohn has well summed up the romantic *Weltanschauung*:

> The romantic individual ... regarded himself not as a representative of universal order but as a unique being and demanded complete freedom, in life and work, for his creative genius. At the same time the romantics, for all their revolt against society, did not accept the titanic loneliness of the Storm and Stress. They longed for a community of like-minded individuals who would live a full life according to their innermost emotions and convictions. The complexity and anguish of their search for this community was heightened by their underlying subjectivism. The unique individual longed for a full gratification of all his desires and yet felt the need for fulfilment in the miracle of a true harmonious union in which all the conflicting opposites of life would be reconciled.[9]

Marx's poems are full of tragic love and talk of human destiny as the plaything of mysterious forces. There is the familiar subjectivism and extreme exaltation of the personality of the creative artist isolated from the rest of society. As a result of his love for Jenny,

> With disdain I will throw my gauntlet
> Full in the face of the world,
> And see the collapse of this pigmy giant
> Whose fall will not stifle my ardour.
>
> Then I will wander godlike and victorious
> Through the ruins of the world
> And, giving my words an active force,
> I will feel equal to the creator.[10]

9. H. Kohn, *The Mind of Germany* (Macmillan, London, 1965) p. 50.
10. *MEGA* I, i (2) 50.

Other poems display a longing for something infinite and a love of death *à la* Novalis, while still others consist entirely in a dream world of mystical imagination. To the aesthetic idealism of these poems was added a series of typically romantic ironical attacks on 'Philistines', people like doctors and mathematicians, who followed utilitarian professions based on an ordered and rational approach to problems. To help him in his composition, Marx had copied out large extracts from Lessing's *Laokoon*, Solger's *Erwin*, and Winckelmann's *History of Art*. Marx's habit of making excerpts from all the books he was reading (and sometimes adding comments of his own) stayed with him all his life, and those notebooks that remain form a valuable guide to the development of his thought.[11] He also wrote a few chapters of a comic novel, *Scorpion and Felix*, in the style of Sterne and then gave that up to compose the first scene of *Oulanem*, a contemporary comic thriller whose hero was a feeble copy of the ageing Faust. Finally there was an interesting series of epigrams on Hegel, whom Marx accuses of being arrogant and obscure. In the first epigram, he says:

Because my meditations have discovered the highest of things
    and also the depths,
I am as crude as a god and cloak myself in darkness as he does,
In my long researches and journeys on the wavy sea of thought,
I found the word and remain firmly attached to my find.[12]

The second epigram has the same theme opening:

I teach words that are mixed up in a devilish and chaotic mess.[13]

11. See M. Rubel, 'Les Cahiers d'études de Karl Marx (1840–1853)', *International Review of Social History* (1957).

12. *MEGA* I, i (2) 41.

13. *MEGA* I, i (2) 42.

The most interesting is the last epigram:

> Kant and Fichte like to whirl into heaven
> And search there for a distant land,
> While my only aim is to understand completely
> What – I found in the street.[14]

The point of this epigram is totally misunderstood if it is taken to be Marx himself speaking.[15] As in the former epigrams, it is Hegel who is speaking, criticized by Marx, the subjective romantic, for being too attached to day-to-day reality. The whole tenor of Marx's poems makes this an obvious criticism of Hegel, and it was a common one among romantic writers.

In general, Marx's first contact with the university brought about a great change in the views he had expressed in his school-leaving essay. No longer was he inspired by the thought of the service of humanity and concerned to fit himself into a place where he might best be able to sacrifice himself for this noble ideal: his poems of 1837, on the contrary, reveal a cult of the isolated genius and an introverted concern for the building of his own personality apart from the rest of humanity.

2. CONVERSION TO HEGELIANISM

It is fortunately very easy to follow Marx's evolution during his first year at the University of Berlin, for he described it in great detail in a letter to his father written in November 1837 (the only letter to have survived from

14. ibid.

15. This is the interpretation of, for example, W. Johnston, 'Marx's verses of 1836–7', *Journal of the History of Ideas* (April 1967) 261; also E. Kamenka, *The Ethical Foundations of Marxism* (Routledge, London, 1962) p. 20, and of S. Avineri, *The Social and Political Thought of Karl Marx* (Cambridge U.P., 1968) p. 8.

Marx's student days).[16] In this letter, from which quotations have already been made, he recounted the course of his ideas and criticized them from his newly-won Hegelian standpoint. Poetry, even during his first year at Berlin, was not Marx's only concern. He also read widely in jurisprudence and felt compelled to 'struggle with philosophy'. The two were, in his mind, closely connected and he tried to work out a philosophy of law. He prefaced this with a metaphysical introduction and the whole grew to a work of three hundred pages before he gave it up. The particular problem which he was unable to overcome in the metaphysical introduction was the conflict between what is and what ought to be, 'a conflict peculiar to idealism, and this gave rise to the following hopelessly inaccurate classification. First of all, what I gratuitously christened "metaphysics of law" – that is, principles, reflections, determinative concepts – was severed from all actual law and from any actual form of law, as in the writing of Fichte, only in my case in a more modern and less substantial fashion.'[17] It was precisely this gap between what is and what ought to be that Marx considered to have been bridged by the Hegelian philosophy. Marx's second objection to the metaphysical system he had constructed was its 'mathematical dogmatism'. Here Marx repeats Hegel's polemic against mathematics contained in the preface to his *Phänomenologie*, where Hegel contrasts mathematical truth unfavourably with historical truth: 'The process of mathematical truth does not belong to that which is its object, but is an activity that remains external to its matter.'[18] According to Marx, the systems of Kant and Fichte, who were the inspiration for his own ideas at this

16. First published, with an introduction by his daughter Eleanor, in *Die neue Zeit*, (1897), XVI, 4 ff.

17. *MEGA* I, i (2) 215; Easton and Guddat, p. 42.

18. Hegel, *Werke* II, 32; translated in Kaufmann, *Hegel*, p. 418.

time, were open to this objection: they were abstract systems that, like geometry, passed from axioms to conclusions. In contrast, 'in the concrete expression of the living world of thought – as in law, the state, nature, philosophy as a whole – the object itself must be studied in its development; there must be no arbitrary classifications; the rationale of the thing itself must be disclosed in all its contradictoriness and find its unity in itself'.[19] Marx then outlines the complicated *schema* of his philosophy of law that comprises the second part of his treatise. The main reason for his dissatisfaction with this classification seems to have been that he did not think, in the Hegelian manner, of the concept as mediator between form and content and thus his classification was empty – a desk, as he put it, into whose drawers he later poured sand.

When he got as far as the discussion of private material law, he realized that his enterprise was mistaken:

I saw the fallaciousness of the whole, which in its fundamental *schema* borders on the Kantian, though differing wholly from Kant in matters of detail. Once more I realized that I could not make my way without philosophy. Hence I was once again able, with good conscience, to throw myself into the arms of philosophy, and I wrote a new basic metaphysical system. Upon its completion I was once again constrained to recognize its futility and that of all my previous endeavours.[20]

This brought Marx to the end of his first semester and he sought refuge from his philosophical problems in writing the poetry discussed above:

At the end of the semester, I once more sought the dance of the muses and the music of the satyrs. Already in the last pages I sent you, idealism plays its part in the form of forced humour

19. *MEGA* I, i (2) 215; Easton and Guddat, p. 43.
20. *MEGA* I, i (2) 217 ff; Easton and Guddat, p. 45.

(*Scorpion and Felix*) and in an unsuccessful dramatic fantasy (*Oulanem*), until at length it takes an entirely different direction and changes into pure formal art, for the most part without any stimulating objects and without any lively movement of ideas.[21]

But this activity, while revealing what poetry could be, at the same time made it impossible for Marx to continue: 'These last poems are the only ones in which suddenly, as if by the wave of a magician's wand – it was shattering at the beginning – the realm of pure poetry flashed open before me like a distant faery palace, and all my creations collapsed into nothing.'[22] Not surprisingly, this period of intense intellectual activity in several fields, often involving his working through the night, ended in a period of severe illness. His doctor advised a change of scene and Marx went to the village of Stralow just outside Berlin. Here his views underwent a big change: 'a curtain had fallen, my holy of holies had been shattered, and new gods had to be found. Setting out from idealism – which, let me say in passing, I had compared to and nourished with that of Kant and Fichte – I hit upon seeking the Idea in the real itself. If formerly the gods had dwelt above the world, they had now become its centre.'[23] Previously Hegel's conceptual rationalism had been rejected by Marx, the follower of Kant and Fichte, the romantic subjectivist who considered the highest being to be separate from earthly reality. Now, however, it began to seem as though the Idea was immanent in the real. 'I had read fragments of Hegel's philosophy and had found its grotesque craggy melody unpleasing. I wished to dive into the ocean once again but with the definite intention of discovering our

21. *MEGA* I, i (2) 218; Easton and Guddat, p. 46.
22. ibid.
23. ibid.

mental nature to be just as determined, concrete, and firmly established as our physical – no longer to practise the art of fencing but to bring pure pearls into the sunlight.'[24]

In order to clarify his mind Marx began to write – a procedure he had adopted before and would adopt many times later. He produced a twenty-four page dialogue entitled 'Cleanthes, or the Starting Point and Necessary Progress of Philosophy'. For this purpose he acquainted himself with natural science, history and a study of the works of Schelling. The influence of the latter is plain in Marx's description of the dialogue as reuniting art and science and comprising a 'philosophical-dialectical discussion of the Godhead manifested as a concept *per se*, as Religion, as Nature, and as History'. This dialogue ended with Marx's conversion to Hegelianism: 'my last sentence was the beginning of the Hegelian system, and this task ... this darling child of mine, nurtured in moonlight, bears me like a false-hearted siren into the clutches of the enemy'.[25] Thus Marx had gone through the same evolution as classical German philosophy itself, from Kant and Fichte through Schelling to Hegel.

This process of giving up his romantic idealism and delivering himself over to 'the enemy' was an extremely radical and painful one for Marx.[26] He describes its immediate results as follows:

Because of my vexation, I was for several days quite unable to think. Like a lunatic I ran around in the garden beside the Spree's dirty water 'which washes the soul and dilutes tea'. I even went out hunting with my host and then returned hotfoot to Berlin wishing to embrace every loafer at the street

24. *MEGA* I, i (2) 218 f.; Easton and Guddat, pp. 46 f.
25. *MEGA* I, i (2) 219; Easton and Guddat, p. 47.
26. cf. *MEGA* I, i (2) 29; Easton and Guddat, p. 47.

corners ... because of the futility of my lost labours, from consuming vexation at having to make an idol of a view I detest. I feel sick.

His conversion to Hegel was completed firstly by a thorough reading of Hegel: while sick he 'got to know Hegel from beginning to end, together with most of his disciples'. Secondly, he joined a sort of Hegelian discussion group: 'through several meetings with friends in Stralow I became a member of a Doctors' Club to which some instructors and my most intimate friend in Berlin, Dr Rutenberg, belong. In discussions many a conflicting opinion was voiced, and I was more and more chained to the current world-philosophy from which I had thought to escape.' This club met regularly in a café in the Französische Strasse and was a hard-drinking and boisterous company. Adolf Rutenberg, whom Marx mentions here, was a geography teacher who had formerly spent some time in prison as a member of the *Burchenschaft* and who regularly wrote for the Hamburg newspaper *Telegraph Deutschlands*. When they were both later on the staff of the *Rheinische Zeitung*, Marx came to regard Rutenberg as a mere cipher. Another member of the club was Karl Friedrich Köppen, a history teacher at a local school who was later to become an acknowledged expert on the origins of Buddhism; Marx mentions him in admiration in the preface to his doctoral thesis.[27] The leading light in the club was Bruno Bauer, who had been lecturing in theology at the university since 1834 and was to be Marx's closest friend for the next four years. He was at that time a disciple of the orthodox Hegelian Marheineke, but soon appeared as spokesman for the radical Young Hegelians.[28]

27. On Köppen, see especially H. Hirsch, *Denker und Kämpfer* (Europäische Verlagsanstalt, Frankfurt-am-Main, 1955) pp. 19–81.

28. On Bruno Bauer, see G. Mayer, 'Die Anfänge des politischen Radikalismus im vormärzlichen Preussen', *Zeitschrift für Politik,* VI

Marx was undoubtedly also strongly influenced by Eduard Gans, Professor of Law at Berlin University, whose lectures he attended more regularly than any others. Gans was a baptized Jew, a liberal Hegelian, who elaborated the master's views in the fields of jurisprudence and history. He was a brilliant lecturer and attracted very large audiences. Progress was his watchword: he very much approved of the French Revolution of 1830 and advocated an English style of monarchy. He appreciated the importance of social questions and sympathized with the Saint-Simonians, whose ideas he publicized in a book that appeared in 1836.

'The Saint–Simonians', wrote Gans,

have rightly observed that slavery has not disappeared and that, even if it has been formally abolished, it nevertheless really exists in a most absolute manner. Just as once master and slave were opposed to each other, and then later patrician and plebeian, then sovereign and vassal, so are opposed today the man who is idle and the man who works. One has only to visit the factories to see hundreds of emaciated and miserable men and women who sacrifice their health for the service and profit of a single man and exchange all the pleasures of life for a meagre pittance. Is it not pure slavery to exploit man like a beast by allowing him only the freedom to die of hunger? Is it not possible to awaken in these miserable proletarians a moral conscience and lead them to take an active part in the work that at present they execute automatically?

(1913); E. Barnikol, *Das entdeckte Christentum im Vormärz* (Jena, 1927); S. Hook, *From Hegel to Marx*, 2nd edn. (Ann Arbor, Michigan, 1962); C. Cesa, 'Bruno Bauer e la filosofia dell' autoscienza (1841–1843)', *Giornale Critico della Filosofia Italiana*, I (Florence, 1960); G. A. van den Bergh van Eysinga, 'Die Tätigkeit von Bruno Bauer in Bonn', *Annali*, 1963 (Milan, 1964); H. Stuke, *Philosophie der Tat* (Ernst Klett Verlag, Stuttgart, 1963); McLellan, *The Young Hegelians and Karl Marx*.

The view that the state should provide for the needs of the most numerous and poorest class is one of the most profound of our time.... Future history will speak more than once of the struggle of the proletarians against the middle classes. The Middle Ages possessed a social organization of work in its corporations. The corporations are destroyed and cannot be re-established. But has not work, now liberated, escaped from the despotism of the corporation and absolute domination of the master to fall under that of the factory-owner? Is there no means of remedying this situation? Yes, there is: the free corporation, socialization.[29]

Although many of these ideas were to reappear in Marx's writings, they had little influence upon him for the present. He was still thinking of a law career: he proposed to his father that, on finishing his studies in Berlin, he would go on to the provincial appeal court at Münster. From there he planned to become an assistant judge and eventually get a university professorship. He also mentions in passing a plan to edit a review of aesthetics, saying that Bruno Bauer and Rutenberg had already obtained the co-operation of 'all the aesthetic notables of the Hegelian school'.

Heinrich Marx's reply to this letter did not take up the philosophical questions raised: it consisted more of renewed complaints about his son's lack of order, neglect of his family, and extravagance. A fatal illness overtook him soon afterwards and he died in March 1838, after which Marx's links with his family became very tenuous.

As a whole, this letter details Marx's conversion to the prevailing philosophy of the day. But it does not contain any criticism of Hegel or any indication of Marx's future intellectual development. Any claim that Marx's concep-

29. E. Gans, *Rückblicke auf Personen und Zustände* (Berlin, 1836) pp. 99 ff. Further on Gans, see H. Reissner, *Eduard Gans. Ein Leben im Vormärz* (Tübingen, 1965).

tions are already here *in nuce* is to read into the text ideas for which at this time there is no evidence.

3. MARX'S DISSERTATION

a. Introductory

In the year after writing this letter to his father, Marx abandoned almost all formal teaching at the university and concentrated on his own reading and discussions with his intimates in the Doctor's Club. The only lectures that he did attend were on philosophical subjects, and his note-books for the next two years were filled with excerpts from Hegel, Aristotle, Spinoza, Leibniz, Hume and Kant. Meanwhile the necessity of earning his living was becoming more pressing: his father, while he lived, urged Karl to lay the foundations of a career that would soon allow him to marry his 'angel of a girl'. His mother took up the same theme: she complained that the Westphalen family despised her, and Jenny herself was increasingly ill at ease in her own family. All these factors led Marx to bring his studies to an end by the composition of a doctoral thesis that he hoped would enable him to obtain a university teaching post.[30]

This thesis, begun towards the end of 1838 and submitted in April 1841, survives in an incomplete state, and is the major source for the knowledge of Marx's ideas in this period. The preliminary notes for the thesis, written during 1839, consist of seven exercise books which Marx entitled 'Epicurean Philosophy' and whose content goes far beyond that of the thesis, dealing with such subjects as the relation between Epicureanism and Stoicism, the con-

30. For the origins of the thesis, see Mehring's introduction to Marx, Engels and Lassalle, *Nachlass*, I, 51 ff.

cept of the sage in Greek philosophy, the views of Socrates and Plato on religion and the prospects of post-Hegelian philosophy. The thesis itself, entitled 'The Difference between the Democritean and the Epicurean Philosophies of Nature', consisted of a criticism of those who had equated the natural philosophies of Democritus and Epicurus and a catalogue of the differences between these philosophies. There was an appendix on Plutarch's criticism of Epicurus and two lengthy notes on Hegel and Schelling.[31]

b. Choice of Subject

Marx's interest in Epicurus seems to have been stimulated by discussions with his fellow Young Hegelians. It is worth while pointing out that since Marx was not a direct disciple of Hegel, his knowledge of Hegel's doctrines was always acquired through, or accompanied by, the commentaries of his disciples. His first serious study of Hegel was undertaken at the same time as that of 'most of his

31. These are all reprinted in *MEGA* I, i (1) 1 ff. The thesis has been re-edited (though without the preliminary notes) in K. Marx, *Die Doktordissertation*, ed. G. Mende (Jena, 1964) and has been translated (equally truncated) as an appendix to: D. Livergood, *Marx's Philosophy of Action* (The Hague, 1967). The MEGA text is fully reproduced in K. Marx, *Texte zu Methode und Praxis*, ed. Hillmann I. There is also an Italian translation by A. Sabbetti, *Sulla fondazione del materialismo storico* (Florence, 1962). There are two book-length discussions of Marx's thesis: R. Sannwald, *Marx und die Antike* (Basel, 1957); Hillmann, *Marx und Hegel*. Useful discussions of the philosophical aspects are contained in H. Popitz, *Der entfremdete Mensch* (Basel, 1953); M. Friedrich, *Philosophie und Ökonomie beim jungen Marx* (Berlin, 1960); M. dal Pra, *La dialettica in Marx* (Laterza, Bari, 1965) pp. 23 ff. There is also useful material in Cornu, *Karl Marx et Friedrich Engels*, I, 179 ff.; C. Wackenheim, *La Faillite de la religion d'après Karl Marx* (P.U.F., Paris, 1963) pp. 90 ff.

disciples'. And it was in discussions at the Doctors' Club that Marx 'was more and more chained to the current world-philosophy'. The Young Hegelians, following Fichte, were in the course of reaffirming the primacy of the subjective over substance and felt a profound sympathy for the post-Aristotelians. The reason was twofold: after the 'total philosophy' of Hegel the Young Hegelians felt themselves in the same position as the Greeks after Aristotle; secondly, they thought that the post-Aristotelian philosophies contained the essential elements of modern thought: they had laid the philosophical foundations of the Roman Empire, had profoundly influenced early Christian morality and also contained rationalist traits of the eighteenth-century Enlightenment. Two in particular of Marx's friends in the Doctors' Club had studied this period: Bruno Bauer, who had recently moved from orthodox Hegelianism to an increasingly radical outlook, viewed post-Aristotelian philosophy as the spiritual basis of early Christianity. He thought that the individualistic philosophers, following on the break-up of the classical world and its objective social ties, had prepared the way for Christianity. In Christianity, however, man was the object of a God he himself had created and thus it fell below the level of human consciousness attained by the atheistic, hellenistic thinkers with their strict separation of philosophy and religion. Karl Friedrich Köppen, too, in his book *Friedrich der Grosse und seine Widersacher* ('Frederick the Great and his Opponents'), which was dedicated to Marx, made connections between the hellenistic thinkers, atheism and the Enlightenment. His book was a eulogy of Frederick William II and the principles of the Enlightenment. Köppen maintained that the king's greatness came from combining the culture of Epicureanism, Stoic devotion to the common good and Sceptic tolerance and lack of dogma.

Marx's presentation of his thesis is along similar lines. He wrote in the preface that the thesis 'should be considered as only the preliminary to a larger work in which I shall describe in detail the cycle of Epicurean, Stoic and Sceptic philosophies in their relationship to the whole of Greek speculation'.[32] Hegel, Marx said, had by and large correctly described the general characteristics of these systems:

But the admirably broad and bold plan of his history of philosophy which really gave birth to the history of philosophy as a subject, made it impossible to enter into details: and also his conception of what he called 'speculative par excellence' prevented this giant of a thinker from recognizing the great importance of these systems for the history of Greek philosophy and the Greek mind in general. These systems are the key to the true history of Greek philosophy.[32a]

In the opening paragraphs of his thesis Marx elaborates on why he thinks these writers hold the key to the history of Greek philosophy and to the contemporary philosophical scene. These philosophers are 'at the origin of the Roman ethos, the form in which Greece became Rome'. They are 'so full of character, so concentrated and essential that the modern world itself must accord them full citizen rights'. 'Is it not', Marx continues, 'a remarkable occurrence that after the total philosophies of Plato and Aristotle, new systems should arise that do not depend on these philosophies, systems that are so rich in spirit, but yet have recourse to the simplest of schools – the natural philosophies in physics and the Socratic school in ethics?'[33] In short, Marx's choice of subject was destined to throw light on the contemporary post-Hegelian situation in philosophy

32. *MEGA* I, i (1) 9. 32a. ibid.
33. *MEGA* I, i (1) 14.

by the examination of a parallel period in the history of Greek philosophy.

c. Marx's Preliminary Notes

The most interesting passage in these notes is one where Marx deals with the philosophical climate following on the world-philosophy of Hegel. Philosophy has now arrived at a turning point:

> Just as there are nodal points in philosophy that in themselves rise to concretion, form abstract principles into a totality, and thus interrupt a straight-line continuation, so there are also moments when philosophy turns its eyes to the external world. No longer reflectively but like a practical person it spins intrigues with the world.... Just as Prometheus, having stolen fire from heaven, begins to build houses and settle on the earth, so philosophy, having extended itself to the world, turns against the apparent world. So now with the Hegelian philosophy.[34]

This and the passage that follows are among the most obscure that Marx ever wrote, partly because they are only personal notes and partly because Marx was probably not sure of his own thought and spoke very metaphorically. A 'nodal point' here was a philosophy that fused into an interlocking whole the principles of the philosophies preceding it. This ended a stage in the development of a philosophy and, while summing up the previous steady progression, compelled future thought to strike out in a fresh direction. In this case, philosophy began a 'practical movement', spinning 'intrigues with the world'. Here, discovering that the world was in the process of changing, it entered into collision with it. Marx goes on to describe this process of opposition between philosophy and the world,

34. ibid. 131; Easton and Guddat, p. 52.

by outlining the position of philosophy at the time of Hegel's death:

As philosophy has closed itself into a complete, total world – the outline of this totality is in general conditioned by its development, the basis of the form which reverses itself in a practical relationship to actuality – the totality of the world is implicitly split, and this split is driven to extremes because spiritual existence has become free, enriched to universality. The heart beat has implicitly become in a concrete way the characteristic of the whole organism. The diremption of the world is not causal while its sides are totalities. Hence, the world is self-divided as opposed to a total philosophy, one in itself.[35]

Put more simply, this means that with Hegel philosophy has, by its very completeness and universality, become unreal and opposed to the world which continues to be divided. Thus philosophy itself became split:

The manifestation of the activity of this philosophy is thereby also split and contradictory; its objective universality reverts to subjective forms of individual consciousness in which it lives. Common harps will sound under any hand; aeolian harps, only when the storm strikes them. But one must not let oneself be misled by the storm that follows a great world-philosophy.[36]

Anyone, Marx continued, who did not understand this necessary development had to deny the possibility of continuing to philosophize after such a total system: to such a man the appearance of Zeno or Epicurus after such a thinker as Aristotle would be incomprehensible.

What was needed was a fundamental change of direction:

35. *MEGA* I, i (1) 132; Easton and Guddat, p. 52.
36. *MEGA* I, i (1) 132; Easton and Guddat, pp. 52 f.

In such times, fearful souls take the reverse point of view of valiant commanders. They believe they are able to repair the damage by decreasing forces, by dispersal, by a peace treaty with real needs, while Themistocles, when Athens was threatened with devastation, persuaded the Athenians to leave it for good and found a new Athens on the sea, on another element.[37]

Marx goes on to say that in such a period two alternatives present themselves: either to imitate feebly what has gone before or to undertake a really fundamental upheaval:

Furthermore, we must not forget that the time following such catastrophes is an iron one, happy if the battles of Titans mark them, lamentable if the time is like the lamely limping centuries of great epochs of art, busied with casting in wax, plaster and copper that which once leapt from the Carraran marble as did Pallas Athena from Zeus's head. Titan-like, however, are the times that follow an implicitly total philosophy and its subjective forms of development, for the diremption – its unity – is tremendous. Thus, Rome came after the Stoic, Sceptic, and Epicurean philosophies. They are unhappy and iron, for their gods are dead, and the new goddess still has immediately the dark form of fate, of pure light or pure darkness. She lacks the day's colours. The kernel of this unhappiness is that the soul of the time, the spiritual Monas, in itself satiated and ideally formed in all aspects, can recognize no actuality which has already developed without it. The happy element in such unhappiness, then, is the subjective form, the modality in which philosophy as subjective consciousness relates itself to actuality.

Thus, for example, the Epicurean, Stoic philosophy was the happy fortune of its time. Similarly the hawk-moth seeks the lamplight of privacy when the sun has set.[38]

Marx finishes this lengthy note by pointing out again that after a total philosophy the new direction taken is determined by the character of that philosophy:

37. *MEGA* I, i (1) 132; Easton and Guddat. p. 53.
38. *MEGA* I, i (2) 132 f.; Easton and Guddat, p. 53.

The other aspect, more important for the historian of philosophy, is the fact that this reversal of the philosophers, their transubstantiation in flesh and blood, is distinguished by the characteristic which an implicitly total and concrete philosophy bears like a birthmark.... But it is important, philosophically speaking, to stress this aspect since from the specific character of this reversal deductions can be made as to the immanent determination and world-historical character of the course of philosophy. What formerly appeared as growth is now determinateness; implicitly existing negativity has become negation. Here we observe, as it were, the *curriculum vitae* of a philosophy focused to the subjective point, just as one can conclude a hero's life story from the way he died.[39]

Marx's language in this note, though often vivid, is very obscure. The general atmosphere of crisis that pervades it was common to all the Young Hegelians. Hegel himself had announced: 'it is something not difficult to see that our time is a time of birth and transition to a new period. The spirit has broken with what was hitherto the world of its existence and imagination, and is about to submerge all this in the past; it is at work giving itself a new form.'[40] Bruno Bauer, with whom Marx kept up a constant correspondence while he was composing his thesis, wrote in 1840: 'The catastrophe will be terrible and must be great. I would almost say that it will be greater and more horrible than that which heralded Christianity's entrance on the world scene.'[41]

d. Marx's Thesis

In the preface to his thesis Marx briefly outlines previous, mistaken interpretations of Epicurus's philosophy and

---

39. *MEGA* I, i (2) 133; Easton and Guddat, p. 54.
40. Hegel, *Werke* II, 10.
41. *MEGA* I, i (2) 241 ff.

mentions the insufficiency of Hegel's treatment of the period. He then justifies his own inclusion of a criticism of Plutarch's attack on Epicurus's atheism, and adds a paean in praise of the supremacy of philosophy over all other disciplines, and in particular over theology. To prove his point, Marx quotes Hume:

'Tis certainly a kind of indignity to philosophy, whose sovereign authority ought everywhere to be acknowledged, to oblige her on every occasion to make apologies for her conclusions, and justify herself to every particular art and science, which may be offended at her. This puts one in mind of a king arraign'd for high treason against his subjects.[42]

Thus Marx makes his own the Young Hegelian criticism of the master's reconciliation of philosophy and religion. He continues:

As long as a single drop of blood pulses in her world-conquering and totally free heart, philosophy will continually shout at her opponents the cry of Epicurus: 'Impiety does not consist in destroying the gods of the crowd but rather in ascribing to the gods the ideas of the crowd.'
Philosophy makes no secret of it. The proclamation of Prometheus: 'In one word – I hate all gods' is her own profession, her own slogan against all gods of heaven and earth who do not recognize man's self-consciousness as the highest divinity. There shall be none other beside it.[43]

Marx thought that it was characteristic of the post-Aristotelian philosophies that in them 'all elements of self-consciousness ... are fully represented'.[44] This 'self-consciousness' was the central concept of the philosophy

42. *MEGA* I, i (1) 10; the quotation is from Hume's *Treatise of Human Nature*, ed. L. Selby-Bigge (Oxford, 1888) p. 250.
43. ibid. p. 10.
44. ibid. p. 14.

that the Young Hegelians, and Bruno Bauer in particular, were elaborating. Hegel, too, had referred to the post-Aristotelian period as that of self-consciousness,[45] but his radical disciples took it out of its carefully circumscribed context and made it into an absolute principle. For them, man's self-consciousness develops continually and realizes that forces it had thought separate from itself – religion for example – are really its own creation. Thus the task of self-consciousness and its principal weapon, philosophical criticism, is to expose all the forces and ideas that stand opposed to the free development of this human self-consciousness.[46]

This enthusiasm for the philosophy of self-consciousness is reflected in the body of the thesis where Marx unfavourably contrasts the mechanistic determinism of Democritus with the Epicurean ethic of liberty.[47] Democritus, a native of Abdera in Thrace, wrote at the end of the fifth century B.C., and summed up, in his theory of atoms and the void, the previous two hundred years of Greek physical speculation. Epicurus taught more than a century later in an Athens marked by the general social chaos of the post-Alexandrine epoch and was concerned to supply principles for the conduct of individuals.[48] Marx begins his account of the relationship of the two philosophers with a paradox: Epicurus held all appearances to

45. Cf. Hegel, *Werke*, II, 131 ff.

46. See in particular on this, C. Cesa, 'Bruno Bauer e la filosofia dell' auto-scienza (1841–1843)', *Giornale Critico della Filosofia Italiana'* I (1960); McLellan, *The Young Hegelians and Karl Marx*, pp. 48 ff.

47. Marx's preference seems to be arrived at solely by comparing their two respective moral philosophies; as philosophers and natural scientists, Democritus is by far the more profound and original thinker. cf. also: C. Bailey, 'Karl Marx on Greek Atomism', *The Classical Quarterly* XXII (1928).

48. See further B. Farrington, *The Faith of Epicurus* (Weidenfeld & Nicolson, London, 1967) pp. 7 f.

be objectively real but at the same time, since he wished to conserve freedom of the will, denied that the world was governed by immutable laws and thus in fact seemed to decry the objective reality of nature. Democritus, on the other hand, was very sceptical about the reality of appearance, but yet held the world to be governed by necessity. From this Marx concludes, rightly, that Epicurus's physics was really only a part of his moral philosophy. He did not merely copy Democritus's physics, as was commonly thought, but introduced the idea of spontaneity into the movement of the atoms, and to Democritus's world of inanimate nature ruled by mechanical laws he added a world of animate nature in which the human will operated. Marx thus prefers the views of Epicurus for two reasons: firstly, his emphasis on the absolute autonomy of the human spirit has freed men from all superstitions of transcendent objects; secondly, the emphasis on 'free individual self-consciousness' shows one way of going beyond the system of a 'total philosophy'.

It was above all this liberating aspect of Epicurus that Marx admired. A few years later in the *German Ideology* he called Epicurus 'the genuine radically enlightened mind of antiquity',[49] and referred to him often in his later writings in similar terms. A counterpart to this enthusiasm for Epicurus is the appendix which attacks Plutarch and particularly his treatise entitled 'It is impossible to live happily by following the principles of Epicurus'.[50] Taking each of Plutarch's arguments separately, Marx demonstrates that the opposite conclusion follows. Marx asserts

49. *MEGA* I, v, 122.
50. This appendix does not survive, but can be reconstructed from the preliminary notes: see *MEGA* I, i, p. xxxi; D. Baumgarten, 'Über den ''verloren geglaubten'' Anhang zu Karl Marx' Doktor-dissertation', in *Gegenwarts-probleme der Soziologie* (Eisermann, Potsdam, 1949).

that belief in gods results from detaching human virtues from their proper subject – man – and attaching them to an illusory subject. Similarly, immortality of the soul reduces itself to the individual's laying claim to the universal. All this is plainly inspired by the first publications of Feuerbach who, as early as 1839, had begun to criticize Hegel's dialectic from a humanist point of view. Marx devotes much space to exposing the fallacies of Plutarch's criticisms of Epicurus, since he considered Plutarch to be typical of the attack on philosophy from a theological point of view. He wrote in the preface: 'We have added as an appendix a criticism of the polemic of Plutarch against Epicurus's theology. The reason for this is that this polemic is not an isolated phenomenon, but represents a whole tradition: it expresses perfectly the attitude of the theological mind to philosophy.'[51]

e. Notes to the Thesis

The idea of the opposition between theology and religion is the main theme of an extended note that Marx added to his thesis at the end of 1841. It was directed primarily against Schelling, who had just been summoned to Berlin by Frederick William IV in order to 'root out the dragonseed of Hegelianism'.[52] In his lectures, entitled *The Philosophy of Revelation*, Schelling drew a distinction between a negative, purely rational philosophy and a positive one whose real content is the evolution of the divine in history and as it is recorded in the various mythologies and religions of mankind. Schelling's lectures were accompanied by much publicity and at first attracted wide attention: Engels, Kierkegaard and Bakunin were all present at his

51. *MEGA* I, i (1) 10.

52. Frederick William IV to Bunsen, in Chr. von Bunsen, *Aus seinen Briefen* (Leipzig, 1869) II, 133.

inaugural lecture. The reaction of the Hegelians was strong and Marx's not least: his technique here was to contrast what Schelling was then saying with his earlier writings. There are often elements in the writings of the Young Hegelians that seem to go back beyond Hegel and in particular to Fichte's ideas on man's dialectical self-creation: Köppen was a declared disciple of Fichte, and both Bruno Bauer and Hess incorporated Fichtean elements into their thought.[53] Marx begins his note by quoting three passages from the early works of Schelling that have a close affinity with Fichte:

Weak reason, however, is not reason which knows no objective God, but wants to recognize one. In general, Herr Schelling would be well advised to recall his first writings. For instance, he says in the piece on the Self as the principle of philosophy: 'If we assume, for example, that in so far as God defined as object is the real basis of our nature, then God himself enters the sphere of our knowledge as object and hence cannot be the ultimate point for us on which this entire sphere depends.' And we remind Herr Schelling of the concluding sentence of his letter mentioned above: 'It is time to acquaint the new humanity with freedom of mind and no longer tolerate its crying about its lost restrictions.' If it was already time in A.D. 1795, how about the year 1841?[54]

Marx then goes on to claim that Hegel inverted the traditional proofs for the existence of God and thereby refuted them. Whereas traditional theology said: 'Since contingency truly exists, God exists', Hegel turned this into: 'Since contingency does not exist, God or the Absolute does.' Marx then posed a dilemma: the first possibility was that the proofs for the existence of God were

53. For an account of the origins of Marxism that lays emphasis on the contribution of Fichte, see R. Garaudy, *Karl Marx: The Evolution of his Thought* (Lawrence & Wishart, London, 1967).

54. *MEGA* I, i (1) 80; Easton and Guddat, p. 64.

tautologies, like the ontological argument which Marx states in the form: 'What I conceive for myself as actual is an actual conception for me.'[55] In that case any gods would have an equal reality. Kant's famous refutation of the ontological proof by comparing one hundred imaginary pound notes with one hundred real ones was not to the point: in fact, paper money was very similar to belief in gods. If you imported paper money into a country where it was not recognized then its value would be purely imaginary. 'If someone had taken a Wendish god to the ancient Greeks, he would have found proof for the non-existence of this god, because this god did not exist for the Greeks. What a certain country is for foreign gods, the country of reason is for God altogether – namely, a place where God no longer exists.[56]

The second possibility was that 'the proofs for the existence of God are nothing but proofs for the existence of the essentially human self-consciousness and logical explications of it. Take the ontological argument. What existence is immediate in being thought? Self-consciousness.'[57] Marx claims that in this sense all proofs for the existence of God are proofs for his non-existence. For a valid proof would have to run: 'Since nature is imperfect, God exists.' But this would amount to saying that non-rationality constituted God's existence.

Marx finished his note with its strange mixture of post-Hegelian philosophy and the simple rationalism of the Enlightenment by quoting two more passages from the early Schelling: 'When you pre-suppose the idea of an objective God, how can you speak of laws which reason

---

55. Marx cites this in its classical, not in its Hegelian, form. His treatment borders on caricature: see Wackenheim, *La Faillite de la religion d'après Karl Marx*, p. 101.

56. *MEGA* I, i (1) 81; Easton and Guddat, p. 65.

57. *MEGA* I, i (1) 81; Easton and Guddat, pp. 65 f.

produces from itself, since autonomy can be attributed only to an absolute free being?'

'It is a crime against humanity to conceal principles which are generally communicable.'[58]

The second important note appended to the thesis takes up the themes already treated in the passage in the preliminary notes on the future of philosophy after Hegel's total system. In the first section of this note, Marx deals with the common charge of Hegel's having 'compromised' with reaction. 'In regard to Hegel ... it is out of mere ignorance that his disciples explain this or that determination of his system by accommodation and the like or, in a word, morally. They forget that a very short time ago they enthusiastically adhered to all aspects of his one-sidedness; clear evidence of this fact is found in their own writings.'[59] Marx defends Hegel by drawing a distinction between the inner mind of the philosopher and the exterior form in which he expresses himself:

It is conceivable that a philosopher commits this or that apparent *non sequitur* out of this or that accommodation. He himself may be conscious of it. But he is not conscious that the possibility of this apparent accommodation is rooted in the inadequacy of his principle or in its inadequate formulation. Hence, if a philosopher has accommodated himself, his disciples have to explain from his inner essential consciousness what for him had the form of an esoteric consciousness. In this way what appears as progress of consciousness is progress of knowledge as well. It is not that the particular consciousness of the philosopher is suspect; rather, his essential form of consciousness is constructed, raised to a particular form and meaning, and at the same time superseded.[60]

This distinction between an esoteric and an exoteric Hegel

58. *MEGA* I, i (1) 81; Easton and Guddat, p. 66.
59. *MEGA* I, i (1) 63; Easton and Guddat, p. 60.
60. *MEGA* I, i (1) 64; Easton and Guddat, p. 61.

was common among the Young Hegelians.[61] Bruno Bauer even went so far as to claim that the real message of Hegel was 'atheism, republicanism and revolution'.[62] Similarly, Marx wished to use Hegelian principles to interpret Hegel.

Marx now turns again to the problem of post-Hegelian philosophy and of what he calls 'the transition from discipline to freedom':

It is a psychological law that the theoretical mind, having become free in itself, turns into practical energy. Emerging as will from Amenthes' shadow world, it turns against worldly actuality which exists outside it. . . . The practice of philosophy, however, is itself theoretical. It is criticism which measures individual existence against essence, particular actuality against the idea. But this direct realization of philosophy is burdened with contradictions in its innermost essence, and this essence manifests itself in appearance and puts its stamp thereon.[63]

This is Marx's first mention of his notion of *praxis* that was to become so central to his later thought. The concept had been originated by August von Cieszkowski, a Polish count who had studied philosophy in Berlin under the orthodox Hegelian Michelet.[64] Cieszkowski had also visited Paris and acquainted himself with socialist ideas, and in 1838 he published a small book, *Prolegomena zur Historiosophie* ('Prolegomena to a Science of History'), that was to prove seminal among the Young Hegelians. For Cieszkowski was the first to talk seriously of a transition from

61. The *locus classicus* is Bruno Bauer, *Die Posaune des jüngsten Gerichts über Hegel den Atheisten und Antichristen* (Leipzig, 1841), reprinted in K. Löwith, *Die Hegelsche Linke* (Stuttgart, 1962).

62. Bauer, op. cit., p. 42.

63. *MEGA* I, i (1) 64; Easton and Guddat, pp. 61 f.

64. For a commentary on Marx's *Dissertation* that lays great emphasis on Cieszkowski's influence, see R. Lauth, 'Einflüsse slawischer Denker auf die Genesis der Marxschen Weltanschauung', *Orientalia Christiana Periodica* (Rome, 1955), XXII, 399 ff.

thought to action. The main theme of his book was that whereas Hegel had only dealt with the present and the past, philosophy should now deal with the future: in much the same way as Cuvier reconstructed the whole animal from a single tooth, so philosophy should attempt to build the future. This philosophy of the future had to be orientated towards society and would thus become practical:

> Philosophy has therefore to resign itself to becoming mainly *applied* philosophy; and just as the poetry of art becomes transformed into the prose of thought, so philosophy must descend from the heights of theory into *praxis*. Practical philosophy, or, more accurately, the philosophy of *praxis* (whose concrete impact on life and social conditions amounts to the employment of both within concrete activity) – this is the future fate of philosophy in general. . . . Just as thought and reflection overcame the *beaux-arts*, so the deed and social activity will now overcome philosophy.[65]

This notion of a transition to a philosophy of action inspired many of the Young Hegelians, particularly Moses Hess, and was even used by Bruno Bauer in an idealist form. Bauer was writing to Marx at the beginning of 1841: 'Theory is now the strongest *praxis* and we cannot say in advance to what extent it will become practical.'[66]

Marx now develops the passage on the relation between philosophy and the world as he had seen it when writing the preliminary notes. He sees two sides to the problem: as regards the objective side, the realization of philosophy, he says:

> While philosophy, as will, turns toward the apparent world, the system is reduced to an abstract totality, that is, it becomes

65. A. von Cieszkowski, *Prolegomena zur Historiosophie* (Berlin, 1838) p. 142.
66. *MEGA* I, i (2) 250.

one side of the world facing another. Its relation to the world is reflexive. Enthusiastic in its drive to realize itself, it enters into tension with everything else. The inner self-contentedness and roundedness is broken down. The former inner light becomes a consuming flame turning outward. The consequence, hence, is that the world's becoming philosophical is at the same time philosophy's becoming worldly, that its realization is at the same time its loss, that what it combats outside is its own inner defect, that just in this combat philosophy itself falls into the faults which it combats in its opponent, and that it transcends these faults only by falling victim to them. Whatever opposes it and what philosophy combats is always the very same thing as philosophy, only with reversed factors.[67]

Interesting here is the theme of the disappearance of philosophy. Cieszkowski had already called Hegel's system 'the beginning of the end of philosophy'[68] and these ideas of Marx are similar to his later ideas on the 'abolition of philosophy by the proletariat'.[69]

There is also, Marx says, a subjective side to the problem. This is:

the relation of the philosophical system which is actualized to its intellectual supporters and to the individual self-consciousnesses in which its progress becomes manifest. The minds of these philosophers occupy a position of mediation between, and opposition to, philosophy and the world. Their liberation of the world from non-philosophy is at the same time their own liberation from the philosophy which fettered it as a definite system.[70]

The post-Hegelian situation reveals two opposing parties. The first, the liberal party, adheres to the concept

67. *MEGA* I, i (1) 64 f.; Easton and Guddat, p. 62.
68. Cieszkowski, *Prolegomena zur Historiosophie*, p. 101.
69. See below, pp. 192 ff.
70. *MEGA* I, i (1) 65; Easton and Guddat, p. 62.

and to philosophy; the second, that of positive philosophy, adheres to the non-concept, to the element of reality.

The activity of the former [says Marx] is criticism; hence, precisely the turning outward of philosophy. The act of the latter is the attempt to philosophize, thus the turning inward of philosophy. It grasps the deficiency as immanent to philosophy, while the former conceives it as a deficiency of the world to be made philosophical. Each of these parties does exactly what the other wants to do and what each one itself does not want to do; but the former, with its inner contradiction, is conscious in general of principle and aim. In the second appears perversity, so to speak, insanity as such. In content only the liberal party makes real progress, because it is the party of the concept while positive philosophy is capable of achieving merely demands and tendencies whose form contradicts its meaning.[71]

Both these parties are within the Hegelian school and it is not difficult to see that Marx's sympathies lie with the liberal party. The 'positive philosophers', who seem to be the same as the 'fearful souls' whom Marx criticized in the parallel passage in the preliminary notes, are the centre of the Hegelian school, men like Michelet and Cieszkowski, who concentrate simply on trying to better philosophy. The liberal or critical school is that group of Young Hegelians influenced by Bruno Bauer.

Marx finishes with a summary of the process that he has been describing: 'What seems to be, first of all, philosophy's wrong relation to and diremption with the world, turns secondly into a diremption of the individual philosophical self-consciousness in itself and finally appears as philosophy's external separation and duality, as two opposed philosophical directions.'[72]

Marx's doctoral thesis and the notes that accompany it

71. *MEGA* I, i (1) 65; Easton and Guddat, p. 63.
72. *MEGA* I, i (1) 65 f.; Easton and Guddat, p. 63.

are typical of the intellectual atmosphere in which he composed it. Many of the themes that Marx was later to elaborate in a unique manner occur here for the first time – in particular the notion of *praxis* and of the abolition of philosophy – but they occur in a form common to Marx and his contemporaries. Marx was not only concerned with writing his thesis during these years; the other projects he was engaged in similarly reflect the Young Hegelian climate and the discussions in the Doctors' Club. Here Marx was not only on the receiving end. His friend Köppen wrote to him that until Marx left Berlin, he had had 'no idea of my own, that I had, so to speak, thought out for myself'[73] and added his opinion that many of the ideas in Bauer's essay 'The Christian State', which was the first Young Hegelian essay to draw political consequences from the criticism of religion, originated in Marx. These were more generally conceived in the spirit of the preface to the thesis: direct opposition between philosophy and religion. In early 1840 Marx was thinking of writing a *Philosophy of Religion* and also of giving a course of lectures at Bonn attacking Hermes, a Catholic theologian who had tried to reconcile religion and Kantian philosophy, a project which he discussed at length with Bruno Bauer, as he did all his plans at this time. Bauer, who had known Hegel personally, was only slowly converted to the Left wing of the Hegelians and only really made up his mind well on in 1840.[74] By the summer of 1840 Marx had finished a book on the subject and sent the manuscript to Bruno Bauer with a covering letter to a publisher. The book was not published, however, and Bauer wrote to Marx concerning the covering letter: 'Perhaps you might write in such terms to your washerwoman, but not to a publisher

73. *MEGA* I, i (2) 257.

74. See the evidence for this quoted in Sens, *Karl Marx. Seine irreligiöse Entwicklung*, pp. 31 f.

from whom you are asking a favour.'[75] At the same time
Marx had the idea of writing a farce entitled *Fischer
Vapulans* against K. P. Fischer's book *Die Idee der Gott-
heit* ('The Idea of the Divinity'), a philosophical attempt
to justify theism.[76] Marx was also preoccupied with logical
problems and wished to devote a work to dialectic: he
took extensive notes on Aristotle and discussed the question in letters to Bauer. He also wished, in this context, to
write a criticism of the contemporary philosopher Trendelenburg and demonstrate that Aristotle was dialectical
whereas Trendelenburg was only formal.

Bauer was meanwhile pressing him hard to finish his
'stupid examination' and join him in Bonn. In April 1841
Marx sent off his thesis to the philosophical faculty at the
University of Jena, and he was granted the degree *in
absentia* very soon afterwards. The whole affair was
managed by Wolff, Professor of Literature there, a friend
of Heinrich Heine and an acquaintance of Marx, who had
probably informed him of the situation inside the faculty
at Jena.[77]

f. Co-operation with Bruno Bauer

As soon as his thesis was accepted Marx went to Trier for
a little time and then in July 1841 he joined Bruno Bauer
in Bonn, where the increasing difficulties of his friend
seemed to be jeopardizing both their chances of a university career. For Bauer was engaged in writing his *Kritik
der Synoptiker* ('Criticism of the Synoptic Gospels'), a

75. *MEGA* I, i (1) 244.

76. Cf. ibid. I, i (2) 237.

77. See Mende, *Karl Marx Doktordissertation*, p. 6. For a fuller
account of the Bauer–Marx correspondence leading to the presentation of the thesis, see Mehring's introduction to Marx, Engels and
Lassalle, *Nachlass*, I, 57 ff.

work which denied the historicity of Christ and portrayed
the Gospels as the mythical inventions of their authors.
The two had planned since March of the same year to
found a review entitled *Atheistic Archives*, which would
take as its foundation Bauer's Gospel criticism.[78] Certainly
Marx's atheism was of an extremely militant kind. Ruge
wrote to a friend: 'Bruno Bauer, Karl Marx, Christiansen
and Feurbach are forming a new *Montagne* and making
atheism their slogan. God, religion, immortality are cast
down from their thrones and man is proclaimed God.'[79]
And Georg Jung, a prosperous young Cologne lawyer and
supporter of the radical movement, wrote to Ruge: 'If
Marx, Bruno Bauer and Feuerbach associate to found a
theological-philosophical review, God would do well to
surround himself with all his angels and indulge in self-
pity, for these three will certainly drive him out of his
heaven.... For Marx, at any rate, the Christian religion is
one of the most immoral there is.'[80] These plans came to
nothing, however, and instead Bauer published in November what appeared to be an arch-conservative pietist
attack on Hegel, entitled *Die Posaune des jüngsten
Gerichts über Hegel den Atheisten und Antichristen* ('The
Trump of the Last Judgement on Hegel the Atheist and
Anti-Christ'). This anonymous tract was designed to show,
under the cover of attacking Hegel, that he was really an
atheist revolutionary. Marx may well have collaborated
with Bauer in writing 'The Trump', and it was thought by
some to be their joint work. In any case they both intended to produce a sequel which was to be entitled
*Hegels Hass gegen die religiöse und christliche Kunst und
seine Auflösung aller positiven Staatsgesetze* (Hegel's

78. Cf. *MEGA* I, i (2) 152.

79. A. Ruge, *Briefwechsel und Tageblätter*, ed. P. Nerrlich (Berlin,
1886) I, 239.

80. *MEGA* I, i (2) 261 f.

Hatred of Religious and Christian Art and his Destruction of all the Laws of the State'). Marx therefore began to read a series of books on art and religion. Bruno Bauer had finished his part in December 1841, but he had to publish it without Marx's contribution, for in January 1842 Baron von Westphalen fell seriously ill and died in March. These events seem also to have prevented Marx's plans for the publication of his thesis. For at the end of 1841 he wrote a new preface in which he said:

The treatise that I am now offering to the public is an old work and should have found its place in a general account of the Epicurean, Stoic and Sceptical philosophies. But now political and philosophical occupations of a totally different character do not allow me to envisage completing this. Only now has the time arrived for the understanding of the systems of the Epicureans, Stoics and Sceptics. They are the philosophers of self-consciousness.[81]

Marx returned to Trier in January and stayed there until April, though he did make a special journey to Bonn, in the company of Moses Hess, to hear Bauer lecture. Marx nevertheless wanted to publish the results of his studies in co-operation with Bauer and wrote to Ruge in March 1842: 'It seems to me that the article on Christian art, which has now become a work on religion and art considered especially with reference to Christian art, must be completely rewritten.'[82] In April Marx wrote that his study had 'almost assumed the proportions of a book',[83] but in July he had to give up the idea completely. Even at this early age (he was only twenty-three) and before he had published anything, Marx made a very strong impression on his contemporaries. Engels reported what he had heard

81. *MEGA* I, i (2) 327.
82. ibid. pp. 271 f.
83. ibid. pp. 273 f.

from his fellow Young Hegelians in a comic poem on the Berlin philosophers:

But who advances here full of impetuosity? It is a dark form from Trier, an unleashed monster, with self-assured step he hammers the ground with his heels and raises his arms in full fury to heaven as though he wished to seize the celestial vault and lower it to earth. In rage he continually deals with his redoubtable fist, as if a thousand devils were gripping his hair.[84]

Georg Jung said of Marx at this time: 'Although a devil of a revolutionary, Dr Marx is one of the most penetrating minds I know.'[85] And Moses Hess, a man of generous enthusiasm, described Marx to his friend Auerbach as

the greatest, perhaps the only, genuine philosopher now alive, who will soon ... attract the eyes of all Germany.... Dr Marx ... will give medieval religion and politics their *coup de grâce*. He combines the deepest philosophical seriousness with the most biting wit. Imagine Rousseau, Voltaire, Holbach, Lessing, Heine, and Hegel fused into one person – I say fused not juxtaposed – and you have Dr Marx.[86]

Marx, however, had no outlet for his talents: Bruno Bauer was dismissed from his teaching post at the end of March 1842 and Marx had to give up all hope of a university career. He soon began to become increasingly engaged in directly political struggles by means of journalism.

84. ibid. pp. 268 f.
85. ibid. p. 262.
86. M. Hess, *Briefwechsel*, ed. Silberner (Moulton, The Hague, 1959) p. 80.

CHAPTER FOUR

Marx the Journalist

1. THE *Hallische Jahrbücher*

Marx's interest in journalism was first aroused by Arnold Ruge, editor of the *Hallische Jahrbücher*, the leading periodical of the Young Hegelians. This was a natural career for Marx; the Young Hegelians were very journalistically-minded and managed to write a total of 20,000 pages in their various reviews.[1] Ruge came from north Prussia, and had studied philosophy at Halle University where he had become a member of the *Burschenschaften* and was subsequently imprisoned for six years. On his release he began lecturing on Plato at Halle, and became a convert to Hegelianism. On being refused a chair owing to his unorthodox views, he resigned from the university and devoted himself entirely to the editorship of the *Hallische Jahrbücher*. For this he was admirably suited: he was a man of independent means, and although no very original mind himself, he wrote quickly and well and had a very wide range of contacts.[2]

The *Hallische Jahrbücher* began appearing in 1838. During the first few months it was far from radical (even religious conservatives like Heinrich Leo contributed) and was mainly devoted to artistic or literary subjects. However, it soon began to defend Strauss and free criticism of religion, discussions which came to a head over

1. See F. Schlawe, 'Die Junghegelsche Publizistik', in *Die Welt als Geschichte* (1960).

2. See further W. Neher, *Arnold Ruge als politiker und politischer Schriftsteller* (Heidelberg, 1933).

the 'Cologne affair',[3] when Leo openly accused the Young
Hegelians of preaching atheism. Although during the early
years the contributions to the *Hallische Jahrbücher* had
in general appealed to an enlightened Prussian state, by
1840 directly political articles were beginning to follow on
the religious ones, a logic implicit in the notion of the
'Christian state'. As a result the *Jahrbücher* were banned
in Prussia in June 1841 and moved to Dresden, where they
appeared under the title *Deutsche Jahrbücher*.[4] During
1840 the Berlin Young Hegelians had begun to contribute,
and by the middle of 1841 Bruno Bauer had become a
regular writer. Marx had been introduced quite early on
to Ruge by Köppen, himself a frequent contributor; in
February 1842 he wrote his first article and sent it to Ruge
with a covering letter offering to review books and put all
his energies at the service of the *Deutsche Jahrbücher*.[5]
Marx's articles have a marked style that recurs in all his
subsequent writings. His radical and uncompromising
disposition, his love of polarization, his method of dealing
with opponents' views by *reductio ad absurdum* all led
him to write very antithetically. Slogan, climax, anaphora,
parallelism, antithesis and chiasmus (particularly the last
two) are all employed by Marx to excess.

Marx's first article dealt with the new censorship instruction issued by Frederick William IV in December
1841. On the fall of Napoleon a free Press had been promised to the Germans, but reaction soon set in: in October
1819, as a result of the Carlsbad decisions, a censorship
edict was issued that was intended to last five years but in

3. See above, p. 20.

4. For the origins and policy of the *Hallische Jahrbücher*, see H.
Kornetski, 'Die revolutionär-dialektische Entwicklung in den Hallis-
chen Jahrbüchern' (unpublished PhD. thesis, Munich, 1955);
McLellan, *The Young Hegelians and Karl Marx*, pp. 11 ff.

5. Cf. 'Letter to Ruge', *MEGA* I, i (2) 266 f.

effect proved much more durable. The censorship was very strict and even newspapers, if they dealt with religion or politics, were subject to control by the Ministries of Foreign Affairs, Interior and Culture. This censorship was slightly relaxed after the July Revolution in France, but Prussian newspapers tended to remain only pale reflections of government opinion. With the death of Frederick William III, there were widespread hopes that all this would change. And indeed the new king was the very opposite of his father. He shared with the bourgeoisie a hatred of regimented bureaucracy: his ideal was a paternalist society in which the German people acted the role of his family. So he agreed with the bourgeoisie's claim to the right to express their opinions in Parliament and the Press, and even emphasized in the censorship instruction 'the value of, and need for, frank and loyal publicity'. Since, however, what the bourgeoisie wanted to campaign for was not a romantically paternalist society, a collision was inevitable.

Marx's article was devoted to pointing out the ambiguous and contradictory character of the royal text. The king was now ordering the censors to apply less strictly the edict of 1819. In Marx's view, then, either the censors had been acting illegally for the past twenty-two years, or the objective mistakes of an institution were perhaps to be blamed on individuals so that a semblance of improvement was achieved without the reality. 'It is this kind of pseudo-liberalism that is apt to make concessions under pressure and that sacrifices persons to maintain the institution, the tools, the object. The attention of a superficial public is thus diverted. External exasperation is turned into exasperation against persons. With a change of personnel one claims to have a change in substance.'[6] The instruction

6. 'Comments on the Latest Prussian Censorship Instruction', *MEGA* I, i (1) 152; Easton and Guddat, p. 69.

said that 'censorship shall not impede any serious and un-
prejudiced pursuit of the truth'. Spinoza, among others,
was quoted to demonstrate the foolishness of trying to set
limits to truth: *verum index sui et falsi*. The only criterion of truth proposed by the king's instruction was the
censor's temperament. 'Furthermore, truth is universal. It
does not belong to me, it belongs to all; it possesses me, I
do not possess it. A style is my property, my spiritual individuality. *Le style, c'est l'homme*. Indeed! The law
permits me to write, only I am supposed to write in a style
different from my own. I may show the profile of my mind,
but I must first show the prescribed mien.'[7] Marx's main
point here is that the new instruction does not meet the
first requirement of any law – that of being precise.

Marx goes on to maintain that the instruction actually
increases the oppression of the old law. He bases this conclusion on the twin principles that religion, being irrational, is essentially incompatible with the state and that
there is no 'general' form of Christianity, only denomina-
tions. The state, according to Marx, should be founded on
'free reason' and he admires the rationalism of the 1819
edict:

Rationalism still prevailed in 1819 and generally viewed
religion as the so-called religion according to reason. This
rationalistic viewpoint is also the viewpoint of the Censorship
Edict which, however, is so illogical as to take an irreligious
point of view while it aims to protect religion. It is contradictory to the fundamental principles of religion to separate those
principles from its positive content and specific quality, for
every religion believes it is different from other illusory religions by virtue of its particular nature, and is the true religion
by virtue of its specific quality.[8]

7. 'Comments on the Latest Prussian Censorship Instruction',
MEGA I, i (1) 154; Easton and Guddat, p. 75.
8. 'Comments on the Latest Prussian Censorship Instruction',
MEGA I, i (1) 158; Easton and Guddat, p. 75.

The old edict did not mention Christianity at all, whereas the new edict forbade attacks on Christianity and thus upheld the principle of the Christian state: 'Nothing will be tolerated which opposes Christian religion in general or a particular doctrine in a frivolous and hostile manner', and went on to oppose 'the fanatical injection of religious convictions into politics and the ensuing intellectual confusion'.[9] The first of these principles made a nonsense of any form of criticism, for the critic was involved in the following dilemma:

Only that part of an attack is frivolous which involves particular surface aspects without being profound and serious enough to get to the substance. The very move against any particular thing is frivolous. As an attack on Christian religion in its fundamentals is forbidden, only a frivolous attack is possible. In reverse the attack on the fundamental principles of religion, on its substance and upon particulars in so far as they are manifestations of that substance is a hostile attack. Religion can be attacked only in a hostile or frivolous way; there is no third way.[10]

The second principle implied a notion of the state that was completely contradictory once one admitted different forms of Christianity:

What does fanatical injection of religious convictions into politics mean? It means that specific religious convictions can determine the state and that the particular nature of religion can become the norm of the state. The old Censorship Edict could rightly oppose this confusion, for it left the particular religion and its specific content to criticism. The old Edict was based on the shallow and superficial rationalism you despise.

9. 'Comments on the Latest Prussian Censorship Instruction', *MEGA* 1, i (1) 158; Easton and Guddat, pp. 75 f.

10. 'Comments on the Latest Prussian Censorship Instruction', *MEGA* 1, i (1) 158 f.; Easton and Guddat, p. 76.

In basing the state on faith and Christianity and wanting a Christian state, how can you expect censorship to prevent this intellectual confusion?[11]

Moreover, half the population must find such a state inimical: 'If your state is only Protestant, it becomes for the Catholic a church to which he does not belong, which he must reject as heretical, and whose essence he finds obnoxious. The reverse would be true if the state were Catholic.'[12] And finally Marx gives this advice to those who wish to fuse religion and politics:

You should forbid that religion be drawn into politics – but you do not want to do that because you wish to base the state on faith rather than on free reason, with religion constituting for you the general sanction of the positive. Or you should permit the fanatical injection of religion into politics. Religion might be politically active in its own way, but you do not want that either. For religion is to support secular matters without the latter's being subject to religion. Once religion is drawn into politics, it becomes an insufferable, indeed an irreligious presumption to want to determine on secular grounds how religion has to operate within politics. If one allies one with religion from religiosity, one must give religion the decisive voice in all matters. Or do you perhaps understand by religion the cult of your own sovereignty and governmental wisdom.[13]

In the same way as he defended the state as being outside the jurisdiction of religion, so Marx defends the autonomy of morality, which the censorship wished to vindicate for itself. 'The specifically Christian legislator cannot recognize morality as an independent sphere sancti-

11. 'Comments on the Latest Prussian Censorship Instruction', *MEGA* I, i (1) 159; Easton and Guddat, pp. 76 f.
12. 'Comments on the Latest Prussian Censorship Instruction', *MEGA* I, i (1) 160; Easton and Guddat, p. 77.
13. 'Comments on the Latest Prussian Censorship Instruction', *MEGA* I, i (1) 160; Easton and Guddat, pp. 77 f.

fied in itself, for he derives the inner universal essence of morality from religion.'[14] But Marx, following the Enlightenment and Feuerbach, believes that morality is independent of religion, autonomous and established on universally true ethical principles:

Morality recognizes only its own universal and rational religion, and religion only its own particular and positive morality. Following the Instruction, censorship will have to repudiate such intellectual heroes of morality as Kant, Fichte, Spinoza for being irreligious and threatening discipline, morals and outward loyalty. All of these moralists proceed from principled opposition between morality and religion, because morality, they claim, is based on the autonomy, and religion on the heteronomy of the human spirit.[15]

Marx devotes the second half of his article to the passage in the instruction that forbade the censoring of opinions because they conflicted with government policy 'so long as their form is decent and their tendency well-intentioned'. Marx finds this passage in clear contradiction to the traditional legal principle that acts and not intentions must be punished: 'Tendentious laws, laws without objective norms, are laws of terrorism, such as those created by Robespierre because of emergencies in the state and by Roman emperors because of the rottenness of the state. Laws that make the sentiment of the acting person the main criterion, and not the act as such, are nothing but positive sanctions of lawlessness.'[16] This sort of legislation could only breed suspicion and serve to divide the state

14. 'Comments on the Latest Prussian Censorship Instruction', *MEGA* I, i (1) 161; Easton and Guddat, p. 78.

15. 'Comments on the Latest Prussian Censorship Instruction', *MEGA* I, i (1) 161; Easton and Guddat, p. 78.

16. 'Comments on the Latest Prussian Censorship Instruction', *MEGA* I, i (1) 162; Easton and Guddat, p. 79.

instead of uniting it – which was absurd, for the state was universal and could not make partisan laws:

A law like that is not a law of the state for the citizenry, but a law of a party against another party. The tendentious law cancels the equality of the citizens before the law. It divides rather than unites; and all dividing laws are reactionary. It is not a law; it is a privilege. In an ethical state the view of the state is subordinated to its members, even if they oppose an organ of the state or the government. But a society in which one organ thinks of itself as the only, exclusive possessor of reason and morality on the state level, a government that in principle opposes the people and assumes that their subversive attitude is universal and normal, the evil conscience of a faction – such a government invents tendentious laws, laws of revenge, against an attitude existing only in the members of the government themselves. Such laws are based on a lack of character and on an unethical and materialistic view of the state.[17]

The state's servants were turned into spies and distrust was bound to be rife – so who could be surprised if the censors were themselves distrusted? The law as it stood necessitated their being universal geniuses, like Chinese bureaucrats. 'All objective norms have been abandoned; the personal relationship is left; and the censor's tact may be called a guarantee. What can the censor violate, then? Tact. But tactlessness is no crime. What is threatened for the writer? His existence. What state ever made the existence of an entire profession dependent upon the tact of individual officials?'[18]

A masterpiece of polemical exegesis, Marx's first political article shows the great pamphleteering talent in the

17. 'Comments on the Latest Prussian Censorship Instruction', *MEGA* I, i (1) 162 f.; Easton and Guddat, p. 80.

18. 'Comments on the Latest Prussian Censorship Instruction', *MEGA* I, i (1) 172; Easton and Guddat, p. 91.

style of Boerne that he exercised all through his life. The article is intransigently liberal and aims at unmasking the pseudo-liberalism of the censorship instruction. Marx is considerably inspired by the *Tractatus* of Spinoza, whose last chapter had a title based on the quotation from Tacitus with which Marx finishes his article: *Rara temporum felicitas, ubi quae velis sentire et quae sentias dicere licet.*[19] Marx had been reading Spinoza very thoroughly during the last half of 1841 and copied out many passages on how misery generates illusion, how religion serves to console and can be exploited politically.[20] The article was too much for the censor and thus could not be published in Ruge's *Jahrbücher*: it appeared in February 1843 in Switzerland in *Anekdota,* a collection of articles suppressed by the censorship and issued in book form by Ruge.

2. THE *Rheinische Zeitung*

a. The Historical School of Law

During the first months of 1842 Marx continued his studies on art and religion. In April he promised Ruge four pieces of work: the first on religious art, the result of the abortive work he had done for the second half of Bauer's *Posaune*; the second on the romantics; the third on the philosophical manifesto of the Historical School of Law; the fourth on the positive philosophers, particularly Schelling, on the lines of his doctoral thesis.[21]

Only the third of these projects, however, was to appear

19. 'Those fortunate times are rare in which you can think what you wish and say what you think.'

20. See further, Wackenheim, *La Faillite de la religion d'après Karl Marx*, pp. 104 ff.

21. Cf. 'Letter to Ruge', *MEGA* I, i (2) 274.

in print. Written in April 1842, this article was occasioned by the appointment of Karl von Savigny as Minister of Justice, who was expected to introduce into the legal system the romantic and reactionary ideas of the new king. Thus it is indirectly an attack on the institutions of the Prussian 'Christian state'. The Historical School of Law had just published a manifesto in honour of their founder Gustav Hugo (1764–1844). Adhering to a complete empiricism, Hugo denied any rational content to political and legal institutions. Hegel, too, had attacked Hugo and his disciples in the introduction to his *Philosophy of Right*, but it was Kant, 'the German theorist of the French Revolution',[22] whom Marx opposed to Hugo. Marx refuted Hugo's claim to be a disciple of Kant:

In calling Herr Hugo a child of the eighteenth century, we are even proceeding in Herr Hugo's spirit, as he himself testifies: he identifies himself as a disciple of Kant and calls his natural law an offshoot of Kantian philosophy. At this point we take up his Manifesto.

Hugo misinterprets the master Kant in saying that since we cannot know what is true, we consequently let pass as entirely valid what is untrue if it merely exists. Hugo is a sceptic concerning the necessary essence of things so that he can be another [E. T. A.] Hoffmann concerning their contingent appearance. In no way does he seek to prove that what is positive is rational; he does seek to prove that what is positive is not rational. With self-satisfied industry he pulls together evidence from all corners of the world to prove that positive institutions such as property, the state, marriage, etc., are not informed by any rational necessity, that they even contradict reason, and that at best one can bicker about them *pro* and *con*.[23]

22. 'Philosophical Manifesto of the Historical School of Law', *MEGA* I, i (1) 254; Easton and Guddat, p. 100.

23. 'The Philosophical Manifesto of the Historical School of Law', *MEGA* I, i (1) 252; Easton and Guddat, pp. 97 f.

In fact Hugo was an absolute sceptic and thus had no criterion of judgement. Against this position Marx employs a rationalism based on Spinoza and Kant, both of whom refused to confuse the positive with the rational: 'Hugo desecrates everything that is sacred to lawful, moral, political man. He smashes what is sacred so that he can revere it as an historical relic; he violates it before the eyes of reason so that he can later honour it before the eyes of history; at the same time he also wants to honour historical eyes.'[24] In short, the Historical School of Law had only one principle – 'the law of arbitrary power'.[25]

Although Marx is rightly pessimistic about the long-term effects of the instruction on the censorship, it did have the short-term effect of permitting considerable liberty of expression during 1842, the year which marked the height of the Young Hegelian movement. The leading manifestation of this radical expression was the *Rheinische Zeitung* ('Rhenish Gazette'). The sub-title of the paper was 'For Politics, Commerce and Industry', and its object at the beginning was to defend the interests of the numerous Rhenish middle class. It was at first regarded favourably by the Prussian Government, who saw it as a possible counterbalance to the *Kölnische Zeitung* ('Cologne Gazette'), an ultramontane and anti-Prussian paper, which at that time had a monopoly in the Rhineland. Already in 1840 a paper with the title *Rheinische Allgemeine Zeitung* ('General Rhenish Gazette') had been founded by a group who considered that the *Kölnische Zeitung* did not adequately defend their social and economic interests. When it was evident that this paper would soon become bankrupt, Georg Jung and Moses Hess

24. 'The Philosophical Manifesto of the Historical School of Law', *MEGA* I, i (1) 252; Easton and Guddat, p. 98.
25. 'The Philosophical Manifesto of the Historical School of Law', *MEGA* I, i (1) 259; Easton and Guddat, p. 105.

persuaded leading rich liberals of the Rhineland, including Camphausen, Mevissen and Oppenheim, to form a company which bought out the *Rheinische Allgemeine Zeitung* (in order to avoid having to renegotiate a concession) and republished it from 1 January 1842 under the title *Rheinische Zeitung.*[26]

Moses Hess had taken the leading part in the founding of the paper and had hoped in consequence for the editorship, but the men who supplied the financial backing were not keen on revolution. Their chief aim was to campaign for measures that would help the expansion of industry and commerce, such as an extension of the customs union, accelerated railway construction and reduced postal charges. So the shareholders chose as editor the protectionist economist Frederick List and, when he was forced to decline for health reasons, Hoeffken, editor of the *Augsburger Zeitung* and a follower of List. Hess had to swallow his pride and accepted a post as sub-editor with special reference to France. Renard, Oppenheim and Jung were appointed directors. Since Oppenheim and particularly Jung had been converted by Hess to Young Hegelian radicalism, a split soon developed between them and Hoeffken: he refused to accept articles from the Berlin Young Hegelians and was driven into resigning on 18 January, declaring himself 'no adept of neo-Hegelianism'.[27]

Hoeffken was replaced by Rutenberg, brother-in-law of Bruno Bauer, who had recently been dismissed from his teaching post for holding unorthodox opinions. He was

26. On the *Rheinische Zeitung*, see in particular H. König, *Die Rheinische Zeitung von 1842–43 in ihrer Einstellung zur Kulturpolitik des Preussischen Staates* (Münster, 1927); *Rheinische Briefe und Akten zur Geschichte der politischen Bewegung 1830–1850*, ed. Hansen (Essen, 1919). For Marx's part, see R. Pascal, *Karl Marx: His Apprenticeship to Politics* (London, 1942).

27. *Rheinische Briefe und Akten*, ed. Hansen, 1, 315.

supported by Karl Marx, who had taken part in discussions on the organization of the paper since September of the previous year. The appointment of Rutenberg made the authorities so anxious as to the tendency of the paper that its suppression was suggested by the central Government. But the President of the Rhineland province feared that this would make a bad impression and only promised closer supervision. Marx had already been asked in January by Bauer why he did not write for the *Rheinische Zeitung*, and in March, pressed by Jung, he put aside the work he was doing for Ruge and decided to devote a series of articles to the debates of the Rhenish Parliament that had held a long session in Düsseldorf in mid 1841.

b. Freedom of the Press

Provincial parliaments had been promised to the Germans on the fall of Napoleon, and though these proposals had been modified after the Carlsbad decisions, these parliaments had functioned quite well in south Germany, largely because the princes wished to play them off against the reactionary central Government.[28] In Prussia, eight provincial parliaments were set up, but their scope was extremely limited: the Government decided when to summon them and how long they would last, and they were under the presidency of a government official; proceedings were secret and their powers were only advisory. Out of 584 votes in all eight parliaments, the aristocracy provided 278, the representatives of the cities 182 and the farmers 124. Since a two thirds majority was necessary to pass a resolution and the aristocracy always had more than one third of the votes, nothing could be done without their agreement. Under Frederick William III the parlia-

28. Cf. F. Mehring, Introduction to Marx, Engels and Lassalle, *Nachlass*, 1, 171 ff.

ment had met only five times in seventeen years, but on his accession in 1841 Frederick William IV summoned the parliaments with the intention of injecting some life into them and having them co-operate with his paternalist government. In order to achieve this he decreed that they should meet every two years, publish their proceedings and elect standing advisory committees. The prospect of these reforms aroused public interest in politics, and this interest was increased by the publication in 1841 of a pamphlet entitled 'Four Questions Answered by an East Prussian'. Its author was Johann Jacoby, a doctor in Königsberg, the city of Kant and centre of East Prussian liberalism, and its thesis was that the people had a right to the constitution promised them back in 1815. These were not the sort of views that the Government wished to foster and Jacoby found himself on trial for treason.

The immediate occasion for Marx's article was the appearance in late March in the official *Preussische Allgemeine Staats-Zeitung* ('Prussian General State Gazette') of articles commenting on the debates of the Parliament 'in order to enlighten the public concerning the true intentions of the Government'.[29] Marx originally conceived a series of five articles on the debates, of which the one written in early April and entitled 'Debates on the Freedom of the Press and on the Publication of the Parliamentary Proceedings' was to be the first: the other four were to deal with the Cologne Affair, the laws on theft of wood, on poaching and 'the really earthy question in all its vital extent, the division of land'.[30] However, only this article on the freedom of the Press and the article on theft of wood were published.

Marx begins his article with what he describes as a

29. Quoted in *MEGA* I, i (1) p. xlvi.
30. 'Letter to Ruge', *MEGA* I, i (2) 278.

'frivolous introduction'[31] mocking the 'confessions' of the official paper and concludes that 'the publication of the parliamentary proceedings will only become true when they are treated as "public facts", that is, when they become matters for the Press'. Marx deals first with the opponents of a free Press. What struck him very forcibly was that the individual speakers did not speak in their own right, but as representatives of classes: 'The debates on the Press show us the specifically class spirit at its clearest, sharpest and fullest. This is especially true of the opposition to a free Press ... the individual interest of the particular class and the natural narrow-mindedness of its character are crudely and recklessly apparent and at the same time show their teeth.'[32]

Marx then takes the representative of each class in order, beginning with the princes, whose representative argued that the merits of the German Press were due to the censorship which was justified by virtue of the authority that imposed it. In England it was, according to the same speaker, only tradition that kept the Press harmless, and in Holland and Switzerland the Press was very detrimental to the life of the nation. Marx refutes these arguments and asserts that the Press is merely the expression of a people's own spirit:

What then is the speaker's complaint against a free Press? That the faults of a people are at the same time the faults of its Press, that its Press is the frank admission and public form of the people's historical spirit. He has shown that every people expresses its spirit in its Press. Shall the philosophically educated spirit of the Germans not obtain what in the speaker's own admission exists among the Swiss, whose horizon does not extend beyond the animal?[33]

31. *MEGA* I, i (2) 274.
32. 'Debates on the Freedom of the Press', *MEGA* I, i (1) 184 ff.
33. ibid., p. 191.

The representative of the nobility discussed the question of whether the proceedings should be published or not. Marx asked in reply whether the Parliament belonged to the province or the province to the Parliament, and whether the province was to be in any way conscious of its representation. It was not surprising that such men had no conception of universal freedom

because they wish to acknowledge freedom not as the natural endowment of the universal light of reason, but as the supernatural gift of a particularly fortunate stellar constellation. They treat freedom only as the individual property of certain persons and classes and are consequently compelled to subsume general reason and freedom under the wayward opinions and day-dreams of 'logically ordered systems'. In order to save the particularity of privilege, they proscribe general freedom of human nature.[34]

Marx goes on to criticize the feudal romanticism of the régime:

Since the *real* situation of these gentlemen in the modern state does not in the least correspond to the idea that they invent for themselves, since they live in a world situated beyond the real world and, consequently, imagination takes the place of head and heart, their practical dissatisfaction obliges them to turn to theory, a theory of the beyond, that is, to religion. This religion, however, acquires in their hands a polemical bitterness impregnated with political tendencies and becomes, in a more or less conscious fashion, merely a sacred cloak that hides aspirations both very profane and also highly imaginative. This then is what we notice in our speaker: to practical needs he opposes a mystico-religious theory stemming from his imagination ... to what is humanly rational he opposes sacred entities, superior to man.[35]

34. ibid. p. 198.
35. ibid., p. 199.

This implicit criticism of the Prussian monarchy, in which Marx uses the language of Spinoza and Feuerbach, no longer criticizes religion as irrational, but as the illusory beyond of a reality that the believer is powerless to transform. There are the beginnings here of a theory of evasion and projection that Marx later developed into a full theory of ideology.

The representative of the nobility goes on to argue that men are imperfect and will be corrupted by a bad Press. Marx replies that even if everything is imperfect this is no argument against a free Press for it is impossible to say that a free Press is bad and a censored Press is good. Indeed, the essence of a free Press was 'the essence of freedom, an essence that is full of character, rational and ethical',[36] whereas censorship was just the opposite. 'The essence of man', Marx claims, 'consists so much in freedom, that even its opponents admit as much.'[37] The nobleman then tries to contrast preventive censorship favourably with a preventive Press law and thus gives Marx an opportunity of painting a picture of what part laws should play in the state. 'A Press law is a true law because it is the positive existence of freedom. It treats freedom as the normal condition of the Press. . . .'[38] Marx goes on to draw conclusions about the nature of law in general: 'Laws are not rules that repress freedom any more than the law of gravity is a rule that represses movement ... laws are rather positive lights, general norms, in which freedom has obtained an impersonal, theoretical existence that is independent of any arbitrary individual. Its law book is a people's bible of freedom.'[39] In this case it was nonsense to speak of preventive laws, for true laws could not prevent

36. ibid. p. 205.
37. ibid. p. 206.
38. ibid. p. 209.
39. ibid. p. 209 f.

the activities of man, but were 'the inner, vital laws of human activity, the conscious mirror of human life'.[40]

Marx does not waste much space on the representative of the cities, who thought a free Press would be a bad influence and cited the example of France which had both a free Press and a turbulent political situation. Marx makes fun of the timidity of the speaker, more *bourgeois* than *citoyen*, saying that it represents the indecision of his class caught between a desire for independence and a fear of change.

Among the defenders of the idea of a free Press, Marx takes issue with the speaker who claimed that a free Press was the concomitant of free trade. Marx agrees that free trade, free property, free Press and so on are all 'types of one and the same species, freedom without qualification'.[41] But the existence of a free Press should not be made conditional on the existence of free trade: it was justified in itself and not as a mere appendix. Nor was it a mere profession among others: anyone who considered writing from an exclusively professional point of view deserved censorship. The only speakers that Marx approved of were the representatives of the farmers, who alone showed some historical sense. They claimed that the human spirit must be free to develop and freely share its experiences. Marx's final conclusion was that the provincial Parliament, in passing judgement against a free Press, had passed judgement on itself.

This article gained Marx a high reputation among his fellow radicals. Jung wrote to him 'your article on the freedom of the Press is superb',[42] and Ruge wrote 'your commentary in the paper on the freedom of the Press is marvellous. It is certainly the best that has been written on

40. 'Debates on the Freedom of the Press', *MEGA* I, i (1) 210.
41. ibid. p. 221.
42. ibid. I, i (2) 275.

the subject.'[43] In May Marx followed it up with the second article in his series on the provincial Parliament which had been debating the 'Cologne affair', but the article was suppressed by the censorship. The only indication as to its contents is given in a letter Marx wrote to Ruge concerning the article: 'I demonstrated in it that the defenders of the state had adopted for their defence a point of view peculiar to the Church, while inversely the men of the Church adopted a position peculiar to the state.'[44] Marx added that he had hoped to gain some Catholic readers through a pseudo-defence of the archbishop.

c. Debate with the *'Kölnische Zeitung'*

By June 1842 the radical tone of the *Rheinische Zeitung* provoked its large rival, the *Kölnische Zeitung*, into launching an attack on its 'dissemination of philosophical and religious views by means of newspapers'.[45] Many of the articles in the *Rheinische Zeitung* were written by Young Hegelians and the general tone of the paper was against Schelling, sympathetic to Ruge's *Deutsche Jahrbücher*, had no good word for the 'Christian state' and emphasized the opposition of philosophy and religion. In the eyes of the Authorities 'The *Rheinische Zeitung* appears to be an organ of Young Hegelian propaganda. Just as in politics it upholds French rationalist ideas, so in religion it openly adopts the atheism of the *Hallische Jahrbücher*, maintaining that contemporary philosophy should replace Christianity.'[46] The existence in Berlin of a radical club of Young Hegelians calling themselves *Die Freien*

43. ibid. p. 276.

44. 'Debates on the Freedom of the Press', *MEGA* i, i (2) 277.

45. 'The Leading Article of the *Kölnische Zeitung*', *MEGA* i, i (1) 233; Easton and Guddat, p. 111.

46. *Rheinische Briefe und Akten*, ed. Hansen; i, 339.

(the free men) had recently been brought to public attention by an article in the *Königsberger Zeitung*, the leading East Prussian newspaper. It was this publicity that led Karl Hermes, editor of the *Kölnische Zeitung*, to attack his rival, though previously the two papers had studiously avoided referring to each other. Hermes took exception to the 'odious attacks on the Christian religion' and called on the Government to enforce the censorship regulation: scientific research was one thing, attacks on religion, which was the foundation of the state, quite another. Marx's next article consists in a critical commentary on Hermes's editorial. He begins by using his recent reading on primitive religions[47] to refute Hermes's arguments condoning fetishism which, according to Marx, was simply a religion of sensual desire. Hermes then asserts that the high point of a people's political life coincides with the greatest development of their religion and that political decadence also involves religious decadence. Marx believes that the reverse is true:

If with the decline of ancient states their religions disappear, this needs no further explanation because the 'true religion' of the ancients for the cult of 'their nationality', of their 'state'. It was not the decline of the ancient religions that brought the downfall of the ancient states but the decline of the ancient states that brought the downfall of the old religions.[48]

Hermes goes on to assert that the best results of scientific inquiry had thus far served only to confirm the myths of the Christian religion. In that case, Marx replied, it was odd that religion should need police protection and odder still that all past philosophies without exception should, at one time or another, have been accused of apostasy by

47. See *MEGA* I, i (2) 115 for details.

48. 'The Leading Article of the *Kölnische Zeitung*', *MEGA* I, i (1) 237; Easton and Guddat, pp. 115 f.

theologians. It was only possible to preserve harmony between reason and religion by calling unscientific anything
that contradicted dogma. But whereas religions changed
from country to country, reason was universal. 'Is there
no universal human nature just as there is a universal
nature of plants and heavenly bodies? Philosophy asks
what is true, not what is accepted as such, what is true for
all men, not what is true for individuals: its metaphysical
truths do not recognize the boundaries of political geography.'[49] Marx also refutes Hermes' claim that all European states are based on Christian religion by quoting
the French constitution and the Prussian civil code. He
then leaves Hermes and turns to the general topic of
whether there should be philosophical discussion of religion in the newspapers, a question which he answers by
a discussion of the relationship of philosophy to the world
in terms that recall the more abstract treatment of the
same question in his doctoral thesis:

Since every genuine philosophy is the spiritual quintessence
of its time, the time must come when philosophy comes into
contact and mutual reaction with the actual world not only
internally by its content, but also externally through its appearance. Then philosophy ceases to be a specific system compared
with other specific systems, it becomes philosophy in general
compared with the world, it becomes the philosophy of the
present world. The formalities which attest that philosophy
has achieved this importance, that it is the living soul of a
culture, that philosophy is becoming worldly and the world
philosophical, have been the same at all times.... Philosophy
is introduced into the world by the yelling of its enemies who
betray their internal infection by their noisy call for help
against the blaze of ideas.[50]

49. 'The Leading Article of the *Kölnische Zeitung*', *MEGA* I, i
(1) 239; Easton and Guddat, pp. 118 f.
50. 'The Leading Article of the *Kölnische Zeitung*', *MEGA* I, i
(1) 243; Easton and Guddat, pp. 122 f.

The argument usually took place on religious matters.

because the public, to which the opponents of philosophy also belong, can touch the ideal sphere of philosophy only with its ideal feelers – and the field of religious ideas is the only one in whose value the public believes almost as much as it believes in the system of material wants – and finally because religion carries on a polemic not against a specific system of philosophy but against philosophy of the specific systems in general.[51]

Marx considered that recent discussions of the latest philosophy in the newspapers had been superficial in the extreme and had completely failed to convey the true spirit of philosophy:

Philosophy speaks differently about religious and philosophical subjects.... You speak without having studied them, it speaks after study. You appeal to passion, it appeals to reason. You curse, it teaches. You promise heaven and earth, it promises nothing but truth. You demand faith in your faith, it demands not faith in its results but the test of doubt. You alarm, it calms.[52]

Moreover, philosophy had every right to comment on political affairs for, being the wisdom of the world, it 'has more right to concern itself with the order of the world, with the state, than the wisdom of the other world, religion'.[53] In fact, only Christianity made a very sharp distinction between Church and state; and the Prussian state was only a hybrid, no genuine religious state which would have to be theocratic, like Byzantium. The whole irration-

51. 'The Leading Article of the *Kölnische Zeitung*', *MEGA* I, i (1) 243; Easton and Guddat, p. 123.
52. 'The Leading Article of the *Kölnische Zeitung*', *MEGA* I, i (1) 244 f.; Easton and Guddat, pp. 124 f.
53. 'The Leading Article of the *Kölnische Zeitung*', *MEGA* I, i (1) 246; Easton and Guddat, p. 126.

ality of the concept of a 'Christian state' could be summed up by the following dilemma:

> Either the Christian state corresponds to the concept of the state as the actualization of rational freedom, and then nothing else can be demanded for it to be Christian than that it be rational; then it suffices to develop the state from reason in human relations, a task philosophy accomplishes. Or, the state of rational freedom cannot be developed out of Christianity; then you will yourselves concede that this development does not lie in the tendency of Christianity, since Christianity does not want a bad state and any state is a bad state which is not the actualization of rational freedom.[54]

Marx finishes his article with an outline of the ideal state according to modern philosophy, i.e. Hegel and after:

> While the earlier philosophers of State Law derived the state from drives of ambition and gregariousness, or from reason – though not reason in society but rather in the individual – the more ideal and profound view of modern philosophy derives it from the idea of the whole. It considers the state as the great organism in which legal, ethical and political freedom has to be actualized and in which the individual citizen simply obeys the natural laws of his own reason, human reason, in the laws of the state. *Sapienti sat.*[55]

Finally, Marx welcomes the idea of the clash of parties, another favourite Young Hegelian topic: 'Without parties there is no development, without division, no progress.'[56]

---

54. 'The Leading Article of the *Kölnische Zeitung*', *MEGA* I, i (1) 248; Easton and Guddat, p. 128.

55. 'The Leading Article of the *Kölnische Zeitung*', *MEGA* I, i (1) 249; Easton and Guddat, p. 130.

56. 'The Leading Article of the *Kölnische Zeitung*', *MEGA* I, i (1) 250; Easton and Guddat, p. 130.

d. The *Rheinische Zeitung* and Communism

This article led the Government to tighten its control over the *Rheinische Zeitung* and Marx wrote to Ruge: 'You need an inflexible tenacity to make a paper like the *Rheinische Zeitung* appear in spite of all the obstacles.'[57] Marx was also having problems with his family. In the same letter, written in July, he says that since April he has only been able to work for four weeks, and even then not without interruption. Another bereavement, following close on the death of Baron von Westphalen in early March, compelled him to stay in Trier for six weeks, and the difficulties caused by his family compelled him to live in very straitened circumstances.[58] In spite of all this, Marx was being drawn more and more into the organization of the *Rheinische Zeitung*, owing mainly to the total incompetence of Rutenberg, of whom Marx declared himself ashamed for having suggested him for the job. Simultaneously with his closer involvement with the paper came the signs of Marx's growing disagreement with his former Berlin colleagues. They had formed themselves into a club known as *Die Freien*, which was a continuation of the old Doctors' Club. The *Freien* were a group of young writers who, disgusted with the servile attitude of the Berliners, lived a style of life whose aim was in many respects simply *épater les bourgeois*. They spent a lot of their time in cafés and even begged in the streets when short of money. The intransigence of their opposition to established doctrines, and particularly to religion, was causing public concern. Their members included Max Stirner, who had published atheist articles in the *Rheinische Zeitung*, as a prelude to his supremely anarcho-individualistic book *Der Einzige und sein Eigentum*

57. 'Letter to Ruge', *MEGA* I, i (2) 277.
58. ibid.

('The Ego and His Own'); Edgar Bauer, whose fervent attacks on any sort of liberal political compromise were taken up by Bakunin; and Engels, who was the author of several polemics against Schelling and liberalism. The article in the *Königsberger Zeitung* that drew public attention to this group of anarchist intellectuals described the programme of the *Freien* as 'the fundamental conviction of modern philosophy: firstly, that all supposed revelations claimed by positive religion are fables; secondly, that the human spirit alone is capable of instructing us correctly about supernatural objects; finally, the transference of this conviction from the limited sphere of science into the wider areas of life and its confirmation there.'[59]

Marx, however, was against these public declarations of emancipation, which seemed to him to be mere exhibitionism. Moreover, because the *Rheinische Zeitung* was associated with the Young Hegelians, he feared that Hermes might be given a further opportunity of attacking the paper. Marx was writing for a business paper in the Rhineland where industry was relatively developed, whereas the *Freien* were philosophizing in Berlin where there was little industry and the atmosphere was dominated by the government bureaucracy. Therefore Marx was in favour of supporting the bourgeoisie in the struggle for liberal reform and against uncompromising criticism. Moreover, it was on Marx's advice that the publisher of the *Rheinische Zeitung*, Renard, had promised the President of the Rhineland to lay less emphasis in the future on religious subjects.[60]

The attitude of the *Freien* raised the question of what the editorial principles of the *Rheinische Zeitung* ought to be. Accordingly, at the end of August Marx wrote to

59. Quoted in R. Prutz, *Zehn Jahre* (Leipzig, 1850) II, 100.
60. Cf. *MEGA* I, i (2) 281 ff.

Oppenheim, whose voice was decisive in determining policy, virtually spelling out his own proposals for the paper, should the editorship be entrusted to him. He wrote:

If you agree, send me the article [by Edgar Bauer] on the *juste-milieu* so that I can review it. This question must be discussed dispassionately. General and theoretical considerations on the constitution of the state are more suitable for learned reviews than for newspapers. The true theory must be expanded and developed in relation to concrete facts and the existing state of affairs. Therefore striking an attitude against the present pillars of state could only result in a tightening of the censorship and even in the suppression of the paper ... in any case we are annoying a large number, perhaps even the majority, of liberals engaged in political activity who have assumed the thankless and painful task of conquering liberty step by step within limits imposed by the Constitution, while we, comfortably ensconced in abstract theory, point out their contradictions to them. It is true that the author of the articles on the *juste-milieu* invites us to criticize, but (1) we all know how the Government replies to such provocations; (2) it is not sufficient to undertake a critique ... the true question is to know whether one has chosen an appropriate field. Newspapers only lend themselves to discussion of these questions when they have become questions that closely concern the state, practical questions. I consider it absolutely indispensable that the *Rheinische Zeitung* should not be directed by its contributors but on the contrary that *it* should direct *them*. Articles like these afford an excellent opportunity of showing the contributors the line of action to follow. An isolated writer cannot, like a newspaper, have a synoptic view of the situation.[61]

In mid October, as a result of this letter, Marx, who had already effectively been running the paper for some months, was made editor-in-chief.

His first task was to answer accusations of communism

61. 'Letter to Oppenheim', *MEGA* i, i (2) 280.

brought against the *Rheinische Zeitung* by the *Augsburger Allgemeine Zeitung*, probably inspired by Hoeffken, one-time editor of the *Rheinische Zeitung*, who had already attacked the *Rheinische Zeitung* in March for printing an article by Bruno Bauer.[62] The basis for the accusation was that in September the *Rheinische Zeitung* had reviewed two articles on housing and communist forms of government, and also that in October it had reported a conference at Strasbourg where followers of Fourier had put forward their ideas. All these items came from Hess. In his reply, Marx criticizes the Augsburg paper for trying to neglect what was an important issue, but denied that the *Rheinische Zeitung* had any sympathy with communism:

The *Rheinische Zeitung*, which cannot even concede theoretical reality to communistic ideas in their present form, and can even less wish or consider possible their practical realization, will submit these ideas to thorough criticism. If the *Augsburger* wanted and could achieve more than slick phrases, the *Augsburger* would see that writings such as those by Leroux, Considérant, and above all Proudhon's penetrating work, can be criticized only after long and deep study, not through superficial and passing notions.[63]

But these notions had to be taken seriously, for ideas were very powerful:

Because of this disagreement, we have to take such theoretical works all the more seriously. We are firmly convinced that it is not the practical effort but rather the theoretical explication of communist ideas which is the real danger. Dangerous practical attempts, even those on a large scale, can be answered with cannon, but ideas won by our intelligence, embodied in our outlook, and forged in our conscience, are chains from which we cannot tear ourselves away without breaking our

62. Cf. *Rheinische Briefe und Akten*, ed. Hansen, I, 323.

63. 'Communism and the *Augsburger Allgemeine Zeitung*', *MEGA* I, i (2) 263; Easton and Guddat, pp. 134 f.

hearts; they are demons we can overcome only by submitting to them.[64]

This reply reflected the general policy of the *Rheinische Zeitung*, which certainly treated poverty as a social and not merely a political question, but which did not see the proletariat as a new social class but only as the innocent victim of bad economic organization.[65]

Although socialism and communism (the terms were generally used interchangeably in Germany at this time) had existed as doctrine in Germany since at least the early 1830s,[66] it was in 1842 that they first attracted widespread attention. This was partly through Moses Hess, who converted both Engels and Bakunin to communism and published much covert communistic propaganda in the *Rheinische Zeitung*, and partly through Lorenz von Stein's book, *Sozialismus und Kommunismus des heutigen Frank-reichs* ('Socialism and Communism in Contemporary France'). This was an investigation into the spread of French socialism among German immigrant workers in Paris, which had been commissioned by the Prussian Government and which, though the author was far from sympathetic to socialists, helped enormously to spread information and even generate enthusiasm.[67] The climate of opinion in Cologne was also favourable to the reception of

64. 'Communism and the *Augsburger Allgemeine Zeitung*', *MEGA* I, i (1) 263; Easton and Guddat, p. 135.

65. See König, *Die Rheinische Zeitung*, pp. 72 ff.

66. See above, pp. 26 ff.

67. For an account of Stein's book claiming that it was an important influence on Marx's conception of the proletariat, see R. Tucker, *Philosophy and Myth in Karl Marx* (Cambridge, 1961) pp. 114 ff. See below, pp. 156 f., on this view. On Stein himself, see K. Mengelberg, 'Lorenz von Stein and his Contribution to Historical Sociology', *Journal of the History of Ideas*, XII (1961); and J. Weiss, 'Dialectical Idealism and the Work of Lorenz von Stein', *International Review of Social History*, VII (1963).

socialist ideas: the Rhenish liberals (unlike the Manchester variety) were very socially-minded and considered that the state had far-reaching duties towards society. Mevissen, for example, had been very struck when visiting England by the decrease in wages, and had become converted to Saint-Simonianism during a stay in Paris. In the offices of the *Rheinische Zeitung* social questions were regularly discussed at the meetings of a group (founded by Moses Hess) which was effectively the editorial committee of the paper. Its members also included Jung, and the future communists Karl d'Ester and Anneke. It met monthly, papers were read, and a discussion followed among the members, who did not necessarily share the same political viewpoint but were all interested in social questions. Marx joined this group when he moved to Cologne in October.[68]

e. The Law against Thefts of Timber

Although the meetings of this group increased Marx's interest in social questions, he was far from being a convert to socialism. In his first important article as editor (the fourth in the planned series of five dealing with the debates in the Rhenish Parliament), he approaches socialism, but does not entirely accept it. A more stringent law was proposed in regard to thefts of timber. The gathering of dead wood had traditionally been unrestricted, but the scarcities caused by the agrarian crises of the 1820s and the growing needs of industry led to legal controls. The situation had become unmanageable: five sixths of all prosecutions in Prussia dealt with wood, and the proportion was even higher in the Rhineland.[69] So it was now being

68. See J. Hansen, *Gustav von Mevissen* (Berlin, 1906) I, 264 ff.

69. See H. Stein, 'Karl Marx und der Rheinscher Pauperismus', *Jahrbuch des kölnischen Geschichtsvereins* (1932) XIV, 131.

proposed that the keeper be the sole arbiter of an alleged offence and that he alone also assess the damages. As the paid servant of the landowner and liable to dismissal, the keeper was naturally not an impartial figure. Moreover, the landowner not only got compensation for his wood, but pocketed the ensuing fine.

Marx discusses these questions from a legal and political standpoint, without much social and historical detail, and claims that the state should defend customary law against the rapacity of the rich. For some things could never become the private property of an individual without injustice; moreover, 'if every violation of property, without distinction or more precise determination, is called theft, is not all private property theft? Do I not, by my private property, deprive another person of this property? Do I not thus destroy his right to property?'[70] Marx here uses the language of Proudhon, but not his spirit, for he confines himself to strictly legal grounds. Marx goes on to claim that the principle of class interest cannot form the basis of the state, for classes represented private interests and thus the state became 'the instrument of private property contrary to the principles of reason and justice'. While it is true that there are elements of Marx's later theory of the state as an instrument of class domination here, in this article he is only concerned with the state as an organization and with the rights of 'the lowest mass of the property-less'.[71] When talking of the supplementary fine payable to the landowner whose wood has been gathered, Marx several times uses the term 'surplus value', a central concept in his later economic writings.[72] Finally, Marx declares that 'any system of the representation of the particular interests ... gives pride of place to an unethical,

70. 'Debate on Thefts of Timber', *MEGA* I, i (1) 269 f.
71. ibid. p. 272.
72. ibid. pp. 293 f.

uncomprehending and insensitive abstraction from a limited material and a limited consciousness that is slavishly subject to it.'[73] This is a brief formulation of the idea of reification: men's social relationships become 'fetishes' – dead things that maintain a secret domination over living men; the natural relationships of domination and possession are reversed, and man is determined by timber, because timber is a commodity that is merely an objectified expression of socio-political relationships. Marx maintains that this dehumanization is a direct consequence of the advice given by the *Preussische Staats-Zeitung* to lawgivers: 'that, when making a law about wood and timber, they are to think only of wood and timber, and are not to try to solve each material problem in a political way – that is, in connection with the whole complex of civic reasoning and civic morality'.[74] Marx concludes his article by comparing an independent observer's impression that wood was the Rhinelanders' fetish with the belief of the Cuban savages that gold was the fetish of the Spaniards.[75]

This article illustrates Marx's growing interest in socio-economic realities. As he himself wrote later: 'In the year 1842–3, as Editor of the *Rheinische Zeitung*, I experienced for the first time the embarrassment of having to take part in discussions on so-called material interests. The proceed-

73. ibid. p. 304.

74. ibid. p. 304. See further K. Löwith, 'Man's Self-alienation in the Early Writings of Marx', *Social Research* (1954) pp. 211 ff., reprinted in Löwith, *Nature, History and Existentialism* pp. 85 ff.

75. 'Debate on the Thefts of Timber', *MEGA* 1, i (1) 304. The concept of 'fetish', quite common in Marx's early writings, recurs in *Capital*, particularly in the first section on the fetishism of commodities. For a comparison of the two contexts, see Ruth-Eva Schulz, 'Geschichte und teleologisches System bei Karl Marx', in *Wesen und Wirklichkeit des Menschen: Festschrift für H. Plessner* (Göttingen, 1957).

ings of the Rhenish Parliament on thefts of wood, etc. . . .
provided the first occasion for occupying myself with the
economic questions.'[76] Engels, too, said later that he had
'always heard from Marx, that it was precisely through
concentrating on the law of thefts of wood and the situation of the Moselle wine-growers, that he was led from
pure politics to economic relationships and so to socialism'.[77]

The circulation of the *Rheinische Zeitung* had been
very modest at 885 copies (only a tenth of that of the
Kölnische Zeitung); it was more than doubled within a
month of Marx's taking over the editorship. The paper's
growing success, together with its criticism of the Rhenish
Parliament, so annoyed the Government that the President of the province wrote in November to the Minister
of the interior that he intended to prosecute the author
of the article on theft of wood. Relations had already been
strained by the publication in the *Rheinische Zeitung* in
October of a secret government project to reform the
divorce law, the first of Frederick William IV's measures
to 'christianize' the law. The *Rheinische Zeitung* followed
up this exposure with three critical articles, the third of
which (in mid December) was by Marx. He agreed that the
present law was too individualistic and did not take into
account the 'ethical substance' of marriage in family and
children. The law still 'thinks only of two individuals and
forgets the family'.[78] But he could not welcome the new
proposal, for it treated marriage not as an ethical, but as a

76. K. Marx, 'Preface to a Critique of Political Economy', in
Marx-Engels, *Selected Works*, 1, 361 f.

77. Letter to R. Fischer, 5 November 1895, quoted in Stein, op.
cit., p. 145.

78. 'On a Proposed Divorce Law', *MEGA* 1, i (1) 317; Easton and
Guddat, p. 139.

religious institution and thus did not recognize its secular nature.

By the end of November the break between Marx and his former colleagues in Berlin was complete. Matters came to a head with the visit of Ruge and the poet Herwegh to Berlin, where they wished to invite the *Freien* to co-operate in the founding of a new university. Ruge (who was always a bit of a Puritan) and Herwegh were revolted by the licentiousness and extravagant ideas of the Berliners. According to Ruge, Bruno Bauer, for example, 'pretended to make me swallow the most grotesque things – e.g. that the state and religion must be suppressed in theory, and also property and family, without bothering to know what would replace them, the essential thing being to destroy everything'.[79] On 25 November Marx made his position clear to everyone by publishing a correspondence from Berlin whose essential points were taken from a letter sent by Herwegh to the *Rheinische Zeitung*.[80] The break was thus final and Marx justified his action as follows in a letter sent a few days later to Ruge:

You know that every day the censorship mutilates our paper so much that it has difficulty in appearing. This has obliged me to suppress quantities of articles by the *Freien*. I allowed myself to annul as many as the censor. Meyen and Co. sent us heaps of scrawls pregnant with world revolutions and empty of thought, written in a slovenly style and flavoured with some atheism and communism (which these gentlemen have never studied). . . . I declared that I considered the smuggling of communist and socialist ideas into casual theatre reviews was unsuitable, indeed immoral, and a very different and more fundamental treatment of communism was required if it was going to be discussed at all. I then asked that religion be criti-

79. Ruge, *Briefwechsel*, ed. Nerrlich, 1 290.

80. Reprinted in *Rheinische Briefe und Akten*, ed. Hansen, 1 382 ff.

cized more through a criticism of the political situation, than that the political situation be criticized through religion. For this approach is more suited to the manner of a newspaper and the education of the public, because religion has no content of its own and lives not from heaven but from earth, and falls of itself with the dissolution of the inverted reality whose theory it is.[81]

f. The Destitution of the Moselle Wine-Growers and the Suppression of the *Rheinische Zeitung*

In January 1843, Marx published a piece of research on poverty that was to be his last substantial contribution to the *Rheinische Zeitung*. The Moselle wine-farmers had suffered greatly from competition after the establishment of the *Zollverein*. Already the subject of considerable public outcry, their impoverishment prompted a report in November 1842 from a *Rheinische Zeitung* correspondent whose accuracy was at once questioned by von Schaper, the President of the Rhineland Province. Judging the correspondent's reply unsatisfactory, Marx prepared to substantiate the report himself. He planned a series of five articles. In the event, only three were written and only two were published before the *Rheinische Zeitung* was banned. Comprising a mass of detail to justify his correspondent's assertions, the two published articles were largely instrumental, in Marx's view, in the suppression of the paper. The conditions in the Moselle valley were due to objectively determined relationships. :

In the investigation of political conditions one is too easily tempted to overlook the objective nature of the relationships and to explain everything from the will of the person acting. There are relationships, however, which determine the actions of private persons as well as those of individual authorities,

81. 'Letter to Ruge', *MEGA* I, i (2) 285 f.

and which are as independent as are the movements in breathing. Taking this objective standpoint from the outset, one will not presuppose an exclusively good or bad will on either side. Rather, one will observe relationships in which only persons appear to act at first.[82]

To remedy these relations, Marx maintains, open public debate is necessary: 'To resolve the difficulty, the administration and the administered both need a third element, which is political without being official and bureaucratic, an element which at the same time represents the citizen without being directly involved in private interests. This resolving element composed of a political mind and a civic heart is a free Press.'[83]

Marx must already have had the impression that the days of the *Rheinische Zeitung* were numbered. On 24 December, the first anniversary of the relaxed censorship, the *Leipziger Allgemeine Zeitung*, one of the most important liberal newspapers, published a letter from Herwegh protesting against the fact that a newspaper he had hoped to edit from Zürich had been forbidden in Prussia. In reply, Herwegh was expelled from Prussia and the *Leipziger Allgemeine Zeitung* was suppressed; on 3 January 1843, under pressure from Frederick William IV, the Saxon Government suppressed the *Deutsche Jahrbücher*; and on 21 January the Council of Ministers presided over by the king decided to suppress the *Rheinische Zeitung*. Marx wrote to Ruge:

Several particular reasons have combined to bring about the suppression of our paper: our increase in circulation, my justification of the Moselle correspondent which inculpated highly-placed politicians, our obstinacy in not naming the person

82. 'On the Distress of the Moselle Wine-Farmers', *MEGA* 1, i (1) 360; Easton and Guddat, pp. 144 f.

83. 'On the Distress of the Moselle Wine-Farmers', *MEGA* 1, i (1) 373; Easton and Guddat, pp. 145 f.

who informed us of the divorce law project, the convocation of the parliaments which we would be able to influence, and finally our criticism of the suppression of the *Leipziger Allgemeine Zeitung* and *Deutsche Jahrbücher*.[84]

The date picked for the final issue of the paper was 31 March, but the censorship was so intolerable that Marx preferred to resign on 17 March.

During the last few months, Marx had certainly been the main force behind the paper. By the end of December its circulation had mounted to 3,500. On 18 March the censor, Saint-Paul, wrote: 'Today the wind has changed. Yesterday the man who was the *spiritus rector*, the soul of the whole enterprise, resigned definitively. . . . I am well content and today I have given to the censorship scarcely a quarter of the time that it usually took'.[85] Marx's views were strongly held, for Saint-Paul wrote that 'Marx would die for his views, of whose truth he is absolutely convinced.'[86] Largely because his views were in transition, but partly because the essence of a good polemicist is to be eclectic, it is impossible to form a systematic idea of Marx's opinions during the year he spent in journalism. Some have maintained, for example, that Marx shows himself here as already practically free from Hegelian influence.[87] Although it is true that Marx has many expressions and lines of argument that are akin to Spinoza and Kant, Marx nevertheless in general declares himself a disciple of Hegel.[88] The following passage, with which Marx ends a

84. 'Letter to Ruge', *MEGA* I, i (2) 293.

85. *Rheinische Briefe und Akten*, ed. Hansen, I, 496.

86. *MEGA* I, i (2) 151.

87. Particularly M. Rubel, *Karl Marx. Essai de biographie intellectuelle* (Paris, 1957) pp. 34 ff. For an account of these articles that stresses the influence of Feuerbach, see W. Schuffenhauer, *Feuerbach und der junge Marx* (Berlin, 1965) pp. 27 ff.

88. See the passage quoted above, p. 120.

short article on the Estates Committees in Prussia, published in the *Rheinische Zeitung* in December 1842, is extremely Hegelian:

In a true state there is no landed property, no industry, no material stuff that in their capacity as raw elements can negotiate an agreement with the state. There are only spiritual powers, and it is only in their civic resurrection, in their political rebirth, that natural powers are capable of influencing the state. The state pervades the whole of nature with spiritual nerves and at each point it necessarily appears that what dominates is not the matter but the form, not nature without the state but the nature of the state, not the unfree object but free humanity.[89]

To Marx, the decision to suppress the *Rheinische Zeitung* came as a release: 'The Government', he said, 'have given me back my liberty.'[90] Although he was still writing, he was certain that his future lay abroad: 'In Germany I cannot start on anything fresh; here you are obliged to falsify yourself.'[91] His decision to emigrate was already taken: his only remaining questions were when and where.

89. 'On the Estates Committees in Prussia', *MEGA* I, i (1) 335.
90. 'Letter to Ruge', *MEGA* I, i (2) 294.
91. ibid.

CHAPTER FIVE

Marx and the Critique of Hegel's Philosophy of the State

1. THE FOUNDATION OF THE *Deutsch-Französische Jahrbücher*

THE decision of the Prussian Government to suppress the liberal Press resulted in a complete split in the Young Hegelian movement. Those in Berlin, led by Bruno Bauer, tended more and more to dissociate themselves from political action. They had imagined their influence to be such that the suppresion of their views would lead to a strong protest among the liberal bourgeoisie. When nothing of the sort happened, they confined themselves increasingly to a purely intellectual criticism that renounced all hope of immediate political influence. The reaction of the group around Ruge was different: they wished to continue the political struggle in an even more practical manner. Since they still thought very much in terms of a journal, their first idea was to base themselves on Julius Froebel's publishing house in Zürich. Froebel was a Professor of Mineralogy at Zürich who had started his business at the end of 1841 in order to publish the poems of Herwegh. He also published a review, edited by Herwegh, that looked for a moment like a successor to the *Deutsche Jahrbücher*, but with Herwegh's banishment from Zürich in March 1843 an obvious gap was waiting to be filled. Ruge was all the more attracted to Zürich as it was, together with Paris, the main centre of German expatriates, both workers and intellectuals. Since the end of 1842 Froebel had dedicated himself full-time to the editorship of a paper that appeared twice weekly and had adopted an increasingly democratic tone, with contributions from Hess, Engels and Bakunin. Ruge's evolution was similar: his last article in the *Deutsche Jahrbücher*, entitled 'Autocritique of Liberalism', rejected liberalism in favour of a democratic humanism that would be realized through the alliance of French and German intellectuals.

Thus it was natural that a review should be started combining the theory of the *Deutsche Jahrbücher* with the more practical ideas of the *Rheinische Zeitung*. Ruge had a great admiration for Marx and wrote to his brother, Ludwig Ruge, in January 1843: 'Marx has great intelligence. He is very worried about his future and particularly his immediate future. Thus the continuation of the *Jahrbücher* with his assistance is something quite natural.'[1] Marx's position was indeed a worrying one; he had been engaged for seven years and wished to get married; yet he was out of a job and was refused all help by his family. He wrote to Ruge in March 1843:

As soon as we have signed the contract, I will go to Kreuznach and get married. Without any romanticism, I can tell you that I am head over heels in love and it is as serious as can be. I have been engaged for more than seven years and my fiancée has been involved on my behalf in the toughest of struggles that have ruined her health. These have been in part against her pietist and aristocratic relations, for whom the Lord in Heaven and the Lord in Berlin are the objects of an equal veneration, and in part against my own family into whom certain radicals and other sworn enemies have insinuated themselves. For years, my fiancée and I have been fighting more useless and exhausting battles than many other persons three

1. Ruge, *Briefwechsel*, ed. Nerrlich, I, 295.

times as old as us who are for ever talking of their 'experience', a word particularly dear to our partisans of the *juste-milieu*.[2]

In June a friend of his father's obtained for Marx an invitation to enter the service of the Prussian state – an invitation he immediately refused.[3] Thus Marx was particularly receptive to the rival invitations of Ruge and Herwegh: the first to start up a new version of the *Deutsche Jahrbücher*, the second to be joint editor of Herwegh's already existing journal.

Marx decided in favour of Ruge. He was hopeful of a revolution in Germany, and in March 1843 wrote to this effect from Holland where he was visiting his mother's relations. This revolution Marx believed to be guaranteed by the backwardness of Germany. 'A shipload of fools', he wrote, 'might drift in the wind for quite a time, but it would meet its doom for the very reason that the fools do not believe this. This doom is the impending revolution.'[4] Ruge, however, was pessimistic. He saw no prospect whatever of a political revolution. The 'eternal submissiveness' of the Germans made it impossible: 'Our nation has no future, so what is the use of our summons to it?'[5] Marx was definitely against simply continuing the *Deutsche Jahrbücher*. 'Even if the *Jahrbücher* were once again permitted, all we could achieve would be a pale imitation of the late review and that is no longer sufficient.'[6] So they decided to give practical expression to the idea of the Franco-German co-operation that had been suggested by most of the Young Hegelians at some time or other during the previous two years. For the influence of French

2. 'Letter to Ruge', *MEGA* I, i (2) 307.
3. cf. *Archiv für die Geschichte des Sozialismus und der Arbeiterbewegung* (1924), x, 64.
4. 'Letter to Ruge', *MEGA* I, i (1) 557; Easton and Guddat, p. 204.
5. 'Letter to Marx', *MEGA* I, i (1) 560.
6. 'Letter to Ruge', *MEGA* I, i (2) 307.

thought made the radicals very internationally-minded, in contrast to the liberals, whom the crises of the 1840s forced into a narrow nationalism. Marx was very enthusiastic: 'Franco-German annals – that would be a principle, an event of importance, an undertaking that fills one with enthusiasm.'[7] Froebel agreed to publish a review of this character, and preparation began. In May, Marx and Froebel went to visit Ruge in Dresden; the three of them decided on Strasbourg as the city of publication. However, Froebel ran into difficulties with the Zürich authorities: books by Weitling and Bruno Bauer that he had published were confiscated, and Froebel himself was condemned to prison for two months. This meant that the annals could not appear before the end of the year at the earliest.

Marx meanwhile settled in Kreuznach where Jenny von Westphalen lived with her mother, and retired into his study to undertake extensive historical reading.[8] He remained in Kreuznach until August, marrying Jenny in June. In a letter to Ruge, written in May and later published in the *Deutsch-Französische Jahrbücher*, he analysed the 'Philistine' German régime at length, a régime that it was essential to shake off once and for all: 'Let the dead bury their dead and mourn them. To be the first among the living to enter into new life, on the other hand, is enviable. This is to be our lot.'[9] Marx was already beginning to envisage the possibility of revolution as consisting in an alliance of 'thinkers' and 'sufferers':

The system of industry and commerce, of property and exploitation of men, however, leads much more rapidly to a

7. ibid.

8. Cf. K. Marx, 'Preface to a Critique of Political Economy', in Marx–Engels, *Selected Works* I, 362.

9. 'Letter to Ruge', *MEGA* I, i (1) 561; Easton and Guddat, p. 205.

rupture within the present society than the increase of the population. The old system cannot heal this rupture because it does not heal and create at all; it merely exists and enjoys itself. The existence of a suffering mankind that thinks, and of a thinking mankind that is suppressed, must necessarily become unpalatable and indigestible for the passive animal kingdom of Philistinism, which is thoughtlessly enjoying itself. It is up to us to expose the old world to full daylight and to shape the new along positive lines. The more time the events allow for thinking men to reflect, and for suffering men to rally, the better will be the product to be born which the present carries in its womb.[10]

It was clear that the *Deutsch-Französische Jahrbücher* would be a *political* review. Thus it was time to come to terms with Hegel's political views and in particular with his *Rechtsphilosophie*. All disciples had sooner or later to do this when it became quite clear that the Prussian Government showed no possibility of becoming Hegel's 'rational state'. Marx had had the idea for at least a year. In March 1842 he wrote to Ruge: 'Another article that I also intend for the *Deutsche Jahrbücher* is a critique of the part of Hegel's natural right where he talks of the constitution. The essential part of it is the critique of constitutional monarchy, a bastard, contradictory and unjustifiable institution'.[11] He went on to say that the article was finished and only wanted rewriting. Six months later he was still talking about publishing it in the *Rheinische Zeitung*.[12] The critique of Hegel's politics that Marx elaborated in the six months he spent at Kreuznach[13]

10. 'Letter to Ruge', *MEGA* I, i (1) 265 f.; Easton and Guddat, pp. 210 f.

11. 'Letter to Ruge', *MEGA* I, i (2) 269.

12. ibid. p. 280.

13. The manuscript seems to have been finished in July–August 1843, according to D. Rjazanov (Introduction to *MEGA* I, i (1) pp. lxxxiv f.), who compares similar passages in the manuscript

is much richer than the purely logical-political approach of the previous year. Many years later, in the preface to his *Critique of Political Economy*, Marx wrote:

The first work which I undertook for the solution of the doubts which assailed me was a critical review of the Hegelian philosophy of law.... My investigation led to the result that legal relations as well as forms of state are to be grasped neither from themselves nor from the so-called general development of the human mind, but rather have their roots in the material conditions of life, the sum total of which Hegel, following the example of the Englishmen and Frenchmen of the eighteenth century, combines under the name of 'civil society', that, however, the anatomy of civil society is to be sought in political economy.[14]

Although this account is too simplified, his experience with the *Rheinische Zeitung* and the rejection of liberal politics by Heine and the socialists, including Hess,

---

and in Marx's notebooks. This dating of the manuscript has been questioned by E. Lewalter, 'Zur Systematik der Marxschen Staats- und Gesellschaftslehre', *Archiv für Sozialwissenschaft und Sozial- politik* LXVIII, 645 ff., and by S. Landshut, *Karl Marx, Die Früh- schriften* (Stuttgart, 1953) p. 20, on two grounds: firstly the letter to Ruge written in March 1842, alluding to an almost finished critique of Hegel's natural right; secondly, the fact that Marx had no time, busied as he was with family matters, to write anything so long and detailed in the summer of 1843. The second point is quite unacceptable: marriage is as often a stimulus to work as a hindrance. As for the first point, in the same letter Marx described other articles, that Ruge never received, as being 'almost finished'. Marx was always more ready to give assurances than to fulfil them. His remarks in the preface to his *Critique of Political Economy*, as well as internal evidence, point conclusively to 1843. The most that could be said is that elements of previous articles may have been used.

14. Karl Marx, 'Preface to a Critique of Political Economy', *Selected Works*, I, 362.

enabled Marx's critique of Hegel to take that much more account of socio-economic factors.

2. THE INFLUENCE OF FEUERBACH

There was another factor, too, that enabled Marx to adopt a new point of view: Feuerbach's 'Preliminary Theses for a Reform of Philosophy'. These had been published in *Anekdota*, a collection of essays originally intended for the *Deutsche Jahrbücher*, but rejected by the censorship. This book, edited by Ruge in Switzerland and published in February 1843, was the last place where Young Hegelians appeared together in print as a coherent group. It also marked the watershed of a movement that was ceasing to be theological and had not yet become political. Feuerbach presented his 'Theses' as a continuation of his *Essence of Christianity*. He wished to apply to speculative philosophy the approach he had already used with regard to religion: theology had still not been completely destroyed; it had a last rational bulwark in Hegel's philosophy, which was as great a mystification as any theology. Since Hegel's dialectic started and ended with the infinite, the finite, i.e. man, was only a phase in the evolution of a superhuman spirit: 'The essence of theology is the transcendence and exteriorized essence of man; the essence of Hegel's logic is transcendent thought, exteriorized human thought.'[15] But philosophy should not start from God or the Absolute, nor even from being as predicate of the Absolute; philosophy had to begin with the finite, the particular, the real, and acknowledge the primacy of the senses. Since this approach had been pioneered by the French, the true philosopher would

15. L. Feuerbach, *Anthropologischer Materialismus. Ausgewählte Schriften* (Frankfurt, 1967) I, 84.

have to be of 'Gallo–Germanic blood'. Hegel's philosophy was the last refuge of theology and as such had to be abolished. This would come about from a realization that 'the true relationship of thought to being is this: being is the subject, thought the predicate. Thought arises from being – being does not arise from thought.'[16]

Marx read Feuerbach's 'Theses' immediately after publication and wrote an enthusiastic letter to Ruge, who had sent him a copy: 'The only point in Feuerbach's aphorisms that does not satisfy me is that he gives too much importance to nature and too little to politics. Yet an alliance with politics affords the only means for contemporary philosophy to become a truth. But what happened in the sixteenth century, when the state had followers as enthusiastic as those of Nature, will no doubt be repeated.'[17] For Marx, the way ahead lay through politics, but a politics which questioned current conceptions of the relationship of the state to society. It was Feuerbach's theses that enabled Marx to operate his particular reversal of Hegel's dialectic. Marx had read Feuerbach as early as the time when he was composing his doctoral thesis, but his *magnum opus*, the *Essence of Christianity*, did not make as great an impression on Marx as it did, for example, on Ruge. It is true that in January 1842 Marx had written a note entitled 'Luther as Arbiter between Strauss and Feuerbach'[18] in which he cited at length a passage from Luther to support Feuerbach's humanist interpretation of miracles as against the transcendent view of Strauss. He finished the note by giving

16. ibid. p. 95.

17. 'Letter to Ruge', *MEGA* I, i (2) 308.

18. It has recently been claimed that Feuerbach, not Marx, was the author of the note. See H.-M. Sass, 'Feuerbach statt Marx', in *International Review of Social History* (1967), XII, 108 ff. The argument is, however, not completely convincing.

this advice to speculative theologians and philosophers: 'Free yourselves from the concepts and prepossessions of existing speculative philosophy if you want to get at things differently, as they are, that is to say, if you want to arrive at the truth. And there is no other road for you to truth and freedom except that leading through the stream of fire [the Feuer-bach]. Feuerbach is the purgatory of the present times.'[19] But it was not until 1843 that Feuerbach's humanism became the outlook that united the group around the *Deutsch-Französische Jahrbücher*.[20]

As far as Marx was concerned in 1843 (and this was true of most of his radical, democratic contemporaries also) Feuerbach was *the* philosopher. Every page of the critique of Hegel's political philosophy that Marx elaborated during the summer of 1843 shows the influence of Feuerbach's method. For Marx, Hegel's approach involves a systematic 'mystification'. This term, taken from Feuerbach's 'Theses', meant to deprive something of its own independent nature by making this nature into a mere emanation of an imaginary entity. Marx gives his criticism a social and historical dimension lacking in Feuerbach, but one point is central to both their approaches: the claim that Hegel had reversed the correct relation of subjects and predicates. Marx says: 'It is important that Hegel always converts the Idea into the subject, and the particular actual subject, such as 'political sentiment', into the predicate. But the development always takes place on the side of the predicate.'[21] And later:

19. 'Luther as Arbiter between Strauss and Feuerbach', *MEGA* I, i (1) 175; Easton and Guddat, p. 95.
20. See particularly McLellan, *The Young Hegelians and Karl Marx*, pp. 85 ff.
21. 'Critique of Hegel's Philosophy of the State', *MEGA* I, i (1) 410; Easton and Guddat, p. 159.

Had Hegel started from real subjects as the basis of the state then he would not have found it necessary to let the state subjectify itself in a mysterious way.... Hegel subjectifies the predicate, the objects, but he objectifies them in separation from their true subject. Consequently the true subject appears as a result, whereas the point is to start with the true subject and deal with its objectification.[22]

Marx's fundamental idea is to take actual political institutions and show thereby that Hegel's conception of the relationship of ideas to reality is mistaken. Hegel had tried to reconcile the ideal and the real by showing that reality was the unfolding of an idea, was rational. Marx, on the contrary, emphasizes the opposition between ideals and reality in the secular world and categorizes Hegel's whole enterprise as speculative, by which he meant that it was based on subjective conceptions that were out of harmony with empirical reality.[23] A note of Marx's on an article by Ranke on the restoration in France shows very clearly the interpenetration of Marx's criticism of Hegel and of his historical analysis:

Under Louis XVIII, the constitution exists by grace of the monarch (grant of royal charter); under Louis-Philippe, the monarch exists by grace of the constitution (royalty granted).

22. 'Critique of Hegel's Philosophy of the State', *MEGA* I, i (1) 426.

23. On Marx's manuscript in general, see L. Dupré, *The Philosophical Foundations of Marxism* (New York, 1966) pp. 87 ff.; S. Avineri, 'The Hegelian Origins of Marx's Political Thought', *Review of Metaphysics* (September 1967); H. Lefebvre, *The Sociology of Marx* (London, 1968) pp. 123 ff.; J. Hyppolite, 'La Conception hégélienne de l'Etat et sa critique par Karl Marx', *Études sur Marx et Hégel*, 2nd edn. (Paris, 1965); J. Barion, *Hegel und die marxistische Staatslehre* (Bonn, 1963). There is now a complete translation with an admirably scholarly introduction: K. Marx, *Critique of Hegel's Philosophy of Right*, ed. J. O'Malley (Cambridge, 1970).

We can, moreover, observe that the transformation of subject into attribute, and attribute into subject ... is always the next revolution. Hegel, in making ... the idea of the state the subject and the old modes of existence of the state the attribute – whereas, in historical reality, it was the opposite that existed, the idea of the state having always been the attribute of its mode of existence – Hegel, I say, is only expressing the general character of his age, its political teleology.[24]

Inspired by Feuerbachian philosophy and historical analysis, this manuscript is the first of many works of Marx (up to and including *Capital*) that were entitled 'Critique' – a term that had a great vogue among the Young Hegelians. The approach it represented – reflecting on and working over the ideas of others – was very congenial to Marx, who preferred to develop his own ideas in opposition to those of other thinkers.

3. MARX AND HEGEL ON THE STATE

The manuscript in which Marx elaborated his thought on Hegel's *Rechtsphilosophie* ('Philosophy of Law') is a very close paragraph-by-paragraph commentary on Hegel's text. It deals with the final part of the *Rechtsphilosophie* which is devoted to the state. The first few pages of Marx's manuscript are missing, and it begins with the paragraph where Hegel explains that concrete freedom consists in the identity of the system of private interests (family and civil society) with the system of general interest (the state) which he describes as both the 'external necessity' and the 'immanent aim'. Marx considers this to be an 'unresolved antinomy' and passes on to the paragraph in which, he says, 'the entire mystery of Hegel's philosophy of law

24. *MEGA* I, i (2) 130.

and of his philosophy in general is laid out'.[25] In this paragraph Hegel says:

The actual Idea, Spirit, divides itself in its finitude into two ideal spheres of its notion, family and civil society, in order to leave behind its ideality and to become explicitly infinite actual Spirit. It lends to these spheres the material of its finite actuality – i.e. individuals as a mass – in such a way that this lending appears mediated in the individual by circumstances, caprice, and his personal choice of his station in life.[26]

Marx finds this odd on two counts: firstly the state is said to predate and produce its own elements. But this involves a reversal of the true relationship:

The Idea is thoroughly subjectivized. The actual relationship of family and civil society to the state is grasped as their inner imaginary activity. Family and civil society are the presuppositions of the state, they are really the active forms. But in speculation this is reversed. As the Idea is subjectivized, the actual subjects – civil society, family, 'circumstances, caprice, etc.' – become unactual, objective moments of the Idea, meaning something else.[27]

Thus Hegel's whole enterprise of reconciling the universal and the particular is a failure: the real elements of the state – family and civil society – are everywhere subordinate to the spirit of the state, whose mystical power infuses the other social spheres with a part of its essence.

25. 'Critique of Hegel's Philosophy of the State', *MEGA* I, i (1) 408; Easton and Guddat, p. 157.
26. 'Critique of Hegel's Philosophy of the State', *MEGA* I, i (1) 405; Easton and Guddat, p. 154.
27. 'Critique of Hegel's Philosophy of the State', *MEGA* I, i (1) 406; Easton and Guddat, p. 155.

4. MONARCHY AND DEMOCRACY

After this general introduction, Marx passes on to the monarchical, executive and legislative powers into which, according to Hegel, the state divides itself. He criticizes Hegel's very strange arguments designed to show that 'the personality of the state and its certainty of itself' are exemplified in the monarch. For Marx such a personified sovereignty cannot be anything but arbitrary. Hegel, says Marx, did admit a sovereignty of the people as antithetical to that of the monarch, but the question should be: is it not rather the sovereignty of the monarch that is an illusion? And if one did talk of sovereignty of the monarch and sovereignty of the people, then this was not the same sovereignty but two completely opposite concepts of sovereignty. The choice between them was an exclusive one, as exclusive as that between the sovereignty of God and that of man.

Marx then elaborates his concept of democracy by contrasting it with monarchy, the essential difference being that monarchy, being one-sided and unilateral, necessarily falsified the roles of all members of the state:

In democracy none of the aspects acquires any other meaning than the appropriate one. Each is actually only an aspect of the whole demos. But in monarchy a part determines the character of the whole. The entire constitution must conform to a fixed point. Democracy is the generic constitution. But monarchy is a modification and indeed a bad one. Democracy is content and form. Monarchy should be only form, but it falsifies the content.[28]

The trouble with monarchy was that it viewed the people as merely an appendix to the political constitution, where-

---

28. 'Critique of Hegel's Philosophy of the State', *MEGA* 1, i (1) 434; Easton and Guddat, p. 173.

as in democracy the constitution was the self-expression of the people. Even constitutional monarchy was not sufficient, in that the constitution affected only a part of the people's life and the political constitution was not coincidental with the state.

To explain his view of the relationship of democracy to previous forms of constitution, Marx invokes a parallel with religion:

Just as religion does not create man, but man creates religion, so the constitution does not create the people but the people create the constitution. In some respects democracy is related to all other forms of state, as Christianity is related to all other religions. Christianity is religion *par excellence*, the essence of religion, deified man as a particular religion. Similarly, democracy is the essence of every constitution, socialized man as a particular constitution.[29]

Hegel presented his political philosophy as a reconciliation of the universal and the particular. But for Marx only democracy was capable of making the formal principle (the political constitution) and the material principle (man's everyday life) into one and the same. In other forms of constitution a man had to lead two distinct lives, a political and an unpolitical one: 'In any other state than democracy the state, the law, the constitution is the dominant factor even without actually dominating, that is, without materially penetrating the content of other non-political spheres. In democracy the constitution, the law, the state itself in so far as it is politically constituted, is only a self-determination of the people and a particular content of the people.'[30]

In order to show that 'all forms of state have democracy

29. 'Critique of Hegel's Philosophy of the State', *MEGA* I, i (1) 434 f.; Easton and Guddat, pp. 173 f.

30. 'Critique of Hegel's Philosophy of the State', *MEGA* I, i (1) 435 f.; Easton and Guddat, p. 175.

for their truth', Marx embarks on a historical analysis very similar to Hegel's in his *Philosophy of History*, though with a much more empirical orientation. In the ancient states of the Graeco-Roman world, people's lives were inescapably political as well as social entities: there was no differentiation between the political and the private spheres, which were completely penetrated by politics. In the Middle Ages, by contrast, it was the socio-economic relations that were considered basic and their political element was an acquired one. It was because 'each private sphere had a political character' that 'the life of the people and the life of the state were identical'. Trade, property and society were all directly political. But, though man was thus the actual principle of the state, it was man who was as yet unfree. Thus the Middle Ages were characterized by the 'democracy of unfreedom'.[31]

The creation of a genuinely political state was a modern invention: 'The abstraction of the state as such belongs only to modern times because the abstraction of private life belongs only to these times. The abstraction of the political state is a modern product.'[32] The modern political state, being a mere abstract form, had little effect on the life of its citizens. This was shown by the fact that the property and legal relationships in Prussia and North America were virtually the same even though the constitutions were very different. The problem of modern times was thus to put an end to the separation of the private spheres from the political state.

Up to now, the political constitution has been the religious sphere, the religion of the people's life, the heaven of their universality in contrast to the particular mundane existence of their actuality. The political sphere was the state's only sphere

31. 'Critique of Hegel's Philosophy of the State', *MEGA* i, i (1) 436 f.; Easton and Guddat, p. 176.
32. ibid.

within the state in which both content and form were a generic content and the genuine universal, but in such a way that its content became formal and particular because these spheres stood in contrast to each other. Political life in the modern sense of the word is the scholasticism of a people's life. Monarchy is the completed expression of this alienation. The republic is the negation of alienation within alienation.[33]

The solution to this problem was 'true democracy'.

Marx does not do much to clarify his conception of democracy. Nevertheless four characteristics are apparent in his sketchy and obviously transitional ideas:

Firstly, his conception is humanist: man is the one and only subject of the political process. 'In a democracy the constitution is always based on its actual foundation, on actual man and the actual people, not only implicitly and in its essence, but in its existence and actuality.'[34] 'In a democracy there is particular human existence while in other forms of state man is the particular juridical existence. This is the basic uniqueness of democracy.'[35]

Secondly, this involved a freedom for mankind that was non-existent in Hegel. For Hegel had downgraded man, who should be the subject, to the status of predicate. Freedom would only be gained when the roles were reversed and man became the free subject with society as his predicate. 'Here [i.e. in democracy] the constitution is man's and the people's own work. The constitution appears as what it is: the free product of man.'[36]

Thirdly, Marx's conception is in some sense socialist.

33. 'Critique of Hegel's Philosophy of the State', *MEGA* I, i (1) 436; Easton and Guddat, p. 176.

34. 'Critique of Hegel's Philosophy of the State', *MEGA* I, i (1) 434; Easton and Guddat, p. 173.

35. 'Critique of Hegel's Philosophy of the State', *MEGA* I, i (1) 435; Easton and Guddat, p. 174.

36. 'Critique of Hegel's Philosophy of the State', *MEGA* I, i (1) 434; Easton and Guddat, p. 173.

It is plain that, like Hegel, he considered the aim to be the realization of an essence. But instead of the realization of the Idea, Marx envisaged the realization of man's 'species-being'.[37] Thus democracy was 'socialized man as a particular constitution'.[38]

Finally, republicanism is not adequate to this new form of society, which involves the disappearance of the state. Thus it is inaccurate to describe Marx as a Jacobin democrat. Referring to French socialist writings, he says: 'Recently the French have conceived of this in such a way that the political state disappears in true democracy. This is correct in so far as the political state as such, as constitution, no longer applies to the whole.'[39]

Marx also describes his democratic ideal in the letter to Ruge mentioned above.[40] The principle of monarchy, and particularly the Prussian monarchy, was man despised, despicable, dehumanized. The effect of Frederick William IV's romanticism was that the only change now possible for Germany was an 'entry into the human world of democracy'.[41] At the same time, Marx's view of the means of effecting this change was still a very idealistic one: 'Freedom, the feeling of man's dignity, will have to be awakened again in these men. Only this feeling, which disappeared from the world with the Greeks and with Christianity vanished into the blue mist of heaven, can

37. This term was popularized by Feuerbach at the beginning of his *Essence of Christianity*, where he defined man, in contrast to other animals, as having consciousness of himself as a member of a species.

38. 'Critique of Hegel's Philosophy of the State', *MEGA* I, i (1) 435; Easton and Guddat, p. 174.

39. 'Critique of Hegel's Philosophy of the State', *MEGA* I, i (1) 435; Easton and Guddat, pp. 174 f.

40. See above, pp. 138 f.

41. 'Letter to Ruge', *MEGA* I, i (1) 564; Easton and Guddat, p. 208.

again transform society into a community of men to achieve their highest purpose, a democratic state.'[42]

5. BUREAUCRACY

Having commented on Hegel's defence of hereditary monarchy, Marx then moves on to the executive power. Marx has some interesting passages on bureaucracy which represent his first attempt to give a sociological definition of state power.[43] Hegel had said that the state mediated between the contradictions of civil society by means of corporations and bureaucracy. The former grouped individual private interests in order to bring pressure to bear upon the state; the latter mediated between the state and private interests thus expressed. By bureaucracy, Hegel meant a body of higher civil servants who were recruited by competition from the middle classes. To them was entrusted the working out of common interests, and the task of securing the unity of the state. Their decisions were prevented from being arbitrary by the sovereign above them and the pressure of the corporations from below. The concept of 'civil society' is one that Marx takes over from Hegel and uses constantly during 1843: in Hegel's political triad the sphere of civil society was the second term, being between the family and the state. In civil society the relationships between men are no longer based on love, as in the family, but on men's self-interest.

42. 'Letter to Ruge', *MEGA* I, i (1) 561; Easton and Guddat, p. 206.

43. For later references to bureaucracy in Marx's writings, see Avineri, *The Social and Political Thought of Karl Marx*, pp. 48 ff.; K. Axelos, *Marx, penseur de la technique* (Paris, 1961) pp. 97 ff.; I. Fetscher, 'Marxismus und Bürokratie', *International Review of Social History*, v (1960).

It is a society akin to that described in Mandeville's *Fable of the Bees*:

> Thus every part was full of vice,
>   Yet the whole mass a Paradise;
> Such were the blessings of that state;
>   Their crimes conspired to make them great.

Hegel formed his concept after reading the English economists Adam Smith and Ricardo, and described it at length in paragraphs 30–40 of the *Rechtsphilosophie*.[44] The purpose of corporations and bureaucracy was to mediate between these discordant aims of civil society and form them into a harmony.

Marx begins by denouncing this attempted mediation that does not resolve, and at best only masks, historically determined oppositions. Hegel had well understood the process of the dissolution of medieval estates, the growth of industry and the economic war of all against all. But in trying nevertheless to construct a formal state unity, he only created a further alienation: man's being, which was already alienated in monarchy, was now even more alienated in the growing power of the executive, the bureaucracy. All that Hegel offered was an empirical description of bureaucracy, partly as it was, and partly as it pretended to be. Indeed, most of Hegel's comment could be taken verbatim from the Prussian civil code. So far from fulfilling a mission of reconciliation, bureaucracy had its origin in the separation of the state and civil society. Marx rejects Hegel's claim that the bureaucracy

44. Hegel's description here to some extent anticipates Marx in that Hegel describes the worker's alienated situation in capitalist society, the polarization of wealth and thus of classes, and even the inherent tendency of capitalism to imperialist expansion. See R. Heiss, 'Hegel und Marx', in *Symposium, Jahrbuch für Philosophie*, I (1948).

is an impartial and thus 'universal' class. He reverses the Hegelian dialectic by asserting that, though their function is in principle a universal one, the bureaucrats have in practice ended by turning it into their own private affair. Certainly in the past the bureaucracy fought on the side of the monarch against the corporations and against separatism: 'When "bureaucracy" is a new principle, when the universal interest of the state starts to become something "apart" by itself and thereby an "actual" interest, bureaucracy conflicts with the corporations just as any consequence conflicts with the existence of its pre-suppositions.'[45] But once the victory had been won, the bureaucracy needed constantly to maintain the appearance of the separation in order to justify its own existence. For

the same spirit that creates the corporation in society creates bureaucracy in the state. The spirit of bureaucracy is attacked along with the spirit of the corporation. If bureaucracy earlier attacked the existence of corporations to make room for its own existence, it now attempts to sustain forcefully the existence of the corporations so as to preserve the corporations' spirit, which is its own spirit.[46]

Thus bureaucracy allocated to itself a particular, closed society within the state, the consciousness, will and power of the state. In the battle against the corporations the bureaucracy was necessarily victorious as each corporation needed it to combat other corporations, whereas the bureaucracy was self-sufficient. In short: 'The corporation is the attempt of civil society to become the state; but bureaucracy is the state which in actuality has become civil

45. 'Critique of Hegel's Philosophy of the State', *MEGA* I, i (1) 455; Easton and Guddat, p. 184.

46. 'Critique of Hegel's Philosophy of the State', *MEGA* I, i (1) 455; Easton and Guddat, p. 184.

society.'[47] Thus bureaucracy, which came into existence to solve problems and then engendered them in order to continue existing, turned into an end in itself and achieved nothing. It was this process that accounted for all the characteristics of bureaucracy: the formalism, the hierarchy, the mystique, the identification of its own ends with those of the state.

Marx sums up these characteristics in a passage whose insight and incisiveness merit a lengthy quotation:

Bureaucracy considers itself the ultimate finite purpose of the state. Since bureaucracy converts its 'formal' purposes into its content, it everywhere comes into conflict with 'real' purposes. It is, therefore, compelled to pass off what is formal for the content and the content for what is formal. The purposes of the state are changed into the purposes of bureaus and vice versa. Bureaucracy is a circle that no one can leave. Its hierarchy is a hierarchy of information. The top entrusts the lower circles with an insight into details, while the lower circles entrust the top with an insight into what is universal, and thus they mutually deceive each other.

Bureaucracy is the imaginary state beside the real state, the spiritualism of the state. Hence everything has a double meaning, a real and a bureaucratic meaning, just as knowledge and also the will are something double, real and bureaucratic. What is real is dealt with in its bureaucratic nature, in its other-worldly spiritual essence. Bureaucracy possesses the state's essence, the spiritual essence of society, as its private property. The universal spirit of bureaucracy is the secret, the mystery sustained within bureaucracy itself by hierarchy and maintained on the outside as a closed corporation. The open spirit and sentiment of patriotism hence appear to bureaucracy as a betrayal of this mystery. So authority is the principle of its knowledge, and the deification of authority is its sentiment. But within bureaucracy spiritualism becomes a crass material-

47. 'Critique of Hegel's Philosophy of the State', *MEGA* 1, i (1) 456; Easton and Guddat, p. 185.

ism, the materialism of passive obedience, of faith in authority, of the mechanism of fixed formal activity, fixed principles, views and traditions. For the individual bureaucrat the state's purposes become his private purpose of hunting for higher positions and making a career for himself. In one respect he views actual life as something material, for the spirit of this life has its separate existence in bureaucracy.[48]

Marx's fundamental criticism of Hegel is the same as that contained in the preceding sections: the attributes of humanity as a whole had been transferred to a particular individual or class, which thus represented the illusory universality of modern political life. Marx calls the spirit of bureaucracy 'theological' and often uses religious parallels to describe this duality. 'Bureaucrats', he says, 'are the state's Jesuits and theologians. Bureaucracy is the priest's republic.'[49] And again, concerning the competitive entry into the bureaucracy: 'The examination is nothing but the bureaucratic baptism of knowledge, the official recognition of the transubstantiation of profane knowledge into sacred knowledge.'[50] The very fact that there has to be an examination condemned the system out of hand: 'The fact that anyone has the chance to acquire the right to another sphere merely proves that his own sphere has not actualized this right. What counts in the genuine state is not the chance of any citizen to devote himself to the universal class as something special, but the capacity of the universal class to be actually universal, that is, to be the class of every citizen.'[51]

48. 'Critique of Hegel's Philosophy of the State', *MEGA* I, i (1) 456 f.; Easton and Guddat, pp. 185 ff.

49. 'Critique of Hegel's Philosophy of the State', *MEGA* I, i (1) 456; Easton and Guddat, p. 185.

50. 'Critique of Hegel's Philosophy of the State', *MEGA* I, i (1) 461.

51. ibid. p. 460; Easton and Guddat, p. 190.

6. THE POLITICAL FUNCTION OF ESTATES

Leaving Hegel's discussion of the executive, Marx proceeds to the legislative power. Here he objects that Hegel saw the functions of the estates as a mediation between the government on the one hand and the people on the other. They constituted the synthesis of the state and civil society. Marx objects to this that the estates are incapable of effecting such a synthesis for two reasons: firstly, they only took part in the legislature and thus were not active in the government as such; secondly, as a consequence, they presupposed the separation of the state and civil society. 'It is not revealed how the estates are to set about uniting in themselves two contrary points of view. The estates are the legal opposition between the state and civil society within the state. They are, at the same time, a summons to dissolve this contradiction.'[52]

Hegel's solution of the problem was thus only an apparent one: 'The element of the estates is the political illusion of civil society.'[53] His merit, Marx went on, was to have described it correctly. 'Hegel is not to be blamed for describing the essence of the modern state as it is, but for pretending that what exists is the essence of the state. That the rational is real is proved even in the contradiction of irrational reality that is at all points the opposite of what it proclaims, and proclaims the opposite of what it is.'[54] One of the most obvious instances of this was precisely Hegel's contention that there could be anything but opposition between civil society (the sphere of private interest) and the state. The advantage of the representative type of constitution lay in clearly having

52. 'Critique of Hegel's Philosophy of the State', *MEGA* I, i (1) 481.

53. ibid. p. 474.

54. ibid. p. 476.

shown this. It was 'the open, unfalsified and consequent expression of the modern type of state. It is unconcealed opposition.'[55] The result of this social division was that members of society were also divided within themselves:

> Civil society and state are separate. Thus the citizen of the state and the member of civil society are separate. Thus man has to undertake an essential separation from himself ... in order to be a real citizen and have political significance and efficacity, he must leave his social reality, abstract himself from it and return from its whole organization into his individuality; for the only existence that he finds for his citizenship is his pure, blank individuality since the existence of the state and government can easily do without him and his existence in civil society can easily do without the state ... The separation of the political state from civil society appears necessarily as a separation of political man, the citizen, from civil society, from his own actual empirical reality.[56]

Marx then gives a historical analysis of estates, an analysis that is based on the extended historical reading he undertook in the summer of 1843. In addition to immersing himself in the political theories of Machiavelli, Montesquieu and Rousseau, Marx took extensive notes on French, English, American and even Swedish history and wrote a chronological table of the period A.D. 600–1589 that covered eighty pages. These readings led Marx to the conclusion that whereas in the Middle Ages the social estates as such also had legislative authority, this authority was destroyed by the absolute monarchies of the sixteenth and seventeenth centuries aided by their centralized bureaucracies. Although this political authority was not at first totally suppressed, and the estates continued to enjoy independent existence, the French Revolution completed the transformation and reduced the

55. ibid. p. 492.   56. ibid. p. 494 f.

political differences of civil society to mere social differences that had no political impact.

'It is a progress of history,' wrote Marx

that turns political estates into social estates, so that the members of the state, equal in the heaven of their political existence, should be unequal in their terrestrial social existence, like Christians who, equal in heaven, are unequal on earth. Strictly speaking, the transformation of political estates into civil estates was brought about by an absolute monarchy.[57]

Thus the estates in countries other than Germany had ceased to have any political significance, and Hegel's idea of their being adequate representatives of civil society was archaic and indicative of German underdevelopment. Hegel's conceptual framework was based on the ideas of the French Revolution, but his solutions were still medieval; this was a mark of how far the political situation in Germany was retarded when compared with German philosophy. Indeed, the only estate in the medieval sense of the word that still remained was the bureaucracy itself. The estates were no longer differentiated by need and work, for social mobility had increased enormously. 'The only general difference, superficial and formal, is merely that between country and town. But in society itself, differences developed in spheres that were constantly in movement with arbitrariness as their principle. Money and education are the main distinguishing characteristics.'[58] Marx breaks off here, noting that the proper place to discuss this will be in later passages (never written) on Hegel's conception of civil society. He does, however, go on to say, in a remark that foreshadows the future importance of the proletariat in his thought, that the characteristic thing about contemporary civil society

57. ibid. p. 497.

58. 'Critique of Hegel's Philosophy of the State', *MEGA* I, i (1) 497.

was precisely that 'the property-less, the class that stands in immediate need of work, the class of material labour, formed not so much a class of civil society as the basis on which its components rest and move'.[59] Marx summarizes his objection to Hegel as follows: 'As soon as civil estates as such become political estates, then there is no need of mediation, and as soon as mediation is necessary, they are no longer political.... Hegel wishes to preserve the medieval system of estates but in the modern context of legislative power; and he wants legislative power, but in the framework of a medieval system of estates! It is the worst sort of syncretism.'[60]

Marx then discusses Hegel's view that one estate in particular is eminently fitted to wield legislative power – the landowners. The system of inalienable properties and primogeniture meant, according to Hegel, that the land-owning aristocracy was firmly rooted in the family, the seat of substantive ethical life. Furthermore, their owner-ship of land not only gave them independence from both the state and civil society but also leisure for political activity. Marx rejects this analysis. The very fact that the landowning class had this independence of the state implied that others did not have it; and thus, since this independence and arbitrariness were the characteristics of private property, land was private property *par excellence*. In Hegel's account, the political constitution was the constitution of private property. Primogeniture was simply the revelation of the inner nature of landowner-ship; its inalienability cut the social links of the land-owners and ensured their isolation from civil society; the fact that the land was not distributed equally among the children was contrary to the social nature of the family. Thus the very class that was based on the family constantly acted in contradiction to the fundamental principle of

59. ibid. p. 497.   60. ibid. pp. 514 f.

the family. Nor was this the only contradiction in Hegel's account: in the sections of the *Rechtsphilosophie* dealing with private law, Hegel had defined private property as essentially alienable and disposable according to the will of the owner. In contrast to the rigid, dead inalienability of primogeniture, even the vices of civil society appeared as at least human vices. Moreover, in a system of primogeniture, there was a group of men who were lawgivers by birth. It was ironical that this group should be of the landed aristocracy who had most laughed at the idea of inborn human rights. But this was merely typical of Hegel's constant oscillation between a political idealism and a crass materialism. Here, once again, Marx discovers the fundamentally antihumanist trend in Hegel that he intends, using Feuerbach's approach, to reverse. 'Hereditary goods, landed property are what remains. It is what is constant in the relationship; it is the substance. The inheritor, the owner is only an accident ... the subject is the thing and predicate is the man. Will becomes a property of property.'[61]

Hegel then discussed the other part of the estates, 'the mobile side of civil society', in contrast to the agricultural class. Their size and the nature of their occupations made it necessary that they should be represented by deputies. In Hegel's view, Marx maintained, the idea that all members of the state had a right to participate in deliberations and decisions on matters of general concern was a facile one, which stopped at the abstract definition of what it was to be a member of the state. It was the 'democratic element without any rational form'.[62] Marx's reply, obviously leaning on Rousseau, is:

61. 'Critique of Hegel's Philosophy of the State', *MEGA* I, i (1) 527.

62. 'Critique of Hegel's Philosophy of the State', *MEGA* I, i (1) 538; Easton and Guddat, p. 196.

In a really rational state one could answer 'It is not the case that all as individuals should participate in deliberation and decision on general political matters', for the 'individuals' participate in deliberating and deciding on political matters of general concern as 'all', that is, within society and as parts of society. Not all as individuals, but the individuals as all.[63]

Hegel's whole problem arose, as before, from the separation of the state from civil society:

The invasion of civil society *en masse*, where possible totally, into legislative power and its will to substitute itself as actual for a fictitious legislative power – this is nothing but the drive of civil society to give itself political existence or to make its political existence actual. The drive of civil society to become political or to make political society actual is evident as a drive toward participation in legislative power as universal as possible.[64]

Marx sees two possibilities: if the state and civil society continue to be separate, then all as individuals cannot participate in the legislature except through deputies, the 'expression of the separation and merely a dualistic unity'.[65] Secondly, if civil society becomes political society, then the significance of legislative power as representative disappears, for it depends on a theological kind of separation of the state from civil society. Hence, what the people should aim for was not legislative power but governmental power. Marx ends his discussion with a passage which makes clear how, in the summer of 1843, he envisaged future political developments:

63. 'Critique of Hegel's Philosophy of the State', *MEGA* I, i (1) 539; Easton and Guddat, p. 197.
64. 'Critique of Hegel's Philosophy of the State', *MEGA* I, i (1) 541; Easton and Guddat, p. 199.
65. 'Critique of Hegel's Philosophy of the State', *MEGA* I, i (1) 542; Easton and Guddat, p. 200.

The essential demand that every social need, law, etc., be politically evolved and determined by the entire state in the social sense, is modified in the state as political abstraction in that the formal stand against another force (content) is attributed to it besides its actual content. This is no French abstraction, but a necessary consequence, because the actual state exists only as the political state-formalism as observed above.... It is not a question whether civil society should exercise legislative power through deputies or through all as individuals. Rather it is the question of the extent and greatest possible universalization of the voting, of active as well as passive suffrage. This is the real bone of contention of political reform, in France as well as in England....

Voting is the actual relationship of actual civil society to the civil society of the legislative power, to the representative element. Or, voting is the immediate, direct relationship of civil society to the political state, not only in appearance but in existence.... Only in unlimited voting, active as well as passive, does civil society actually rise to an abstraction of itself, to political existence as its true universal and essential existence. But the realization of this abstraction is also the transcendence of the abstraction. By making its political existence actual as its true existence, civil society also makes its civil existence unessential in contrast to its political existence. And with the one thing separated, the other, its opposite, falls. Within the abstract political state the reform of voting is a dissolution of the state, but likewise the dissolution of civil society.[66]

Thus Marx arrives here at the same conclusion as in his discussion of 'true democracy'. Democracy implied universal suffrage, and universal suffrage would lead to the dissolution of the state. It is clear from this manuscript that Marx was adopting the fundamental humanism of Feuerbach and with it Feuerbach's reversal of subject and predicate in the Hegelian dialectic. Marx considered it

66. 'Critique of Hegel's Philosophy of the State', *MEGA* I, i (1) 543 f.; Easton and Guddat, pp. 201 f.

evident that any future development was going to involve a recovery by man of the social dimension that had been lost ever since the French Revolution levelled all citizens in the political state and thus accentuated the indivi-dualism of bourgeois society. He was explicit that private property must cease to be the basis of social organization, but it is not obvious that he was arguing for its abolition, nor did he make clear the various roles of classes in the social evolution. This is not at all surprising in that Marx's manuscript represents only a preliminary survey of Hegel's text. The manuscript is incomplete and there are references to elaborations either not undertaken by Marx or since lost. It was written at a very transient stage in the intellectual evolution of both Marx and his colleagues.[67] The different attitudes and conceptual vague-ness of the Young Hegelians are well brought out in the following extract from a letter of Julius Waldeck, a lead-ing Berlin radical:

How often do I tell these people, that basically we are all really ... communists and atheists. The only difference is that some see the impossibility of immediately attaining this goal of ours, and therefore try for something realizable; while the others, the Bauers, Buhl, etc., consider that hypocritical and affirm that ... we must prove the necessity of an upheaval, or rather of a rebuilding, in theory and then it will come about in practice of its own accord. I think that, so long as the balance of power is on the side of reaction, these people do more harm than good; but that is their opinion, for unfortunately they are pessimists.[68]

67. Evidence for this is to be found in Marx's manuscript itself. For example, in a phrase about 'starting from self-conscious, real Spirit', he subsequently deleted the word 'self-conscious' which was, no doubt, too reminiscent of Bauer's idealism. See 'Critique of Hegel's Philosophy of the State', *MEGA* I, i (1) 418.

68. Quoted in G. Mayer, 'Die Anfänge des politischen Radikalismus im vormärzlichen Preussen', *Zeitschrift für Politik*, VI (1913).

Marx himself was very conscious of the intellectual disarray among the radicals and wrote to Ruge soon after finishing his critique of Hegel: 'Even though there is no doubt about the "whence", there does prevail all the more confusion about the "whither". It is not only the fact that a general anarchy has broken out among the reformers; each one will have to admit to himself that he has no exact idea of what is to happen.'[69]

7. THE POSSIBILITIES OF A GERMAN REVOLUTION

A letter of Marx to Ruge, written in September 1843 and later published in the *Deutsch-Französische Jahrbücher*, gives a good impression of Marx's intellectual and political position immediately before leaving Germany, and of how much importance he attached to what he called the 'reform of consciousness'. Things might not be very clear, he wrote, but 'that is exactly the advantage of the new direction, namely, that we do not anticipate the world dogmatically, but rather wish to find the new world through criticism of the old.'[70] What was clear was that all dogmatisms were unacceptable, and that included the various systems of communism:

Especially communism is a dogmatic abstraction; I have in mind the actually existing communism, as Cabet, Dezamy, Weitling, etc., teach it, not some other imagined or possible one. This communism is itself only a separate phenomenon of the humanistic principle, infected by its opposite, private advantage. Dissolution of private property, therefore, is in no way identical with communism, and communism saw the origin of other socialistic doctrines like those of Fourier, Proudhon, etc., not accidentally but necessarily in opposition to itself,

69. 'Letter to Ruge', *MEGA* I, i (1) 573; Easton and Guddat, p. 212.
70. ibid.

because communism itself is only a special, one-sided realization of the socialistic principle. And the entire socialistic principle, in turn, is only one side of the reality of human nature.[71]

In Germany, the realization of this human nature depended above all on a critique of religion and politics, for in Germany these were the focal points of interest; ready-made systems were no use; criticism had to take as its starting-point contemporary attitudes. Marx asserts, in terms that recall Hegel's account of the progress of Reason in history: 'Reason has always existed, but not always in rational form.'[72] Rational goals were already inherent in any form of practical or theoretical consciousness, and awaited their uncovering by the critic. It is in these terms that Marx justifies his previous lengthy examination of Hegel: social truth could be made to emerge from the contradictory nature of the political state.

Just as religion is the table of contents of the theoretical struggles of mankind, the political state is that of the practical ones. The political state, therefore, expresses all social struggles, needs, and truths within its form *sub specie rei publicae*. By no means, then, is the most specific political problem – such as the difference between the estate system and the representative system – to be the object of our critique on account of the *hauteur des principes*. For this question merely expresses in a political way the difference between the control of man and the control of private property. The critic not only can but must enter into these political problems, which crass socialists regard as below their dignity. By developing the advantage of the representative system over the estate system a critic gets a large party interested practically.[73]

71. 'Letter to Ruge', *MEGA* I, i (1) 573; Easton and Guddat, pp. 212 f.
72. 'Letter to Ruge', *MEGA* I, i (1) 574; Easton and Guddat, p. 213.
73. 'Letter to Ruge', *MEGA* I, i (1) 574; Easton and Guddat, pp. 243 f.

And once this interest had been aroused, the very logic of progress would, as Marx showed in his critique of Hegel, lead to the state's dissolution: 'By elevating the representative system from its political context to a general context and by claiming the true significance that is due to it, he [i.e. the critic] at the same time forces his party to go beyond itself, for its victory is simultaneously its loss.'[74]

Thus Marx saw no objection to starting from actual political struggles and explaining why they took place. The point was to demystify religious and political problems by instilling an awareness of their exclusively human dimensions. Marx ends his letter:

Our slogan, therefore, must be: reform of consciousness, not through dogmas, but through analysis of the mystical consciousness that is unclear about itself, whether in religion or politics. It will be evident, then, that the world has long dreamed of something of which it only has to become conscious in order to possess it in actuality. It will be evident that there is not a big blank between the past and the future, but rather it is a matter of realizing the thoughts of the past. It will be evident, finally, that mankind does not begin any new work but performs its old work consciously.

Therefore, we can express the aim of our periodical in one phrase: a self-understanding (critical philosophy) of the age concerning its struggles and wishes. This is a task for the world and for us. It must be the work of united forces. It is a confession, nothing else. To have its sins forgiven, mankind has only to declare them for what they are.[75]

74. ibid., p. 214.
75. 'Letter to Ruge', *MEGA* I, i (1) 575; Easton and Guddat, pp. 214 f.

CHAPTER SIX

Marx and the *Deutsch-Französische Jahrbücher*

While Marx was studying at Kreuznach, the plan for the *Deutsch-Französische Jahrbücher* had been making progress. Ruge and Froebel were active in trying to get German participation but the liberal writers refused, and of the Berlin Young Hegelians only Bruno Bauer agreed, and in the end even he contributed nothing. So the collaborators were reduced to those who were already interested in Froebel's Zürich publications: Hess, Engels, Bakunin and Herwegh. Their views were very diverse: Hess and Bakunin proclaimed their own brand of eclectic anarcho-communism, while Froebel, Herwegh and Ruge vaguely called themselves democrats and emphasized the importance of popular education. As French influence on the Young Hegelians increased and, with it, their political awareness, the term 'democracy' began to replace the vaguer 'radicalism'. But the unity of Ruge's group went no further than a wish to further political application of Feuerbach's philosophy. Marx suggested in May 1843 that Feuerbach contribute to the review a critique of Schelling:

Schelling's sincere early thought . . . has become for you truth and reality, full of strength and weight. That is why Schelling is an anticipatory caricature of you. But once a caricature is faced with the reality, it necessarily vanishes into thin air. Thus I consider you the necessary and natural adversary of Schelling, the adversary summoned by their majesties Nature and History. The struggle that opposes you is the struggle that opposes the image of philosophy to philosophy itself.[1]

1. 'Letter to Feuerbach', *MEGA* I, i (2) 316 f.

Feuerbach, however, refused to write for the journal: in his opinion, the time was not yet ripe for a transition from theory to practice, for the theory had still to be perfected; Marx and Ruge were too impatient for action.

The practical side of the review was more easily settled. In order to finance it, Ruge tried to float a large loan in Germany, but when this failed completely he bore virtually the whole cost of publication himself. As a place of publication Strasbourg (which they had previously favoured) was rejected, and Froebel proposed that he and Ruge go to Brussels and Paris to see which of the two would be more suitable. At the end of July Ruge travelled west, stopped at Kreuznach to see Marx, and then, joining forces with Hess and Froebel at Cologne, went on to Brussels. Brussels, too, proved unsatisfactory, for though the Press was very free there, the city was too small and not politically-minded. So in August Hess and Ruge moved on to Paris.

All the contributors to the *Deutsch-Französische Jahrbücher* viewed Paris as both a haven and an inspiration. Ruge wrote:

We are going to France, the threshold of a new world. May it live up to our dreams! At the end of our journey we will find the vast valley of Paris, the cradle of the new Europe, the great laboratory where world history is formed and has its ever fresh source. It is in Paris that we shall live our victories and our defeats. Even our philosophy, the field where we are in advance of our time, will only be able to triumph when proclaimed in Paris and impregnated with the French spirit.[2]

These expectations were justified in so far as Paris was the undisputed centre of socialist thought. The revolutions of 1789 and 1830 had made Paris the centre of political thinking. The 'bourgeois monarchy' of Louis-

2. A. Ruge, *Zwei Jahre in Paris* (Leipzig, 1846 I, 4 ff.

Philippe was drawing to its close and becoming more conservative; the censorship laws had been tightened in 1835, and from 1840 onwards the anti-liberal Guizot dominated the Government. But political commitment was none the less lively for being semi-clandestine, and there was a bewildering variety of sects, *salons* and newspapers all proclaiming some form of socialism.[3] As soon as he arrived in Paris Ruge set out to make contacts, piloted by Hess, who was familiar with the political scene from his days as correspondent of the *Rheinische Zeitung*. His account of his tour of the *salons* is a catalogue of one misunderstanding after another.[4] Each party thought the other a century out of date. Amazed that Ruge appeared so little versed in communism, the French were equally surprised by his being a disciple of atheism and materialism, watchwords of the pre-1789 French thought. Ruge could not understand how the French could be so attached to religion, which German philosophy had spent such long and involved efforts in neutralizing. Lammenais, Blanc, Lamartine, Leroux, Cabet, Considérant, all refused their participation, and in spite of every effort the *Deutsch-Französische Jahrbücher* appeared without a single French

3. For an excellent account of current political groupings and publications, see P. Kägi, *Genesis des historischen Materialismus* (Vienna, 1965) pp. 157 ff.

4 Ruge, op. cit. A Parisian intellectual's impression of Hess seems to have been the general one produced by German philosophers: 'Hess is very effective in converting the highly educated: but he talks in concepts and not directly, and so is unintelligible to those who are not highly educated. So far all German philosophers are the same. He realizes this and says he will improve. . . . The Young German philosophical school likes this exaggeration in theory as much or even more than the Jacobins do in practice. In general all such words are a genuine obstacle. . . . But apart from these weaknesses Hess is very good.' Quoted in J. C. Bluntschli, *Die Kommunisten in der Schweiz* (Zürich, 1843) pp. 83 f.

contribution. By November, Ruge began to be anxious even about the number of his German contributors: Herwegh was honeymooning and Bakunin was leading an errant life after expulsion from Zürich. This gap was filled by Heine, who, having been increasingly sympathetic to socialist ideas during his three-year stay in Paris, agreed to contribute some poems, and by Ferdinand Bernays, recently expelled from Bavaria after being the editor of the *Mannheimer Abend-Zeitung*. Marx himself arrived in Paris on 11 October with Jenny already pregnant. They lodged at 38 Rue Vaneau, on the Left Bank near the Invalides, together with Herwegh, Mäurer, a leader of the German workers' League of the Just, and Ruge, who conceived of the house as an experiment in community living.

1. 'ON THE JEWISH QUESTION'

It is difficult to tell how quickly Marx was affected by his stay in Paris. Of his two essays published in February 1844 in the *Deutsch-Französische Jahrbücher*, the first, 'On The Jewish Question', was in large part written before his arrival and often merely summarizes passages of his 'Critique of Hegel's Philosophy of the State' and the reading on France and America that he had undertaken at Kreuznach in July and August. The result is to replace political emancipation by social emancipation, by rejecting Hegel's notion of 'objective spirit', which here becomes incarnate in society and not in the state. Starting from the question of Jewish emancipation, he further develops the problem of the separation in modern politics of the state and civil society with which he had already dealt at some length. Since 1816 the Prussian Jews had enjoyed rights far inferior to those of Christians; recently liberals had strongly supported the Jews in their demands for equality.

The approaches of both Bauer and Marx stem from the disillusion they felt with the liberals, who had done nothing to help the radicals in 1842–3 when under government pressure. Bauer criticized the liberals' claim in two articles. The first, published in the *Deutsche Jahrbücher* in November 1842, and then in a separate pamphlet in 1843, asserted that the opponents of Jewish emancipation were superior to its advocates: their only fault was that they stopped short of subjecting the Christian state to the same criticism as Judaism. What neither party had realized was that, in order to be able to live together, both Jews and Christians had to renounce what separated them. Neither Christians nor Jews as such could have human rights: so it was not only Jews but all men who needed emancipation. Civil rights were inconceivable in an absolute state. Religious prejudice and religious separation would vanish when civil and political castes and privileges were done away with.

Marx had been thinking about this question for some time. In August 1842 he had asked a friend to send him all anti-semitic articles by Hermes so that he could publish a reply.[5] At the beginning of his stay at Kreuznach, the president of the Jewish community there asked Marx to present a petition to the Rhineland Diet in favour of the Jews. Marx agreed, writing to Ruge: 'However detestable I find the Jewish religion, Bauer's conception seems to me too abstract',[6] an incidental criticism that by the end of his stay in Kreuznach he had worked up into a full-scale attack. Bauer was accused of subjecting to his criticism only the 'Christian state' and not the state as such, and thus failing to examine the relationship of

5. Cf. 'Letter to Oppenheim', *MEGA* I, i (2) 279.
6. 'Letter to Ruge', *MEGA* I, i (2) 308.

political emancipation, that is, the granting of political rights, to human emancipation. To prove the insufficiency of a merely political emancipation attained by atheist propaganda, Marx points out that the Jewish question is formulated in terms that vary according to the degree of laicization achieved by various states. In the Christian state of Germany the question was a purely theological one, for the Jew found himself in religious opposition to the state. In the constitutional state of France, with its incomplete political emancipation and its state religion (the religion of the majority), the Jewish question was a political problem retaining a theological appearance. Whereas in the free states of North America the problem was a purely secular one, and accordingly any criticism had to be political, and thus Bauer's solution ceased to be relevant. Marx quotes several authorities to show the extent of religious practice in North America and goes on:

If we find even in a country with full political emancipation that religion not only exists but is fresh and vital, we have proof that the existence of religion is not incompatible with the full development of the state. But since the existence of religion implies a defect, the source of this defect must be sought in the nature of the state itself. We no longer take religion to be the basis but only the manifestation of secular narrowness. Hence we explain religious restriction of free citizens on the basis of their secular restriction. We do not claim that they must transcend their religious restriction in order to transcend their secular limitations. We do claim that they will transcend their religious restriction once they have transcended their secular limitations. We do not convert secular questions into theological ones. We convert theological questions into secular questions. History has long enough been resolved into superstition, but now we can resolve superstition into history. The question of the relation of political emancipation to religion becomes for us a question of the relation of political emancipation to human emancipation. We criticize the religious weakness of the political state by criticizing the political state in its secular constitution apart from the religious defects.[7]

Thus political emancipation from religion did not free men from religious conceptions, for political emancipation was not the same as human emancipation. For example, citizens might still be bound by the limitations of a religion from which a state had shaken itself free. What Bauer had not realized was that the political emancipation he advocated embodied an alienation similar to the religious alienation he had just criticized. Man's emancipation, because it passed through the intermediary of the state, was still abstract, indirect and partial. 'Even when man proclaims himself an atheist through the medium of the state – that is, when he declares the state to be atheistic – he is still captive to religion since he only recognizes his atheism indirectly through an intermediary. Religion is merely the indirect recognition of man through a mediator. The state is the mediator between man and the freedom of man.[8]

Marx then moves on to a closer examination of the relationship between the abstract political state and civil society. He begins by drawing a parallel between emancipation from religion and emancipation from private property. The state abolished private property as far as the constitution was concerned by declaring that no property qualification was necessary for voting. But this, far from really abolishing private property, actually presupposed it. The state 'is aware of itself as a political state and makes

7. 'On the Jewish Question', *MEGA* I, i (1) 581 f.; Easton and Guddat, p. 222. For an examination of Marx's ideas on secularization and politics, see E. Weil, 'Sekularisation des politischen Denkens', *Marxismusstudien*, IV (1962) 144 ff.

8. 'On the Jewish Question', *MEGA* I, i (1) 583; Easton and Guddat, p. 224.

its universality effective only in opposition to these elements',[9] that is, in opposition to private property, education, occupation and so on.

The result was that man's being was profoundly divided. Whereas his social being was fulfilled in the abstract sphere of the state, the material conditions of his life remained unchanged:

By its nature the perfected political state is man's species-life[10] in opposition to his material life. All the presuppositions of this egoistic life remain in civil society outside the state, but as qualities of civil society. Where the political state has achieved its development, man leads a double life, a heavenly and an earthly life, not only in thought or consciousness but in actuality. In the political community he regards himself as a communal being; but in civil society he is active as a private individual, treats other men as means, reduces himself to a means, and becomes the plaything of alien powers. The political state is as spiritual in relation to civil society as heaven is in relation to earth.... Here, where he counts as an actual individual to himself and others, he is an illusory phenomenon. In the state, where he counts as a species-being, on the other hand, he is an imaginary member of an imagined sovereignty, divested of his actual individual life and endowed with an unactual universality.[11]

To describe this dual personality, Marx uses the terms – already popularized by Hergel in his *Rechtsphilosophie* – of *bourgeois* and *citoyen* (indeed he had already used them in his article on the freedom of the Press in May 1842 in the *Rheinische Zeitung*). Returning to the subject of religion, Marx points out that in civil society it was just be-

9. 'On the Jewish Question', *MEGA* I, i (1) 584; Easton and Guddat, p. 225.

10. See note above, p. 151.

11. 'On the Jewish Question', *MEGA* I, i (1) 584; Easton and Guddat, pp. 225 f.

cause of this dichotomy that religion flourished there so much. For religion, which was nothing but idealization of this division, found its best basis in political emancipation, the perfection of this division; and the forms of religion were but a function of the types of political organization. Instead of being the spirit of the state, as in Germany, religion became the spirit of civil society, the spirit of egoism and division – and Marx pointed to the infinite number of sects in North America. It was true that the French revolutionary state tried to affirm itself in opposition to civil society by abolishing religion and private property, and attempted to set itself up as the real species-life of man. But this state of affairs, being in direct opposition to the state's own presuppositions, could only be maintained by violence and was therefore bound to come to an end.[12]

This analysis enables Marx to open a parenthesis on the Christian Germanic state, the object of so much of his criticism when writing for the *Rheinische Zeitung*. This state, he says, is far from being the political realization of Christianity. In it, Christianity was merely a political tool and betrayed its own principles, for the true Christian state was 'the atheistic state, the democratic state, the state that relegates religion to the level of other elements of civil society. The state that is still theological and still officially prescribes belief in Christianity, has not yet dared to declare itself to be a state and has not yet succeeded in expressing in secular and human form, in its actuality as a state, those human foundations of which Christianity is the sublime expression.'[13] Germany was alienation incorporated into a political régime: its relations were hier-

12. This analysis draws on Hegel's views on the French Revolution. On Hegel, see Plamenatz, *Man and Society*, II, 168 f.

13. 'On the Jewish Question', *MEGA* I, i (1) 587; Easton and Guddat, p. 228.

archical relations of faith in which the religious spirit had not been secularized. Nor, indeed, could it be secularized in such circumstances. For since it was merely derivative, its secularization depended on political secularization. This was what happened in the democratic state: 'The basis of the democratic state is not Christianity but the human ground of Christianity. Religion remains the ideal, unsecular consciousness of its members because it is the ideal form of the stage of human development attained in the democratic state.'[14]

Political democracy was not, however, to be denigrated. For it was a great step forward and 'the final form of universal human emancipation within the prevailing order of things'.[15] Political democracy could be called Christian in that it had man as its principle and regarded him as sovereign and supreme. But unfortunately this meant

man in his uncivilized and unsocial aspect, in his fortuitous existence and just as he is, corrupted by the entire organization of our society, lost and alienated from himself, oppressed by inhuman relations and elements – in a word, man who is not yet an actual species-being. The sovereignty of man – though as alien and distinct from actual man – which is the chimera, dream, and postulate of Christianity, is a tangible and present actuality, a secular maxim, in democracy.[16]

Having shown that religion is more than compatible with *civil* rights, Marx now contests Bauer's refusal to acknowledge the Jewish claim to *human* rights, the rights of man. Bauer had said that neither the Jew nor the Christian could claim universal human rights because

14. 'On the Jewish Question', *MEGA* I, i (1) 590; Easton and Guddat, p. 231.
15. 'On the Jewish Question', *MEGA* I, i (1) 587; Easton and Guddat, p. 227.
16. 'On the Jewish Question', *MEGA* I, i (1) 590; Easton and Guddat, p. 231.

their particular and exclusive religions necessarily contradicted any such claims. Marx refutes Bauer's view by referring to the French and American Constitutions. Firstly, he discusses the distinction between the rights of the *citizen* and the rights of *man*. The rights of the citizen were of a political order; they expressed man's participation in the universality of the state and, as had been shown, by no means presupposed the abolition of religion. These rights contained the social essence of man – though in a totally abstract form – and the reclaiming of this essence would give rise to human emancipation. Not so the rights of man in general: being expressions of the division of bourgeois society they had nothing social about them.[17] As exemplified in the French Constitutions of 1791 and 1793 and in the Constitutions of New Hampshire and Pennsylvania, the rights of man did not deny the right to practise religion; on the contrary, they expressly recognized it, and Marx quotes chapter and verse to prove it.

Marx then asks: why are these rights called the rights of *man*? Because they were the rights of man regarded as a member of civil society. And why was the member of civil society identified with man? Because the rights of man were egoistic and anti-social. This was the case with all the constitutions in question, even the most radical; none succeeded in subordinating 'man' to the 'citizen'. All the rights of man that they proclaimed had the same character. Liberty, for example, 'the power belonging to each man to do anything which does not impair the rights of others', was, according to Marx, 'not based on the association of man with man but rather on the separation of man from man. It is the right of this separation, the right

17. See the passages in the *Holy Family* where Marx enlarges on this and other aspects of the Jewish question; see also E. Bloch, 'Man and Citizen according to Marx', in *Socialist Humanism*, ed. E. Fromm (London, 1967) pp. 200 ff.

of the limited individual limited to himself.'[18] Property, the right to dispose of one's possessions as one wills without regard to others, was 'the right of self-interest. . . . It lets every man find in other men not the realization, but rather the limitation of his own freedom.'[19] Equality was no more than the equal right to the liberty described above, and security was the guarantee of egoism. Marx concludes:

Thus none of the so-called rights of men goes beyond the egoistic man, the man withdrawn into himself, his private interest and his private choice, and separated from the community as a member of civil society. Far from viewing man here in his species-being, his species-life itself – society – rather appears to be an external framework for the individual, limiting his original independence. The only bond between men is natural necessity, need and private interest, the maintenance of their property and egoistic persons.[20]

These considerations make it strange, Marx continues, that these egoistic rights had been proclaimed most forcefully by men in revolutionary France who had been bent on founding a political community and awaking men's patriotism to fend off foreign aggression. For in their theory citizenship and the political community were merely the means to protect natural, human rights. Of course, the practice of the revolutionaries had often contradicted their theory and the state power had intervened to curtail men's liberties, but the problem still remained. It had an easy solution: political emancipation was the dissolution of the old civil society – feudalism – all of

18. 'On the Jewish Question', *MEGA* I, i (1) 594; Easton and Guddat, p. 235.
19. 'On the Jewish Question', *MEGA* I, i (1) 594; Easton and Guddat, p. 236.
20. 'On the Jewish Question', *MEGA* I, i (1) 595; Easton and Guddat, pp. 236 f.

whose elements had a directly political character (Marx here summarizes the long and detailed analyses in the 'Critique of Hegel's Philosophy of the State). This unity was destroyed when feudalism disappeared: 'The political revolution thereby abolished the political character of civil society. It shattered civil society into its constituent elements – on the one hand individuals and on the other the material and spiritual elements constituting the vital content and civil situation of these individuals. It released the political spirit, which had been broken, fragmented, and lost, as it were, in the various cul-de-sacs of feudal society.'[21] But the transition from feudal to bourgeois society had not brought human emancipation: 'Thus man was not freed from religion; he received religious freedom. He was not freed from property. He received freedom of property. He was not freed from the egoism of trade but received freedom of trade.'[22] Marx does not go into detail about the human emancipation that he proposes in place of political emancipation. He defines political emancipation as 'a reduction of man to a member of civil society, to an egoistic independent individual on the one hand and to a citizen, a moral person, on the other', and declares:

Only when the actual, individual man has taken back into himself the abstract citizen and in his everyday life, his individual work, and his individual relationships has become a species-being, only when he has recognized and organized his own powers as social powers so that social force is no longer separated from him as political power, only then is human emancipation complete.[23]

21. 'On the Jewish Question', *MEGA* I, i (1) 597; Easton and Guddat, p. 239.

22. 'On the Jewish Question', *MEGA* I, i (1) 598; Easton and Guddat, p. 240.

23. 'On the Jewish Question', *MEGA* I, i (1) 599; Easton and Guddat, p. 241.

The second part of Marx's review article is devoted to Bauer's essay entitled 'The Capacity of Present-Day Jews and Christians to Become Free', which was published in Herwegh's *Twenty-one Sheets from Switzerland*. Bauer's theme was that the Jew was further removed from emancipation than the Christian for, whereas the Christian had only to break with his own religion, the Jew had also to break with the completion of his religion, that is, Christianity. The Christian had only one step to make, the Jew two. Taking issue again with Bauer's theological formulation of the problem, Marx develops a theme that he had already touched on in the first part of his article: religion as the spiritual façade of a sordid and egoistic world. For Marx, the question of Jewish emancipation had become the question of what specific *social* element needs to be overcome in order to abolish Judaism. He defines the secular basis of Judaism as practical need and self-interest, the Jew's worldly cult as barter, and his worldly god as money. The conclusion is:

An organization of society that would abolish the preconditions of bargaining and thus its possibility would render the Jew impossible. His religious consciousness would dissolve like a dull mist in the actual life-giving air of society. On the other hand, when the Jew recognizes this practical nature of his as futile and strives to eliminate it, he works away from his previous development towards general human emancipation and opposes the supreme practical expression of human self-alienation.[24]

The Jew had, however, already emancipated himself in a Jewish way. This had been possible because the Christian world had become impregnated with the practical Jewish spirit. Their deprivation of theoretical political rights

24. 'On the Jewish Question', *MEGA* I, i (1) 601; Easton and Guddat, p. 243.

mattered little to Jews, who in practice wielded great financial power. 'The contradiction existing between the practical political power of the Jew and his political rights is the contradiction between politics and financial power in general. While politics ideally is superior to financial power, in actual fact it has become its serf.'[25]

The basis of civil society was practical need and the god of this practical need was money, the secularized god of the Jews:

> Money is the jealous god of Israel before whom no other god may exist. Money degrades all the gods of mankind – and converts them into commodities. Money is the general, self-sufficient value of everything. Hence it has robbed the whole world, the human world as well as nature, of its proper worth. Money is the alienated essence of man's labour and life, and this alien essence dominates him as he worships it.[26]

Judaism could not develop further as a religion, but had succeeded in installing itself in practice at the heart of civil society and the Christian world:

> Judaism reaches its height with the perfection of civil society, but civil society achieves perfection only in the Christian world. Only under the reign of Christianity, which makes all national, natural, moral and theoretical relationships external to man, was civil society able to separate itself completely from political life, sever all man's species-ties, substitute egoism and selfish need for those ties, and dissolve the human world into a world of atomistic, mutually hostile individuals.[27]

Thus Christianity, which arose out of Judaism, had now dissolved itself back into Judaism.

25. 'On the Jewish Question', *MEGA* I, i (1) 602 f.; Easton and Guddat, p. 245.

26. 'On the Jewish Question', *MEGA* I, i (1) 603; Easton and Guddat, pp. 245 f.

27. 'On the Jewish Question', *MEGA* I, i (1) 604 f.; Easton and Guddat, p. 247.

Marx's conclusion outlines the idea of alienated labour that he will shortly develop at length:

As long as man is captivated in religion, knows his nature only as objectified, and thereby converts his nature into an alien illusory being, so under the domination of egoistic need he can only act practically, only practically produce objects, by subordinating both his products and his activity to the domination of an alien being, bestowing upon them the significance of an alien entity – of money.[28]

Many of the themes of this article, particularly that of money and the Jewish–Christian relationship, are taken directly from an article by Hess entitled 'On the Essence of Money'.[29] Hess submitted this article for publication in the *Deutsch–Französische Jahrbücher,* but the review collapsed before it could appear. Hess's influence here is important, as Marx's criticism of Bauer's second article contains his first tentative application to the field of economics of Feuerbach's idea of alienation. Hess had converted both Engels and Bakunin to communism, but his influence on Marx was a much slower process: in 1842–3, when Hess's proselytizing was at its most active, Marx was no communist, and by the time Marx did become a communist, in Paris, Hess was only one among many new points of reference. Nevertheless, at this particular juncture, Marx seems to have leaned very heavily on Hess.[30]

It is largely this article that has given the impression

28. 'On the Jewish Question', *MEGA* I, i (1) 605; Easton and Guddat, p. 248.

29. See further McLellan, *The Young Hegelians and Karl Marx,* pp. 153 ff.

30. On the relationship of Hess to Marx, see Kägi, *Genesis des historischen Materialismus,* pp. 145 ff.; McLellan, *The Young Hegelians and Karl Marx,* pp. 137 ff. For a view emphasizing the 'eschatological' elements peculiar to both, see E. Thier, *Das Menschenbild des jungen Marx* (Göttingen, 1957) pp. 41 ff.

that Marx was an anti-semite.[31] This is inaccurate. In the passages already referred to in the *Holy Family* which deal with the Jewish question, Marx tends to side with the Jews more than with Bauer. Marx also makes clear there that he judges the political maturity of a state by the degree to which the Jews in it are emancipated, and considers it illogical of civil society not to grant the Jews equal rights.[32] Equally important, *Judentum*, the German word for Judaism, had the derivative meaning of 'commerce', and it is this meaning which is uppermost in Marx's mind throughout the article. 'Judaism' has very little religious, and still less racial, content for Marx and it would be little exaggeration to say that this latter part of Marx's review is an extended pun at Bauer's expense.

2. 'INTRODUCTION TO THE CRITIQUE OF HEGEL'S PHILOSOPHY OF LAW'

The perspective of the second of Marx's articles published in the *Deutsch-Französische Jahrbücher* is noticeably different. Whereas with regard to the Jewish question Marx criticizes Bauer within the framework of Feuerbach's philosophy, the 'Introduction to the Critique of Hegel's Philosophy of Law' contains much more dispassionate historical analysis. It was written as an introduction to a proposed rewriting of his 'Critique of Hegel's Philosophy of the State' of which the 'Jewish Question' had already elaborated several themes. Being only an introduction, it is in the nature of a summary, ordering its themes in a way that reflected the different stages of Marx's own de-

31. See, as an extreme, D. Runes's edition of this article entitled *A World without Jews* (New York, 1959).

32. See S. Avineri, 'Marx and Jewish Emancipation', *Journal of the History of Ideas*, xxv (1964).

velopment: religious, philosophical, political, revolutionary. The result is a manifesto whose incisiveness and dogmatism recall the *Communist Manifesto* of 1848. All the elements of the article are already contained in the 'Critique of Hegel's Philosophy of the State', though there is quite a new emphasis on the proletariat as future emancipator of society. Although written in Paris, the whole article is orientated towards Germany and the possibility of a German revolution. Accordingly Marx starts with religion and goes on to politics, the two most pressing subjects in Germany according to his programmatic letter to Ruge of September 1843.[33]

Marx begins by alluding to the whole work of the Young Hegelian school from Strauss to Feuerbach. 'For Germany', he wrote, 'the criticism of religion has been essentially completed, and criticism of religion is the premise of all criticism.'[34] It can be inferred that for Marx criticism of religion was 'the premise of all criticism'[35] for two reasons: in Germany, religion was one of the chief pillars of the Prussian state and had to be knocked away before any political change could be thought of; more generally, he believed that religion was the most extreme form of alienation and the point where any process of secularization had to start, and this supplies him with a model for criticism of other forms of alienation. The next sentences are a summary of Feuerbach's (and Hegel's) views on religion:

The profane existence of error is compromised when its heavenly *oratio pro aris et focis* [defence of altar and hearth] has been refuted. Man, who has found only the reflection of

33. See above, pp. 165 ff.

34. 'Introduction to a Critique of Hegel's Philosophy of Law', *MEGA* I, i (1) 607; Easton and Guddat, p. 249.

35. 'Introduction to a Critique of Hegel's Philosophy of Law', *MEGA* I, i (1) 607; Easton and Guddat, p. 249.

himself in the fantastic reality of heaven where he sought a supernatural being, will no longer be inclined to find the semblance of himself, only the non-human being, where he seeks and must seek his true reality.[36]

But then Marx shows where he differs from Feuerbach. It was not simply a question of reduction, of reducing religious elements to others that were more fundamental. Religion's false consciousness of man and the world existed as such because man and the world were radically vitiated: 'The basis of irreligious criticism is: man makes religion, religion does not make man. But man is not an abstract being squatting outside the world. Man is the world of man, the state, society. This state and this society produce religion, which is an inverted consciousness of the world because they are an inverted world.'[37] Religion was the necessary idealistic completion of a deficient material world and Marx used a cascade of images here: 'Religion is the generalized theory of this world, its encyclopedic compendium, its logic in popular form, its spiritualistic *point d'honneur*, its enthusiasm, its moral sanction, its solemn complement, its general ground of consolation and justification.'[38] Marx continues with a series of brilliant metaphors to show that religion, while being the symptom of a deep social malaise, was at the same time a protest against this malaise. Religion nevertheless stood in the way of any cure of social evils since at the same time it tended to justify them.

The struggle against religion is therefore indirectly the struggle against that world whose spiritual aroma is religion.

36. 'Introduction to a Critique of Hegel's Philosophy of Law', *MEGA* I, i (1) 607; Easton and Guddat, pp. 249 f.

37. 'Introduction to a Critique of Hegel's Philosophy of Law', *MEGA* I, i (1) 607; Easton and Guddat, p. 250.

38. 'Introduction to a Critique of Hegel's Philosophy of Law', *MEGA* I, i (1) 607; Easton and Guddat, p. 250.

Religious suffering is the expression of real suffering and at the same time the protest against real suffering. Religion is the sigh of the oppressed creature, the heart of a heartless world, as it is the spirit of spiritless conditions. It is the opium of the people. . . . The criticism of religion is thus in embryo a criticism of the vale of tears whose halo is religion.[39]

Marx did not write much about religion (Engels wrote much more) and this is the most detailed passage in all his writings. What he says here – that religion is a fantasy of alienated man – is representative of his early thought. In later remarks, the element of class ideology was much more dominant. Marx thought religion at once important and unimportant. Important, because the purely spiritual compensation that it afforded men frustrated efforts at material betterment. Unimportant, as he considered that his colleagues and particularly Feuerbach had fully exposed the true nature of religion. It was only a secondary phenomenon and, being dependent on socio-economic circumstances, merited no independent criticism.

Attempts to characterize Marxism as a religion, although plausible within their own terms, confuse the issue, as also do attempts to claim that Marx was not really an atheist. This is the approach usually taken by writers who stress the parallel between Marxism and the Judaeo–Christian history of salvation[40] – though some say that Marx took over this tradition when already secularized by Schelling or Hegel into an aesthetic or philosophical revelation.[41] It is true that Marx has in mind the religion of contemporary Germany dominated by a dogmatic and over-spiritual Lutheranism, but he writes about 'religion'

39. 'Introduction to a Critique of Hegel's Philosophy of Law', *MEGA* I, i (1) 607; Easton and Guddat, p. 250.

40. See, for example, Tucker, *Philosophy and Myth in Karl Marx*.

41. See Popitz, *Der entfremdete Mensch*.

in general and his rejection is absolute. Unlike so many early socialists (Weitling, Saint-Simon, Fourier), he would brook no compromise. Atheism was inseparable from humanism, he maintained; indeed, given the terms in which he posed the problem, this was undeniable. It is, of course, legitimate to change the meaning of 'atheism' in order to make Marx a believer *malgré lui*, but this tends to make the question senseless by blurring too many distinctions.[42]

Marx then turns from a summary of past results to the current progress of criticism:

Criticism has plucked imaginary flowers from the chain, not so that man will wear the chain that is without fantasy or consolation but so that he will throw it off and pluck the living flower. The criticism of religion disillusions man so that he thinks, acts, and shapes his reality like a disillusioned man who has come to his senses, so that he revolves around himself and thus around his true sun. Religion is only the illusory sun that revolves around man so long as he does not revolve about himself.[43]

The result was that criticism must turn to a deeper alienation, that of politics:

Thus it is the task of history, once the other-worldly truth has disappeared, to establish the truth of this world. The immediate task of the philosophy which is in the service of history is to unmask human self-alienation in its unholy forms now that it has been unmasked in its holy form. Thus the criticism of heaven turns into the criticism of the earth, the criticism of

42. The best general discussions of this topic are the two books by H. Desroches, *Marxisme et religions* (Paris, 1962); *Socialismes et sociologie religieuse* (Paris, 1965).

43. 'Introduction to a Critique of Hegel's Philosophy of Law', *MEGA* I, i (1) 608; Easton and Guddat, pp. 250 f.

religion into the criticism of law, and the criticism of theology into the criticism of politics.[44]

The body of Marx's article consists of two parts: an analysis of contemporary German politics as opposed to German philosophy; and the possibilities of revolution arising from this contrast. Marx begins by pointing out that even the necessary negation of Germany's present is anachronistic and would still leave Germany fifty years behind France. 'Indeed,' he continues

German history plumes itself on a development no nation in the historical firmament previously exhibited or will ever copy. We have in point of fact shared in the restorations of the modern nations without sharing in their revolutions. We have been restored, first because other nations dared to make revolutions, and secondly because other nations suffered counter-revolutions – on the one hand because our masters were afraid, and on the other because they were not afraid. Led by our shepherds, we found ourselves in the company of freedom only once, on the day of its burial.[45]

This state of chronic underdevelopment found its intellectual counterpart, according to Marx, in two schools of thought which he briefly characterizes. The first – the Historical School of Law which 'legitimizes today's infamy by yesterday's'[46] – Marx had already criticized at length two years previously in the *Rheinische Zeitung*,[47] the second, consisting of 'good-natured enthusiasts, German chauvinists by extraction and liberals by reflection ... seek our history of freedom beyond our freedom in the prim-

44. 'Introduction to a Critique of Hegel's Philosophy of Law', *MEGA* I, i (1) 608; Easton and Guddat, p. 251.
45. 'Introduction to a Critique of Hegel's Philosophy of Law', *MEGA* I, i (1) 608 f.; Easton and Guddat, p. 251.
46. 'Introduction to a Critique of Hegel's Philosophy of Law', *MEGA* I, i (1) 609; Easton and Guddat, p. 251.
47. cf. *MEGA* I, i (1) 251 ff.; Easton and Guddat, pp. 96 ff.

eval Teutonic forests.'[48] But what was wanted was not a freedom only to be found in forests, but one created by that 'relentless criticism of all existing conditions'[49] which Marx had advocated in his letter to Ruge. Marx shows in detail what he meant by this criticism by applying it to Germany. The situation there, he wrote, was really beneath any criticism, though an attack could serve to give the final blow to what had already been condemned and destroy what had already been refuted. 'Criticism is no longer an end in itself but simply a means. Its essential pathos is indignation, its essential task, denunciation.'[50] Marx then paraphrases, in two short paragraphs, the criticism of German society that he had so frequently elaborated over the last two years.

It is a matter of describing the pervasive, suffocating pressure of all social spheres on one another, the general but passive dejection, the narrowness that recognizes but misunderstands itself – this framed in a system of Government that lives on the conservation of all meanness and is nothing in Government.[51]

The purpose of this criticism was the same as that of the criticism of religion with which he began:

The point is to permit the Germans not even a moment of self-deception and resignation. We must make the actual pressure more pressing by adding to it the consciousness of pressure and making the shame more shameful by publicizing it. . . . The people must be taught to be terrified of themselves to give them courage. This will fulfil an imperative need of

48. 'Introduction to a Critique of Hegel's Philosophy of Law', *MEGA* I, i (1) 609; Easton and Guddat, p. 252.

49. 'Letter to Ruge', *MEGA* I, i (1) 573; Easton and Guddat, p. 212.

50. 'Introduction to a Critique of Hegel's Philosophy of Law', *MEGA* I, i (1) 609; Easton and Guddat, p. 252.

51. 'Introduction to a Critique of Hegel's Philosophy of Law', *MEGA* I, i (1) 609 f.; Easton and Guddat, p. 252.

the German nation, and the needs of nations are themselves the ultimate grounds of their satisfaction.[52]

This criticism, Marx continues, could also be of interest to those modern nations who were still burdened with reminders of their past. But whereas for them the downfall of the *ancien régime* could justly be called tragic, 'the modern *ancien régime* is merely the comedian in a world where real heroes are dead.'[53] Under the impact of French socialists like Saint-Simon and Proudhon who had considered the political implications of industrial development, Marx gives an example of how impossible it is to discuss 'truly human problems' within the framework of German conditions. 'The relation of industry and the world of wealth in general to the political world is a major problem of modern times. In what form is this problem beginning to preoccupy the Germans? In the form of protective tariffs, the system of prohibition, and political economy.'[54] Referring to Freidrich List, the chief exponent of the protectionist economics that he is criticizing, Marx continues:

Whereas the problem in France and England reads: political economy or the rule of society over wealth, in Germany it reads: political economy or the rule of private property over nationality. Thus in France and England it is a question of abolishing monopoly that has developed to its final consequences; in Germany it is a question of proceeding to the final consequences of monopoly. There it is a question of solution; here, still a question of collision. This is an adequate example of the German form of modern problems, an example of how

52. 'Introduction to a Critique of Hegel's Philosophy of Law', *MEGA* I, i (1) 610; Easton and Guddat, p. 253.

53. 'Introduction to a Critique of Hegel's Philosophy of Law', *MEGA* I, i (1) 611; Easton and Guddat, p. 254.

54. 'Introduction to a Critique of Hegel's Philosophy of Law', *MEGA* I, i (1) 611; Easton and Guddat, p. 254.

our history, like a raw recruit, still has had to do extra drill on matters threshed over in history.[55]

But there was one aspect in which Germany was actually in advance of other nations and which afforded her the opportunity for a radical revolution: her philosophy. This view, shared by all the contributors to the *Deutsch-Französische Jahrbücher,* made them appear to the French to be some sort of missionaries. It had been current in the Young Hegelian movement since Heine in his *History of Religion and Philosophy in Germany,* written in 1835, had drawn the parallel between German philosophy and French politics and prophesied a radical revolution for Germany as a consequence. In order to be at the heart of contemporary questions it was German philosophy that had to be criticized. For in Germany it was only political philosophy that was abreast of modern conditions. The result of this analysis was that:

The German nation must therefore join its dream-history to its present conditions and criticize not only these present conditions but also their abstract continuation. Its future can be limited neither to the direct negation of its real political and legal conditions nor to their direct fulfilment, for it has the direct negation of its real conditions in its ideal conditions and has almost outlived the direct fulfilment of its ideal conditions in the view of neighbouring countries.[56]

Marx then clarifies his own position by pointing to two different attitudes both of which seem to him to be inadequate. The first, which in some respects recalls the views of Feuerbach, Marx calls the 'practical political party'. This party

55. 'Introduction to a Critique of Hegel's Philosophy of Law', *MEGA* I, i (1) 611 f.; Easton and Guddat, pp. 254 f.

56. 'Introduction to a Critique of Hegel's Philosophy of Law', *MEGA* I, i (1) 612 f.; Easton and Guddat, pp. 255 f.

rightly demands the negation of philosophy. It is wrong not in its demand but in stopping at the demand it neither seriously fulfils nor can fulfil. It supposes that it accomplishes that negation by turning its back on philosophy.... You demand starting from actual germs of life but forget that the actual life-germ of the German nation has so far sprouted only inside its cranium. In short: you cannot transcend philosophy without actualizing it.[57]

The second attitude, characteristic of the theoretical party – by which Marx means Bruno Bauer and his followers – commits the same error but from the opposite direction:

In the present struggle the theoretical party saw only the critical struggle of German philosophy against the German world. It did not consider that previous philosophy itself belongs to this world and its complement, although an ideal one.... Its main defect may be summarized as follows: it believed that it could actualize philosophy without transcending it.[58]

Bauer's philosophy, because it refused any mediation with the real, was undialectical and condemned to sterility. What Marx proposes is a synthesis of the two views he condemns: a mediation with the real that would abolish philosophy 'as philosophy' while realizing it.[59] This is akin to Marx's later 'unity of theory and practice' and takes up a theme that had been in his mind since his thesis if not before – that of the secularization of philosophy. From Cieszkowski's *praxis* in 1838 to Hess's 'Philosophy of

57. 'Introduction to a Critique of Hegel's Philosophy of Law', *MEGA* I, i (1) 613; Easton and Guddat, p. 256.
58. 'Introduction to a Critique of Hegel's Philosophy of Law', *MEGA* I, i (1) 613; Easton and Guddat, p. 256.
59. The word that Marx uses for 'abolish' is the Hegelian term *aufheben*, on the meaning of which see above, pp. 33 f.

Action' in 1843,[60] this is a theme central to Hegel's disciples trying to break loose from their master's system to get a grip on political events. It is along these lines that Marx sees the only possible way of solving Germany's problems.

Marx then turns, in the second part of his article, to an exploration of the possibility of a revolution that would not only eliminate Germany's backwardness, but also make her the first nation to have achieved an emancipation that was not merely political. Thus Marx puts the question 'Can Germany reach a practice *à la hauteur des principes,* that is, a revolution which will raise it not only to the official level of modern nations, but to the human level which will be their immediate future?'[61] By way of a preliminary answer, Marx recapitulates his previous conclusion:

The weapon of criticism obviously cannot replace the criticism of weapons. Material force must be overthrown by material force. But theory also becomes a material force once it has gripped the masses. Theory is capable of gripping the masses when it demonstrates *ad hominem,* and it demonstrates *ad hominem* when it becomes radical. To be radical is to grasp things by the root, but for man the root is man himself. The clear proof of the radicalism of German theory and hence of its political energy is that it proceeds from the decisive positive transcendance of religion. The criticism of religion ends with the doctrine that man is the highest being for man, hence with the categorical imperative to overthrow all conditions in which man is a degraded, enslaved, neglected, contemptible being.[62]

60. See Hess's articles in *Twenty-One Sheets from Switzerland,* reprinted in *M. Hess. Philosophische und sozialistische Aufsätze,* ed. Cornu and Mönke, pp. 220 ff.

61. 'Introduction to a Critique of Hegel's Philosophy of Law', *MEGA* I, i (1) 614; Easton and Guddat, p. 257.

62. 'Introduction to a Critique of Hegel's Philosophy of Law', *MEGA* I, i (1) 614 f.; Easton and Guddat, pp. 257 f.

The importance of the 'weapon of criticism' for Germany is shown by Luther's theoretical revolution – the Reformation. Of course this revolution was an incomplete one: Luther had merely internalized man's religious consciousness; he had 'shattered faith in authority by restoring the authority of faith'.[63] But although Protestantism had not found the true solution, at least its formulation of the problem had been correct. The present situation of Germany was similar to that which preceded the Reformation; the only difference was that philosophy took the place of theology and the result would be a human emancipation instead of one that took place entirely within the sphere of religion.

In the last few pregnant pages of the article, Marx draws from his sombre review of the German scene the optimistic conclusion that the revolution in Germany, as opposed to France, could not be partial and must be radical. Only the proletariat, in alliance with philosophy, would be capable of carrying it out.

Marx begins with the difficulties that seem to stand in the way of a radical German revolution. 'Revolutions require a passive element, a material basis. Theory is actualized in a people only in so far as it actualizes their needs.'[64] The question was whether practical needs in Germany complemented theoretical needs. 'It is not enough that thought should seek its actualization; actuality must itself strive toward thought.'[65] But German reality was many stages behind the political development of such countries as France and it was not at all clear how it could

63. 'Introduction to a Critique of Hegel's Philosophy of Law', *MEGA* I, i (1) 615; Easton and Guddat, p. 258.
64. 'Introduction to a Critique of Hegel's Philosophy of Law', *MEGA* I, i (1) 615 f.; Easton and Guddat, p. 259.
65. 'Introduction to a Critique of Hegel's Philosophy of Law', *MEGA* I, i (1) 616; Easton and Guddat, p. 259.

transcend not only its own limitations but those of other nations too. 'A radical revolution can only be a revolution of radical needs whose preconditions and birthplaces appear to be lacking.'[66]

But the very fact that Germany was so deficient politically indicated the sort of future that awaited her. The enormous and increasing gap between, on the one hand, modern political states together with their counterpart – German philosophy – and, on the other, the political situation inside Germany created a state of affairs that demanded radical measures. German governments 'are driven to combine the civilized deficiencies of the modern political order (whose advantages we do not enjoy) with the barbarous deficiencies of the *ancien régime* (which we enjoy in full). Hence Germany must participate more and more if not in the sense at least in the nonsense of those political forms transcending its *status quo*.'[67] This tendency, which ensured that 'as the gods of all nations were found in the Roman Pantheon, the sins of all forms of the state will be found in the Holy German Empire',[68] was enhanced by the character of Frederick William IV, whose indecisive nature denied to his many vices even the virtue of consistency. The result of this was that 'as the deficiency of the political present erected into a system, Germany will not be able to shed these specifically German limitations without shedding the general limitations of the political present.'[69]

66. 'Introduction to a Critique of Hegel's Philosophy of Law', *MEGA* I, i (1) 616; Easton and Guddat, p. 259.

67. 'Introduction to a Critique of Hegel's Philosophy of Law', *MEGA* I, i (1) 616; Easton and Guddat, p. 259.

68. 'Introduction to a Critique of Hegel's Philosophy of Law', *MEGA* I, i (1) 617; Easton and Guddat, p. 260.

69. 'Introduction to Critique of Hegel's Philosophy of Law', *MEGA* I, i (1) 617; Easton and Guddat, p. 260.

What was utopian for Germany was not a radical revolution that would achieve the complete emancipation of mankind but a partial revolution, a revolution that was merely political, a revolution 'that leaves the pillars of the house standing'.[70] Marx then characterizes a purely political revolution, obviously taking the French Revolution as his paradigm. The basis of this revolution was 'part of civil society emancipating itself and attaining universal supremacy, a particular class by virtue of its special situation undertaking the general emancipation of society. This class emancipates the whole of society, but only on the condition that the whole of society is in the same position as this class, for example, that it has or can easily acquire money and education.'[71] No class could occupy this 'special situation' in society without arousing an impulse 'of enthusiasm in itself and in the masses, an impulse in which it fraternizes and merges with society at large, identifies itself with it, and is experienced and recognized as its general representative, an impulse in which its claims and rights are truly the claims and rights of society itself and in which it is actually the social head and the social heart.'[72] And for a class to be able to seize this emancipatory position, there must be a polarization of classes: 'A particular class must be the class of general offence and the incorporation of general limitation. A particular social sphere must stand for the notorious crime of society as a whole so that emancipation from this sphere appears as general self-emancipation. For one class to be the class of emancipation *par excellence*, conversely another must be the obvious class of

70. 'Introduction to a Critique of Hegel's Philosophy of Law', *MEGA* I, i (1) 617; Easton and Guddat, p. 260.
71. 'Introduction to a Critique of Hegel's Philosophy of Law', *MEGA* I, i (1) 617; Easton and Guddat, p. 260.
72. 'Introduction to a Critique of Hegel's Philosophy of Law', *MEGA* I, i (1) 617; Easton and Guddat, p. 260.

oppression.'[73] This, according to Marx, was the situation in France before 1789 when 'the negative, general significance of the French nobility and clergy determined the positive, general significance of the bourgeois standing next to and opposing them.'[74]

In Germany, however, the situation was very different. For there every class lacked the cohesion and courage that could cast it for the role of the negative representative of society and also the imagination to identify itself with the people at large. Class consciousness sprang from the activity of oppressing a lower class rather than from defiant protest against oppression from above. Progress was thus impossible, for every class was engaged in a struggle on more than one front:

Hence princes struggle against kings, the bureaucrat against the nobility, and the bourgeoisie against them all, while the proletariat is already beginning to struggle against the bourgeoisie. The middle class hardly dares to conceive the idea of emancipation from its own perspective. The development of social conditions and the progress of political theory show that perspective to be already antiquated or at least problematic.[75]

Marx then summarizes the contrast he has been elaborating between France and Germany:

In France it is enough to be something for one to want to be everything. In Germany no one can be anything unless he is prepared to renounce everything. In France partial emancipation is the basis of universal emancipation. In Germany universal emancipation is the *conditio sine qua non* of any partial emancipation. In France it is the actuality, in Germany the

73. 'Introduction to a Critique of Hegel's Philosophy of Law', *MEGA* I, i (1) 618; Easton and Guddat, p. 261.

74. 'Introduction to a Critique of Hegel's Philosophy of Law', *MEGA* I, i (1) 610; Easton and Guddat, p. 261.

75. 'Introduction to a Critique of Hegel's Philosophy of Law', *MEGA* I, i (1) 619; Easton and Guddat, p. 262.

impossibility, of gradual emancipation which must give birth to complete freedom. In France every class of the nation is politically idealistic and experiences itself first of all not as a particular class, but as representing the general needs of society. The role of emancipator thus passes successively and dramatically to different classes of people until it finally reaches the class which actualizes social freedom, no longer assuming certain conditions external to man and yet created by human society but rather organizing all the conditions of human existence on the basis of social freedom. In Germany by contrast, where practical life is as mindless as mental life is impractical, no class in civil society has any need or capacity for general emancipation until it is forced to it by its immediate condition, by material necessity, by its very chains.[76]

This passage shows the importance of his study of the French Revolution in the formation of Marx's views. The Rhineland, where he was born, brought up and edited the *Rheinische Zeitung*, had been French until 1814, and had taken part in the gains of the French Revolution where civil emancipation was a genuine experience and not a possession of foreigners only, to be envied from afar. To all German intellectuals the French Revolution was *the* revolution, and Marx and his Young Hegelian friends constantly compared themselves to the heroes of 1789. It was his reading of the history of the French Revolution in the summer of 1843 that showed him the role of class struggle in social development. While at Kreuznach Marx read, and took many extracts from, the works of Wachsmuth, Condorcet, Madame Roland, Madame de Staël, Mignet, Thiers, Buchez and Roux, Bailleul and Levasseur.[77] In 1852 Marx wrote to Weydemeyer: 'No credit is

76. 'Introduction to a Critique of Hegel's Philosophy of Law', *MEGA* I, i (1) 619; Easton and Guddat, p. 262.

77. For a short analysis of the content of each of these books and suggestions as to their effect on Marx, see Kägi, *Genesis des historischen Materialismus*, pp. 169 ff.

due to me for discovering the existence of classes in modern society, nor yet the struggle between them. Long before, the bourgeois historians had described the historical development of the class struggle.'[78] This reading continued until the summer of 1844. Ruge wrote in May 1844: 'Marx wishes ... to write the history of the Convention; he has assembled the necessary documentation for this and arrived at new and fruitful conceptions.'[79] Marx even sketched out the table of contents of a book he intended to call *The Genetic History of the Modern State or The French Revolution*.[80]

Marx now arrives at the denouement of his article, which he introduces with the question: 'Where, then, is the positive possibility of German emancipation?' His answer is:

in the formation of a class with radical chains, a class in civil society that is not of civil society, a class that is the dissolution of all classes, a sphere of society having a universal character because of its universal suffering and claiming no particular right because no particular wrong but unqualified wrong is perpetrated on it; a sphere that can invoke no traditional title but only a human title, which does not partially oppose the consequences but totally opposes the premises of the German political system; a sphere, finally, that cannot emancipate itself without emancipating itself from all the other spheres of society, thereby emancipating them; a sphere, in short, that is the complete loss of humanity and can only redeem itself through the total redemption of humanity. This dissolution of society as a particular class is the proletariat.[81]

78. Marx–Engels, *Selected Correspondence* (London, 1934) p. 37.
79. Ruge, *Briefwechsel und Nachlass*, ed. Nerrlich 1 343; see also ibid., p. 362.
80. *MEGA* 1 v 532; Easton and Guddat, p. 399.
81. 'Introduction to a Critique of Hegel's Philosophy of Law', *MEGA* 1, i (1) 619 f.; Easton and Guddat, p. 262.

This passage raises an obvious question as to the reasons for Marx's sudden adhesion to the cause of the proletariat. Some have claimed that Marx's description of the proletariat is non-empirical and thus that its ultimate source is Hegel's philosophy. It has, for example, been maintained that 'The insight into the world-historical role of the proletariat is obtained in a purely speculative manner by a 'reversal' of the connections that Hegel had established between different forms of objective spirit.'[82] Or, more recently: 'It is evident that Marx ... arrives at his idea of the proletariat not through an economic study or an historical analysis, but through a series of arguments and confrontations all of which are within the Hegelian tradition and relate to the Hegelian idea of a universal class.'[83] Another author claims to find here the exemplification of the dual Hegelian dialectic of master and slave and universal and particular.[84] A further refinement claims that Hegel's insights are fundamentally those of a German Protestant and thus that Marx's underlying *schema* here is the Christian conception of salvation – the proletariat plays the role of Isaiah's suffering servant:

Through Hegel, the young Marx links up, no doubt unconsciously, with the soteriological *schema* underlying the Judaeo–Christian tradition: the idea of the collective salvation obtained by a particular group, the theme of salvific destitution, the opposition of injustice that enslaves and generosity that frees. The proletariat, bringing universal salvation, plays a role analogous to that of the Messianic community or personal saviour in biblical revelation.[85]

82. Friedrich, *Philosophie und Ökonomie beim jungen Marx*, p. 81, following Popitz, *Der entfremdete Mensch*, p. 99.

83. S. Avineri, 'The Hegelian Origins of Marx's Political Thought', *Review of Metaphysics* (September 1967) p. 41.

84. Cf. Wackenheim. *La Faillite de la religion d'apres Karl Marx*, p. 200.

85. ibid.

Or, even more explicitly: 'That the *universality* of the proletariat echoes the claims of the *universal* Christ is confirmed by Marx's insistence that the proletariat will exist, precisely at the point when it becomes universal, in a scourged and emptied condition – and this, of course, is Marx's variant of the divine *kenosis*.'[86] Others have claimed that, since Marx's views are not empirically based, this shows that they have their origin in an ethical indignation at the condition of the proletariat.

These views, at least as a total explanation, are mistaken. Marx's proclamation of the key role of the proletariat is a contemporary application of the analysis of the French Revolution he had outlined earlier in his article, when he talked of a particular social sphere having to 'stand for the notorious crime of society as a whole so that emancipation from this sphere appears as general self-emancipation'.[87] The proletariat was now in the position the French bourgeoisie had occupied in 1789. It was now the proletariat which could echo the words of Sièyès,[88] 'I am nothing and I should be everything'. The context thus shows that Marx's account of the role of the proletariat was drawn from his study of the French Revolution, however much his language may be that of Young Hegelian journalism.

To this historical base was added a distillation of contemporary French socialist ideas. For three months already Marx had lived and worked with prominent socialists in Paris. The view of the proletariat contained in his article was not unique even in Young Hegelian circles, but it was of course commonplace in Paris. It is surprising,

86. E. Olssen, 'Marx and the Resurrection', *Journal of the History of Ideas* (1968) p. 136.

87. 'Introduction to a Critique of Hegel's Philosophy of Law', *MEGA* I, i (1) 618; Easton and Guddat, p. 261.

88. Not noted for having been a Hegelian before the event.

then, that some have argued that Lorenz von Stein's book *Socialism and Communism in Contemporary France* was instrumental in his conversion.[89] (The book had first appeared eighteen months previously when Marx was not responsive to socialist ideas; though it had wide influence on the German radical circles in which he moved, it had apparently made no impact on him at that time.) Indeed, far from being elaborations of bookish material studied at second or third hand,[90] Marx's sudden espousal of the proletarian cause can be directly attributed to his first-hand contacts with socialist intellectuals in France. Instead of editing a paper for the Rhenish bourgeoisie or sitting in his study in Kreuznach, he was now at the heart of socialist thought and action. From October 1843 Marx was breathing a socialist atmosphere and even living in the same house as Germain Mäurer, one of the leaders of the League of the Just whose meetings Marx frequented. It is not surprising that his surroundings made a swift impact on Marx.

Marx admitted that the proletariat he described was only just beginning to exist in Germany. For what characterized it was not natural poverty (though this had a part to play) but poverty that was artificially produced and resulted particularly in the disintegration of the middle class. The proletariat would achieve the dissolution of the old order of society by the negation of private property, a negation of which it was itself the embodiment. This was the class in which philosophy could finally realize itself: 'As philosophy finds its material weapons in the proletariat, the proletariat finds its intellectual weapons in philosophy. And once the lightning of thought has deeply

89. On Stein's books, see above, p. 125.

90. See Tucker, *Philosophy and Myth in Karl Marx*, p. 114, who goes as far as to say that the only proletarians Marx knew were those in books.

struck the unsophisticated soil of the people, the Germans will emancipate themselves to become men.'[91] The signal for this revolution would come from France: 'When all the inner conditions are fulfilled, the day of German resurrection will be announced by the crowing of the French rooster.'[92]

In spite of the originality of many of the articles it contained, the *Deutsch-Französische Jahrbücher* met with little success. In Paris, the French were not interested in an exclusively German publication and in Germany government reaction was swift. Warrants were issued in Prussia for the arrest of Ruge, Marx, Heine and Bernays immediately they should set foot on Prussian soil, and the confiscation of the periodical inside Prussia was ordered. Hundreds of copies were seized at the frontier and this aggravated the financial difficulties of the review. When Froebel decided to withdraw his backing, its fate was virtually sealed. There were also financial problems among the contributors themselves: Hess had to borrow money from Ruge and had difficulty in paying it back; and Ruge only paid Marx for his contributions with copies of the *Deutsch-Französische Jahrbücher*. Finally, the political opinions of Marx and Ruge began to diverge more and more. For during his stay in Paris Ruge became more and more bitter about German communists, arriving, by the spring of 1844, at the conclusion that they were money-grasping individuals who advocated a slavery and a police state that would only generalize the misery of the proletariat. The occasion of the definitive break between Ruge and Marx was a quarrel about Herwegh, whom Ruge criticized for his dissolute life. But whereas in the

91. 'Introduction to a Critique of Hegel's Philosophy of Law', *MEGA* I, i (1) 620; Easton and Guddat, pp. 263 f.

92. 'Introduction to a Critique of Hegel's Philosophy of Law', *MEGA* I, i (1) 621; Easton and Guddat, p. 264.

case of the *Freien* Marx had agreed with Ruge, now he took the opposite side. On 15 May, Ruge wrote to Feuerbach: 'Marx broke formally with me by letter, taking advantage for this of my having expressed myself perhaps a little too harshly on the sybaritism and cynicism of Herwegh that contrasted with his public character. Marx defended Herwegh by saying that he was a genius with a great future in front of him.'[93]

Marx later found an opportunity of publicly breaking with Ruge by violently attacking an article that Ruge wrote in July in *Vorwärts*, a German socialist paper published in Paris and edited by Bernays who had contributed to the *Deutsch-Französische Jahrbücher*. Apropos of the revolt of the Silesian weavers in the summer of 1844, Ruge had claimed that no social revolt could succeed in Germany since political consciousness was extremely underdeveloped and social reform sprang from political revolution. Marx, in his reply, favourably contrasted the scale of the Silesian weavers' revolt with workers' revolts in England. A political consciousness was not sufficient to deal with social poverty: England had a very developed political consciousness, yet it was the country with the most extended pauperism. The British Government had an enormous amount of information at its disposal, but after two centuries of legislation on pauperism could find nothing better than the workhouse. In France, too, the Convention and Napoleon had unsuccessfully tried to suppress beggary. Thus the fault was not in this or that form of the state, as Ruge believed, and the solution could not be found in this or that political programme. The fault lay in the very nature of political power:

The state and the organization of society are not, from the political standpoint, two different things. The state is the

93. Ruge, *Briefwechsel und Nachlass*. ed. Nerrlich, 1 345.

organization of society. So far as the state admits the existence of social evils, it attributes them either to natural laws, which no human power can change, or to private life, which is independent of the state, or to the inadequacy of the administration, which is dependent on it. Thus England finds poverty rooted in the natural law according to which population continuously exceeds the means of subsistence. From another side, England explains pauperism as a consequence of the ill will of the poor, just as the King of Prussia explains it by the unchristian spirit of the rich and the Convention explains it by the counter-revolutionary and equivocal attitude of property owners. Hence England punishes the poor, the King of Prussia admonishes the rich, and the Convention decapitates property owners.[94]

Thus if the state wanted to transcend the impotence of its administration it would have to abolish itself, for

it is based on the contradiction between public and private life, and on the contradiction between general interests and particular interests. The administration, therefore, must confine itself to a formal and negative activity because its power ceases where civil life and its work begin.... This dismemberment, this debasement, this slavery of civil society is the natural foundation on which the modern state rests, just as the civil society of slavery was the foundation of the state in antiquity. The existence of the state and the existence of slavery are indivisible.[95]

This was confirmed by the fact that the more powerful the state and the more developed the political consciousness of a nation, the less it was disposed to seek the cause of social ills in the state itself. Marx once again substantiates his point by reference to the French Revolution, whose heroes

94. 'Critical Notes on "The King of Prussia and Social Reform" ', K. Marx and F. Engels, *Werke* (Berlin, 1965 ff.) I, 401 (hereafter referred to as *MEW*); Easton and Guddat, p. 348.

95. 'Critical Notes on "The King of Prussia and Social Reform" ' *MEW* I, 401 f.; Easton and Guddat, p. 349.

'far from perceiving the source of social defects in the principle of the state, rather saw the source of political evils in social defects'.[96]

Thus for Marx it was not 'political consciousness' that was important. The Silesian revolt was even more important than revolts in England and France, because it showed a more developed class consciousness. After favourably comparing Weitling's works with those of Proudhon and the German bourgeoisie,[97] Marx repeats his prediction in the *Deutsch-Französische Jahrbücher* of the role of the proletariat and the chances of a radical revolution:

The German proletariat is the theorist of the European proletariat, just as the English proletariat is its economist and the French proletariat its politician. It must be admitted that Germany, though incapable of political revolution, has a classical summons to social revolution.... Only in socialism can a philosophical people find its suitable practice, thus only in the proletariat can it find the active element of its emancipation.[98]

Marx finishes his article with a passage that gives a concise summary of his studies on social change:

We have seen that a social revolution involves the standpoint of the whole because it is a protest of men against dehumanized life even if it occurs in only one factory district, because it proceeds from the standpoint of the single actual individual, because the community against whose separation from himself the individual reacts is the true community of man, human existence. The political soul of a revolution, on the other hand,

96. 'Critical Notes on "The King of Prussia and Social Reform"', *MEW* I, 402; Easton and Guddat, p. 350.

97. Marx is somewhat inaccurate in claiming that there existed a specifically German form of socialism; for Weitling, like the other German socialists, had got his socialism from French sources, having lived several years in Paris.

98. 'Critical Notes on "The King of Prussia and Social Reform"', *MEW* I, 405; Easton and Guddat, p. 353.

consists in the tendency of politically uninfluential classes to end their isolation from the state and from power. Its stand-point is that of the state, an abstract whole, which exists only through the separation from actual life and which is unthink-able without the organized antithesis between the universal idea and the individual existence of man. Hence a revolution of the political soul also organizes, in accordance with the narrow and split nature of this soul, a ruling group in society at the expense of society.[99]

Thus Ruge's idea that social revolution necessarily had a political soul was the opposite of the truth:

Any revolution breaks up the old society; to that extent it is social. Any revolution overthrows the old ruling power; to that extent it is political.... Revolution in general – the overthrow of the existing ruling power and the dissolution of the old conditions – is a political act. Without revolution, however, socialism cannot come about. It requires this political act so far as it needs overthrow and dissolution. But where its organizing activity begins, where its own aim and spirit emerge, there socialism throws the political hull away.[100]

This article marked the end of Marx's collaboration with his Young Hegelian colleagues. Of the old company, only Hess remained, though Marx made the closer ac-quaintance of another Young Hegelian – Frederick Engels. It was partly under his influence that Marx began to undertake exclusively economic studies.

99. 'Critical Notes on "The King of Prussia and Social Reform"', *MEW* 1, 408; Easton and Guddat, pp. 356 f.

100. 'Critical Notes on "The King of Prussia and Social Reform"', *MEW* 1, 409; Easton and Guddat, p. 357.

CHAPTER SEVEN

The 'Paris Manuscripts'

1. THE PREFACE

During the summer of 1844, Marx began to compose a
critique of political economy that was, in effect, the first of
several drafts preceding *Capital* in 1867. In a preface that
he sketched out for this work he explained that he could
not fulfil the promise made in the *Deutsch-Französische
Jahrbücher* of publishing a critique of Hegel's philosophy
of law. For

> preparing this for publication, I found that the combination of
> criticism directed solely against speculation with criticism of
> various subjects would be quite unsuitable; it would impede
> the development of the argument and render comprehension
> difficult. Moreover, the wealth and diversity of the subjects to
> be dealt with could have been accommodated in a single work
> only in a very aphoristic style, and such aphoristic presentation
> would have given the impression of arbitrary systematization.[1]

He therefore proposed to deal with the various subjects –
law, morals, politics etc. – in independent 'brochures', beginning with political economy, and ending with a general
treatise showing their interrelationship and criticizing the
speculative treatment of the material – indeed, he had already signed a contract for this work with Leske, a publisher in Darmstadt. In this project for a lifetime's work,
Marx never got beyond the first stage, *Capital* and its

1. Paris Manuscripts', *Frühe Schriften*, ed. H.-J. Lieber and P.
Furth (Stuttgart, 1962) I, 504 (hereafter referred to as *Frühe Schriften*); Easton and Guddat, p. 284.

predecessors being the first and also the last of these 'brochures'.

Four of the manuscripts which were to form the basis of this critique of political economy have survived, though in an incomplete form. The first, twenty-seven pages long, consists largely of excerpts from classical economists on wages, profit and rent, followed by Marx's own reflections on alienated labour. The second manuscript is a fragment of four pages on the relationship of capital to labour. The third is forty-five pages long and comprises a discussion on private property, labour and communism; a critique of Hegel's dialectic; a section on production and the division of labour; and a short section on money. The fourth manuscript, four pages long, is a summary of the final chapter of Hegel's *Phenomenology*.

The form of these manuscripts is similar to that of Marx's 'Critique of Hegel's Philosophy of Law' of the previous summer – extracts from the authors under discussion accompanied by a critical commentary. The style and degree of elaboration are, however, very varied. In the excerpts from the classical economists Marx, as he says himself,[2] uses their own language, and speaks in plain, short sentences; Marx's own reflections on society recall the rhetorical language of his previous articles; while his discussions of Hegel's philosophy have the same involvement and obscurity as their subject.

In the preface, Marx mentions his sources. The first was a 'thorough critical study of political economy'.[3] Before beginning his first manuscript, Marx had read and excerpted fifteen works on economics, including Adam

2. 'Paris Manuscripts', *Frühe Schriften*, p. 559; Easton and Guddat, p. 287.

3. 'Paris Manuscripts', *Frühe Schriften*, p. 507; Easton and Guddat, p. 284.

Smith, Ricardo and Say. The second debt that Marx acknowledged was to German socialists, though he adds that, apart from Weitling, 'the significant and original German contributions on this subject ... amount to no more than the essays by Hess in *Twenty-one Sheets* and Engel's 'Outlines of a Critique of Political Economy' in the *Deutsch-Französische Jahrbücher*.[4] It was above all Engels who directed Marx's attention to economics and Engels's article in the *Deutsch-Französische Jahrbücher* was the first work on economics from which Marx took notes. The two had met before in Cologne in November 1842, but Marx had received Engels coldly, seeing in him a representative of the Berlin *Freien* with whom he had just broken. Engels had been converted to communism by Hess and spent most of 1843 working in his father's factory at Manchester. There he had been in contact with English socialists and studied Smith, Owen, Mill, Malthus and Ricardo. Herwegh invited him to write something for the *Deutsch-Französische Jahrbücher* and Engels replied with two articles: 'The Situation in England' and 'Outlines of a Critique of Political Economy'. Having interpreted continental movements to the English in the Owenite paper *New Moral World*, Engels did the reverse in the *Deutsch-Französische Jahrbücher*. The first of his articles was a critique of Carlyle's book *Past and Present*. Engels sympathized with Carlyle's criticism of the inhuman society created by capitalism, but denied that the solution consisted in a return to religious idealism: what Engels advocated was a thorough Feuerbachian humanism. His second article was a summary of his reading on economics. Central to it was an indictment of private property and of the spirit of competition that it engendered. The recurrent

4. 'Paris Manuscripts', *Frühe Schriften*, p. 507; Easton and Guddat, p. 285.

crises were the result of anarchy in production; the growth and accumulation of capital involved a lowering of salaries and accentuated the class struggle. Science and technology, which could afford immense possibilities under communism, only served, in a capitalist society, to increase the oppression of the workers. This article made a great impression on Marx (who called it a 'sketch of genius')[5] and marked the beginning of his interest in economic questions. Marx and Engels began their long correspondence immediately after the appearance of the *Deutsch-Französische Jahrbücher*. And Marx wrote later that, when Engels came to Paris in the summer of 1844, 'We realized that our views were in complete harmony in all theoretical fields and it is from that time that our cooperation dates.'[6]

The third source that Marx mentions are the French and English socialists. Among these it was certainly Proudhon with whom Marx had the most contact. Marx had already singled out from among French socialists Proudhon's 'penetrating work'.[7] They saw a lot of each other while Marx was in Paris. Marx wrote: 'In the course of lengthy debates, often lasting all night, I infected him to his great injury with Hegelianism which, owing to his lack of German, he could not study properly.'[8] Engels, too, recalled when 'the two of them in Paris spent whole nights discussing economic questions'.[9] What Marx most ap-

5. K. Marx, 'Preface to A Critique of Political Economy', in Marx–Engels, *Selected Works*, I, 364.

6. F. Engels, 'History of the Communist League', in Marx–Engels, *Selected Works* II, 3; II, 344.

7. 'Communism and the *Augsburger Allgemeine Zeitung*', *MEGA* I, i (1) 263; Easton and Guddat, p. 135.

8. Marx to Schweitzer, in Marx–Engels, *Selected Correspondence*, p. 171.

9. F. Engels, Introduction to K. Marx, *The Poverty of Philosophy* (New York, 1963) p. 7.

preciated in Proudhon was his thoroughgoing critique of private property and his conception of economics as the determining factor in social evolution.

Underlying all Marx's notes is Feuerbach's humanism (Hess and Engels, too, would have described themselves as disciples of Feuerbach). Marx says that positive criticism, and thus also German positive criticism of political economy, is founded on Feuerbach's discoveries in his 'Thesen' and *Grundsätze*. 'Positive humanistic and naturalistic criticism begins with Feuerbach. The less vociferous Feuerbach's writings are, the more certain, profound, extensive, and lasting is their influence – the only writings since Hegel's *Phenomenology* and *Logic* containing a real theoretical revolution.'[10]

2. ALIENATED LABOUR

The first part of Marx's first manuscript consists largely of extracts or paraphrases from the books on economics that he was reading at that time. He divided these extracts into three sections on wages, capital and rent, each occupying one of the three vertical columns into which Marx had divided his pages. In the first, drawing on Adam Smith, Marx notes that the bitter struggle between capitalist and worker, which determined wages, also reduced the worker to the status of a commodity. The worker could not win: if the wealth of society were diminishing, it was he who suffered most; if it was increasing, then this meant that capital was being accumulated and the product of labour was increasingly alienated from the worker. In short, 'In a declining state of society, increasing misery of

10. 'Paris Mauscripts', *Frühe Schriften*, p. 508; Easton and Guddat, p. 285.

the worker; in a progressive state, complicated misery; and in the final state, stationary misery.'[11]

Political economy, says Marx, dealt with man in much the same terms as it dealt with, say, a house. It did not deal with man 'in his free time, as a human being'; this aspect it left to other disciplines. Marx continues:

Let us now rise above the level of political economy and seek from the foregoing argument, which was presented almost in the words of the economists, answers to two questions –

1. What is the significance, in the development of mankind, of this reduction of the greater part of mankind to abstract labour?
2. What errors are committed by the advocates of piecemeal reform, who either want to raise wages and thereby improve the conditions of the working class, or (like Proudhon) regard equality of wages as the aim of social revolution?[12]

To answer these two questions Marx amasses a series of quotations from three sources: firstly from the German liberal writer Wilhelm Schulz on the workers' pauperization, the dehumanizing effect of machinery and the number of women and children working;[13] secondly from Constantin Pecqueur on the dependence and degradation forced on workers under capitalism;[14] thirdly from Eugène Buret on the misery and exploitation of the proletariat.[15]

11. 'Paris Manuscripts', *Frühe Schriften*, p. 515: K. Marx, *Early Writings*, ed. Bottomore (London, 1963) p. 74 (hereafter referred to as Bottomore).

12. 'Paris Manuscripts', *Frühe Schriften*, p. 518; Bottomore, pp. 76 f.

13. Cf. W. Schulz, *Die Bewegung der Produktion. Eine geschichtlich-statistische Abhandlung* (Zürich, 1843).

14. C. Pecqueur, *Théorie nouvelle d'économie sociale et politique* (Paris, 1842). Pecqueur advocated a democratic, fairly centralized socialism and criticized capitalism as contrary to religion and morality.

15. E. Buret, *De la misère des classes laborieuses en Angleterre et en France* (Paris, 1840). Buret's book is a well-documented account

In his second section Marx notes a number of passages under the heading 'Profit of Capital'. First, quoting Adam Smith, he defines capital as the power of command over labour and its products. He then describes the means by which capitalists make a profit both from wages and from raw materials advanced; the motives that inspire the capitalist; and the accumulation of capital and competition among capitalists. In this last section Marx quotes from Ricardo, Schulz and Pecqueur as well as from Adam Smith.

Marx's third section is on rent as one instance of the perpetual opposition of interests that is characteristic of capitalist society. Marx quotes from Adam Smith here, but comments:

It is absurd to conclude, however, as Smith does, that since the landlord exploits everything which benefits society, the interest of the landlord is always identical with that of society. In the economic system under the domination of private property, the interest that an individual has in society is in exactly inverse proportion to the interest which society has in him – just as the interest of the moneylender in the spendthrift is by no means identical with the interest of the spendthrift.[16]

Marx outlines the similarities between landlord and capitalist: in the last analysis there was no distinction between them and society was divided into two classes only – workers and capitalists. The character of landed property had been utterly transformed since feudal times and

---

both of the horrors of the Industrial Revolution and of the positive possibilities it offers to men. For the influence of Buret on Marx's economic conceptions, see G. Cottier, *Du romantisme au marxisme* (Paris, 1961).

16. 'Paris Manuscripts', *Frühe Schriften*, p. 549; Bottomore, p. 109.

neither the preservation of large estates nor their division into small properties could avoid precipitating a crisis.[17]

At this point in his manuscript Marx breaks off writing in three parallel columns and begins to write straight across the page. He also changes his style, writing in his own person with no quotation from other writers. This passage on alienated labour is the best-written part of the manuscripts. In it Marx criticizes the concept of labour found in the classical economists, from whom he had just been quoting, on the general grounds that their conceptions were superficial and abstract whereas his own gave a coherent account of the essential nature of economics. Having started from their presuppositions Marx claims to show that the more the worker produces, the poorer he becomes. But this analysis remained superficial:

> Political economy proceeds from the fact of private property. It does not explain private property. It grasps the actual, material process of private property in abstract and general formulae which it then takes as laws.... Political economy teaches us nothing about the extent to which these external, apparently accidental circumstances are simply the expression of a necessary development. We have seen our political economy regards exchange itself as an accidental fact. The only wheels which political economy puts in motion are greed and the war among the greedy, competition.[18]

But because the classical economists had failed to understand the necessary connection and development of different economic factors, they could give no coherent account

17. On Marx's commentary on the classical economists, see further: J. Maguire, *Marx's Paris Writings,* chapter II (Dublin, 1972).

18. 'Paris Manuscripts', *Frühe Schriften,* p. 559; Easton and Guddat, p. 287. The last sentence of the quotation is mistranslated by Tucker, *Philosophy and Myth in Karl Marx,* p. 138, as: 'The only wheels that set political economy in motion, are greed and the war between the greedy – competition.' The difference between the two versions is of the first importance.

of economics. Marx, on the contrary, aims 'to grasp the essential connection among private property, greed, division of labour, capital and land ownership, and the connection of exchange with competition, of value with the devaluation of men, of monopoly with competition, etc., and of this whole alienation with the money-system'.[19] The usual method of the economist is to suppose a fictitious primordial state and to go on from there; but this simply accepted as a fact what it was supposed to be explaining: 'In such a manner theology explains the origin of evil by the fall of man. That is, it asserts as a fact in the form of history what it should explain.'[20]

Before introducing his main point, Marx once more asserts its empirical basis. 'We proceed', he says, 'from a present fact of political economy.'[21] This fact is the general impoverishment and dehumanization of the worker. Marx develops the implications of this, thus introducing the theme of this section:

This fact simply indicates that the object which labour produces, its product, stands opposed to it as an alien thing, as a power independent of the producer. The product of labour is labour embodied and made objective in a thing. It is the objectification of labour. The realization of labour is its objectification. In the viewpoint of political economy this realization of labour appears as diminution of the worker, the objectification as the loss of and the subservience to the object, and the appropriation as alienation, as externalization.[22]

19. 'Paris Manuscripts', *Frühe Schriften*, p. 560; Easton and Guddat, p. 288.
20. 'Paris Manuscripts', *Frühe Schriften*, p. 560; Easton and Guddat, p. 289.
21. 'Paris Manuscripts', *Frühe Schriften*, p. 560; Easton and Guddat, p. 289.
22. 'Paris Manuscripts', *Frühe Schriften*, p. 561; Easton and Guddat, p. 289. It is interesting to note that the situation of the alienated worker in capitalist society was described by Hegel in his

Put very simply and roughly, what Marx means when he talks of alienation is this: it is man's nature to be his own creator; he forms and develops himself by working on and transforming the world outside him in co-operation with his fellow men. In this progressive interchange between man and the world, it is man's nature to be in control of this process, to be the initiator, the subject in which the process originates. However, this nature has become alien to man; that is, it is no longer his and belongs to another person or thing. In religion, for example, it is God who is the subject of the historical process. It is God who holds the initiative and man is in a state of dependence. In economics, according to Marx, it is money or the cash nexus that manoeuvres men around as though they were objects instead of the reverse. The central point is that man has lost control of his own evolution and has seen this control invested in other entities. What is proper to man has become alien to him, being the attribute of something else.[23]

The fact that the worker is related to the product of his labour as to an alien object means that the more the worker produces the more he approaches loss of work and

---

Realphilosophie in terms that are almost word for word the same as Marx's. The big difference is that Hegel, unlike Marx, offered no solution to the problem that he so accurately stated.

23. Marx uses two German words to express his ideas of alienation: they are *Entäusserung* and *Entfremdung*. Strictly speaking, the first emphasizes the idea of dispossession and the second the idea of something being strange and alien. Marx seems to use the two term indiscriminately, sometimes using both together for rhetorical emphasis. Further, see the articles by Bell, Braybrooke and O'Neill mentioned in the Bibliography.

starvation. Once more, Marx draws a parallel with religion:

> It is the same in religion. The more man attributes to God, the less he retains in himself. The worker puts his life into the object; then it no longer belongs to him but to the object. ... The externalization of the worker in his product means not only that his work becomes an object, an external existence, but also that it exists outside him independently, alien, an autonomous power, opposed to him. The life he has given to the object confronts him as hostile and alien.[24]

The worker is here deprived in a dual way: his contact with nature, the sensuous external world, is so necessary for him that alienation deprives him both of objects on which to work and also of objects from which to live.

Marx then returns to the attitude of classical economics which enunciates the law of alienation as follows: 'The more the worker produces, the less he has to consume; the more values he creates the more worthless and unworthy he becomes; the better shaped his products, the more misshapen is he.'[25] Classical economics dwelt long on the wealth produced under capitalism, but ignored the poverty, mutilation and cretinism that it imposed upon the workers. The relation of the worker to the objects of his production was the crucial dimension from which to judge the quality of labour.[26]

24. 'Paris Manuscripts', *Frühe Schriften*, p. 562; Easton and Guddat, p. 290.

25. 'Paris Manuscripts', *Frühe Schriften'*, p. 563; Easton and Guddat, p. 291.

26. On the theme of the alienation of labour caused by the introduction of machinery, there are striking anticipations of Marx's views in Hegel's *Rechtsphilosophie* and even in his *Realphilosophie* of 1803–6. See H. Marcuse, *Reason and Revolution* (London, 1941), pp. 77 ff., and more broadly, Alastair Clayre, *Machinery and Imagination* (London, 1972), chapters iv and vi. This point has been admirably treated by Shlomo Avineri in a paper entitled 'The Roots

Having discussed this relationship of the worker to the objects of his production, Marx defines and analyses a second, third and fourth characteristic of alienated man. The second is his alienation in the act of production. 'How could the worker', asks Marx, 'stand in an alien relationship to the product of his activity if he did not alienate himself from himself in the very act of production?'[27] Marx distinguishes three aspects of this type of alienation: firstly, labour was external to the labourer and no part of his nature; secondly, it was not voluntary, but forced labour; and thirdly, man's activity here belonged to another, with once more the religious parallel: 'In religion the spontaneity of human imagination, the spontaneity of the human brain and heart acts independently of the individual as an alien, divine or devilish activity. Similarly, the activity of the worker is not his own spontaneous activity. It belongs to another. It is the loss of his own self.'[28] The result of this was to turn man into an animal, for he only felt at ease when performing the animal functions of eating, drinking and procreating – in his distinctly human functions he was made to feel like an animal.

Marx has analysed man as alienated from the product of his labour and also as alienated in the act of production (this second he also calls 'self-alienation'). He now derives his third characteristic of alienated labour from the two previous ones: man is alienated from his species, from his fellow men. Marx now defines what he means by 'species',

of Hegel's *Rechtsphilosophie* in his *Jenenser Realphilosophie*' presented at the Marquette Hegel symposium 1970 and to be published in the *Proceedings*.

27. 'Paris Manuscripts', *Frühe Schriften*, p. 564; Easton and Guddat, p. 291.

28. 'Paris Manuscripts', *Frühe Schriften*, p. 565; Easton and Guddat, p. 292.

a term he took over from Feuerbach. The two chief characteristics of a species-being were self-consciousness and universality: 'Man is a species-being not only in that he practically and theoretically makes his own species as well as that of other beings his object, but also – and this is only another expression for the same thing – in that as present and living species he considers himself to be a universal and consequently free being.'[29] This universality consisted in the fact that man could appropriate for his own use the whole realm of inorganic nature.

The universality of man appears in practice in the universality which makes the whole of nature his inorganic body: (1) as a direct means of life, and (2) as the matter, object, and instrument of his life activity. Nature is the inorganic body of man, that is, nature in so far as it is not the human body. Man lives by nature. This means that nature is his body with which he must remain in perpetual process in order not to die. That the physical and spiritual life of man is tied up with nature is another way of saying that nature is linked to itself, for man is a part of nature.[30]

It was true that animals also produced – but only what was immediately necessary for them. It was man's nature, on the other hand, to produce universally and freely: he was able 'to produce according to the standard of any species and at all times knows how to apply an intrinsic standard to the object. Thus man creates also according to the laws of beauty.'[31] Marx sums up the results of his discussion as follows:

29. 'Paris Manuscripts', *Frühe Schriften*, p. 566; Easton and Guddat, p. 293.
30. 'Paris Manuscripts', *Frühe Schriften*, p. 566; Easton and Guddat, p. 293.
31. 'Paris Manuscripts', *Frühe Schriften*, p. 568; Easton and Guddat, p. 295.

In alienating (1) nature from man, and (2) man from himself, his own active function, his life-activity, alienated labour also alienates the species from him; it makes species-life the means of individual life. In the first place it alienates species-life and the individual life, and secondly it turns the latter in its abstraction into the purpose of the former, also in its abstract and alienated form.[32]

Man was a species-being in that he lived by consciously transforming inorganic nature, by producing. This 'life-activity' was his essence. And since this 'life-activity' was alienated and turned into a mere means of existence, man had lost his species-being. For since labour was the objectification of man's species-life and man was deprived of the objects he produces, it followed that he was deprived of his objective species-life.

Marx then completes his picture by drawing a fourth characteristic of alienation out of the first three: man is alienated from other men. 'In general,' he says

the statement that man is alienated from his species-existence means that one man is alienated from another just as each man is alienated from human nature. The alienation of man, the relation of man to himself, is realized and expressed in the relation between man and other men. Thus in the relation of alienated labour every man sees the others according to the standard and the relation in which he finds himself as a worker.[33]

Having reiterated that he is solely analysing concepts derived from economic facts, Marx now poses the question: If the product of my labour is alien to me, and belongs to someone else, who is this other person? At the

32. 'Paris Manuscripts', *Frühe Schriften*, pp. 566 f.; Easton and Guddat, p. 294.
33. 'Paris Manuscripts', *Frühe Schriften*, p. 569; Easton and Guddat, p. 296.

beginning of the passage he had touched on this question: 'The relationship of the rich to the objects of production and to production itself is only a consequence of this first relationship and confirms it.'[34] Now he takes his point further: the produce of man's labour did not belong to gods, nor to nature; it could only belong to man himself. 'That the product of labour does not belong to the worker and an alien power confronts him is possible only because this product belongs to a man other than the worker. If his activity is a torment for him, it must be the pleasure and the life-enjoyment for another. Not gods, not nature, but only man himself can be this alien power over man.'[35] Marx here refers back to his discussion of the fourth characteristic of man's alienation.[36] The fact that both the product of man's labour and the activity of production

34. 'Paris Manuscripts', *Frühe Schriften*, pp. 563 f.; Easton and Guddat, p. 291.

35. 'Paris Manuscripts', *Frühe Schriften*, p. 570; Easton and Guddat, pp. 296 f. This does not mean, according to Marx, that the capitalist is not alienated. Both capitalist and worker partake of the same alienation, though in different ways. See G. Cohen, 'Bourgeois and Proletarians', *Journal of the History of Ideas* (January 1968).

36. Tucker, *Philosophy and Myth in Karl Marx*, p. 149, mistranslates this passage. He says: 'Marx was at least obscurely aware of the shakiness of his position, for he made a note in the manuscript saying: "We must think over the previously made statement that the relation of man to himself first becomes objective and real through his relation to another man." ' The translation should be: 'Let us consider the statement previously made . . .' Marx is here simply reiterating his fourth characteristic of alienation. Tucker is led to make this mistake by postulating (with no evidence from the text) that Marx conceives of self-alienation (which Tucker refers to as 'alienated self-relation' – a very different thing) as primarily a phenomenon of the individual psyche: he then points out that this is in contradiction with what Marx says about self-alienation being essentially social and describes this as theoretically untenable. But the 'contradiction' is between Tucker and Marx, not between Marx and Marx.

had become alien to him meant that another man had to control his product and his activity.

Every self-alienation of man, from himself and from nature, appears in the relationship which he postulates between other men and himself and nature. Thus religious self-alienation appears necessarily in the relation of laity to priest, or also to a mediator, since we are here now concerned with the spiritual world. In the practical real world self-alienation can appear only in the practical real relationships to other men.[37]

Marx now draws a few practical conclusions with regard to private property and wages. Since, according to Marx's analysis, it was the relation of the worker to his labour that produced the relation of the capitalist to labour, 'private property is thus product, result and necessary consequence of externalized labour'.[38] It was true that private property seemed to come first, but 'the analysis of this idea shows that though private property appears to be the ground and cause of externalized labour, it is rather a consequence of externalized labour, just as gods are originally not the cause but the effect of an aberration of the human mind. Later this relationship reverses.'[39] This has been called a *petitio principii*, and, strictly speaking, this is correct: the idea of alienated labour presupposes private property just as much as it gives rise to it. What Marx wishes to bring out, however, is that social labour is the source of all value and thus of the distribution of wealth.

Marx uses his conclusion to answer two contemporary problems.

37. 'Paris Manuscripts', *Frühe Schriften*, pp. 570 f.; Easton and Guddat, p. 297.

38. 'Paris Manuscripts', *Frühe Schriften*, p. 571; Easton and Guddat, p. 298.

39. 'Paris Manuscripts', *Frühe Schriften*, p. 572; Easton and Guddat, p. 298.

The first arose from the fact that whereas classical economics treated labour as the basis of production, it gave nothing to labour and everything to private property. Here again, classical economics had only formulated the laws of alienated labour. 'Wages and private property are identical: for when the product, the object of labour, pays for the labour itself, wages are only a necessary consequence of the alienation of labour.'[40] Labour thus became the servant of wages and an increase in wages would be unable to restore to labour its human meaning and significance. Marx concludes:

Even the equality of wages, as advanced by Proudhon, would only convert the relation of the contemporary worker to his work into the relation of all men to labour. Society would then be conceived as an abstract capitalist. Wages are a direct result of alienated labour, and alienated labour is the direct cause of private property. The downfall of one is necessarily the downfall of the other.[41]

The second of the problems that Marx mentions is that of the achievement of universal human emancipation. Marx thinks (and here he repeats his views at the end of his 'Introduction to a Critique of Hegel's Philosophy of Law') that this will be brought about by the emancipation of the workers. Universal human emancipation 'is contained in their emancipation because the whole of human servitude is involved in the relation of worker to production, and all relations of servitude are only modifications and consequences of the worker's relation to production'.[42]

Marx next planned a discussion of all aspects of classical

40. 'Paris Manuscripts', *Frühe Schriften*, p. 572; Easton and Guddat, p. 298.

41. 'Paris Manuscripts', *Frühe Schriften*, p. 573; Easton and Guddat, p. 299.

42. 'Paris Manuscripts', *Frühe Schriften*, p. 573; Easton and Guddat, p. 299.

economics – barter, competition, capital, money – based on the twin factors of alienated labour and private property. But first he tries to determine 'the general nature of private property in its relation to truly human property'. Having summarized his previous conclusions, he proposes to consider the relation of the alien person, under whose domination production has fallen, to the worker, to labour and its object. Marx makes three preliminary remarks. Firstly, everything that with the worker appeared as an activity of alienation, with the non-worker appeared as a condition of alienation; secondly, the practical attitude of mind of the worker to his product and work appeared as a theoretical attitude in the non-worker; thirdly, the non-worker did everything against the worker that the worker did against himself, but he did not do against his own self what he did against the worker. Marx writes: 'Let us consider more closely these three relationships', and there the manuscript breaks off, unfinished.

In spite of the incompleteness of the manuscript, it is possible to reconstruct what the continuation would have looked like. In his notebooks of this time, Marx put down his own reflections on his reading of the classical economists and his note on James Mill's *Elements of Political Economy* is exceptionally long and rich. In it Marx deals with the categories of classical economics that he had planned to discuss in the unfinished part of his manuscript on alienated labour – barter, competition, capital and money. He concentrates on the dehumanizing effect of money and private property, finishing with an account of his conception of unalienated labour which is the positive side of his critique of alienated labour.

Marx begins his note by criticizing Mill's attempt to formulate precise 'laws' in economics, a field so chaotic and open to constant fluctuation. He then comments on Mill's description of money as the medium of exchange.

Money alone gave significance to man's relationship to his fellow men and even to his products:

The essence of money is not primarily that it externalizes property, but that the mediating activity or process – the human and social act in which man's products reciprocally complement one another – becomes alienated and takes on the quality of a material thing, money, external to man. By externalizing this mediating activity, man is active only as he is lost and dehumanized. . . . Through this alien mediation, man regards his will, his activity, and his relationships to others, as a power independent of himself and of them – instead of man himself being the mediator for man. . . . Apart from this mediation, objects lose their value. They have value only in so far as they represent it while originally it appeared that the mediation would have value in so far as it represents objects.[43]

After drawing a (not very clear) parallel between the mediation of money and the mediation of Christ, Marx explained that money was necessary under a régime of private property, for men must exchange and exchange must end up in value. People, it was true, were still superstitious and hung on to their money bags. Enlightened economists had tried to combat this by introducing bills of exchange, cheques and various forms of credit. Even the followers of Saint-Simon had been misled into thinking that in a credit system (a fully organized banking system was their ideal) the alienation of man from man would be gradually overcome and human relationships restored. This restoration was only apparent, however, for here the alienation, instead of being purely exterior, lodged itself inside man's moral and social existence, for

. . . Credit is the economic judgement of man's morality. In credit, man himself instead of metal and paper has become the medium of exchange, but not as man, but rather as the

43. 'Excerpt-notes of 1844', K. Marx, *Texte zu Methode und Praxis*, ed. Hillmann, II, 166 f. (Hereafter referred to as *Texte*); Easton and Guddat, p. 266.

existence of capital and interest.... Human individuality and human morality have become an article of trade and the material in which money exists. Instead of money and paper, my very personal existence, my flesh and blood, my social virtue and reputation is the matter and the substance of the monetary spirit.[44]

The credit system, according to Marx, had four main characteristics. Firstly, it increased the power of the wealthy, for credit was more readily accorded to those who already had money; secondly, it added a moral judgement to an economic one, implying that a man without credit was also untrustworthy; thirdly, it compelled people to try to obtain credit by lying and deceit; fourthly, credit reached its perfection in the banking system.

It is in contrast to this society based on money and credit that Marx outlines his idea of man's authentic social existence:

As human nature is the true common life of man, men through the activation of their nature create and produce a human common life, a social essence which is no abstractly universal power opposed to the single individual, but is the essence or nature of every single individual, his own activity, his own life, his own spirit, his own wealth. Authentic common life arises not through reflection; rather it comes about from the need and egoism of individuals, that is, immediately from the activation of their very existence. It is not up to man whether this common life exists or not. However, so long as man does not recognize himself as man and does not organize the world humanly, this common life appears in the form of alienation, because its subject, man, is a being alienated from itself. Men as actual, living, particular individuals, not in an abstraction, constitute this common life.[45]

44. 'Excerpt-notes of 1844', *Texte*, p. 170; Easton and Guddat, p. 270.

45. 'Excerpt-notes of 1844', *Texte*, p. 171; Easton and Guddat, pp. 271 f.

Classical economists, Destutt de Tracy and Adam Smith, for example, considered this common life of man to consist in commerce and exchange. But if exchange and barter was the social, generic act, then even private property took on an impersonal character. For in the first place, it had been taken from the man who produced it and acquired by someone for whom it had not such personal significance.

In the second place, it has been related to and equated with another private property. A private property of a different nature has taken its place, just as it itself takes the position of a private property of a different nature. On both sides, then, private property appears as a representative of private property of a different nature, as the equivalence of another natural product. Both sides are so related that each represents the existence of the other and they mutually serve as substitutes for themselves and the other. The existence of private property as such has thus become a substitute, an equivalent.[46]

This results inevitably in the transformation of labour into wage-labour. In primitive barter men only exchanged the surplus of their own produce. But soon men produced in order to exchange and finally 'It becomes entirely incidental and unessential whether the producer immediately enjoys and needs his product and whether the activity, the action of labour itself, is his self-satisfaction and the realization of his natural dispositions and spiritual aims.'[47] This process was only enhanced by the division of labour that increased with civilization.

Thus while man in a barbaric state produced just as much as he needed, the overproduction in advanced stages of society was

46. 'Excerpt-notes of 1844', *Texte*, p. 174; Easton and Guddat, p. 274.

47. 'Excerpt-notes of 1844', *Texte*, p. 175; Easton and Guddat, p. 275.

only an indirect way of satisfying a need which finds its objectification in the production of another person.... Our mutual product, therefore, is the means, the intermediary, the instrument, the acknowledged power of our mutual needs. Your demand and the equivalent of your property are terms which for me are synonymous and equally valid, and your demand is effective only when it has an effect on me. Without this effect your demand is only an unsatisfied effort on your part and without consequence for me. You have no relationship to my object as a human being because I myself have no human relation to it.[48]

The conclusion was that 'Our mutual value is the value of our mutual objects for us. Man himself, therefore, is mutually valueless for us.'[49] Marx finishes his note on money with a description of unalienated labour that is one of the few passages where he describes in any detail his picture of the future communist society. It is worthwhile quoting at length:

Suppose we had produced things as human beings: in his production each of us would have twice affirmed himself and the other. (1) In my production I would have objectified my individuality and its particularity, and in the course of the activity I would have enjoyed an individual life; in viewing the object I would have experienced the individual joy of knowing my personality as an objective, sensuously perceptible and indubitable power. (2) In your satisfaction and your use of my product I would have had the direct and conscious satisfaction that my work satisfied a human need, that it objectified human nature, and that it created an object appropriate to the need of another human being. (3) I would have been the mediator between you and the species and you would have experienced me as a redirection of your own nature and a necessary part of

48. 'Excerpt-notes of 1844', *Texte*, pp. 178 f.; Easton and Guddat, p. 279.

49. 'Excerpt-notes of 1844', *Texte*, p. 180; Easton and Guddat, p. 280.

yourself; I would have been affirmed in your thought as well as your love. (4) In my individual activity, I would have immediately confirmed and realized my true human and social nature.

Our productions would be so many mirrors reflecting our nature.

What happens so far as I am concerned would also apply to you....

My labour would be a free manifestation of life and an enjoyment of life....

Furthermore, in my labour the particularity of my individuality would be affirmed because my individual life is affirmed. Labour then would be true, active property. Under the presupposition of private property my individuality is externalized to the point where I hate this activity and where it is a torment for me. Rather it is then only the semblance of an activity, only a forced activity, imposed upon me only by external and accidental necessity and not by any internal and determined necessity.[50]

Marx's basic thesis is thus that man's objectification of himself in capitalist society denies his species-being instead of confirming it. Marx asserts that this is a judgement based purely on a study of economic fact; he claims to be using the conclusions of the classical economists themselves and only criticizing their premises. Several times Marx claims merely to be giving expression to economic facts; and in the introduction to the manuscripts as a whole, he says: 'It is hardly necessary to assure the reader familiar with political economy that my conclusions have been obtained through an entirely empirical analysis based on a thorough, critical study of political economy.'[51] However, his use of terms like 'alienation' and 'the realization of the

50. 'Excerpt-notes of 1844', *Texte*, pp. 180 f.; Easton and Guddat, p. 281.

51. 'Paris Manuscripts', *Frühe Schriften*, pp. 506 f.; Easton and Guddat, p. 284.

human essence' plainly show that Marx's analysis is not a purely scientific one. Nor is it empirical, if this is taken to mean devoid of value judgements. For Marx's description is full of dramatically over-simplified pronouncements that border on the epigrammatic. And while the economic analysis is taken over from classical economics, the moral judgements are inspired by the reading (noted above) of Schulz, Pecqueur, Sismondi, and Buret. It is important to realize, in order to understand Marx's claims, that 'empirical' for him did not involve a fact-value distinction (an idea which he would have rejected) but merely that the analysis (wherever it might lead) started in the right place – with man's material needs.[52]

3. COMMUNISM

Of Marx's second manuscript only four pages towards the end survive. Here Marx is describing the attitude of the capitalist to the worker.

The worker is only a worker when he exists as capital for himself, and he only exists as capital when capital is there for him. The existence of capital is his existence, his life, since it determines the content of his life independently of him. Political economy thus does not recognize the unoccupied worker, the working man so far as he is outside this work relationship.[53]

The existence of private property implied both the production of human activity as alienated labour and the

52. For a closely argued analysis of the empirical features of Marx's doctrine of alienation, see D. Braybrooke, 'Diagnosis and Remedy in Marx's Doctrine of Alienation', in *Social Research* (autumn 1958). There are several pieces of research that take Marx's doctrine as a basis. One of the best-known is R. Blauner, *Alienation and Freedom* (Chicago, 1964).

53. 'Paris Manuscripts', *Frühe Schriften*, p. 576; Bottomore, p. 137.

production of capital which made all natural and social characteristics irrelevant; Marx praises classical economics for having abolished the romantic illusions of the land-owner and transformed him into a prosaic capitalist. He analyses recent economic developments and concludes that 'There follows the necessary victory of the capitalist, i.e. of developed private property, over undeveloped, immature private property, the landowner.'[54] The manuscript finishes with short passages on the development of the relationships of capital to labour.

The third manuscript begins with two long notes referring to a manuscript that has been lost. The first of these notes deals with private property and labour. It is only the economics of Adam Smith and his followers, says Marx, that 'can be considered as both a product of modern industry, and a force which has accelerated and extolled the dynamism and development of industry and had made it a power in the domain of consciousness'.[55] Engels was right in calling Adam Smith 'the Luther of economics'.[56] Just as Luther internalized religion, so in modern economics man was recognized as the essence of private property. But this recognition was only apparent, for economics was caught in the contradiction of making labour the sole essence of wealth and yet demonstrating that this had consequences that were inimical to man. The rest of the note is a criticism of Quesnay and the physiocrats for defending feudal conceptions in the language of modern economics.

The second of Marx's notes outlines his conception of communism. The path towards the overcoming of self-alienation followed the same stages as the process of alienation. Previous attempts to formulate this transition

54. 'Paris Manuscripts', *Frühe Schriften*, p. 583; Bottomore, p. 143.
55. 'Paris Manuscripts', *Frühe Schriften*, p. 585; Bottomore, p. 147.
56. 'Paris Manuscripts', *Frühe Schriften*, p. 585; Bottomore, p. 147.

had been unsatisfactory. Proudhon, for example, had advocated the abolition of capital and Fourier and Saint-Simon had traced the alienation of labour to a particular form of labour. As a result, Fourier had advocated a return to agricultural labour, while Saint-Simon considered the correct organization of industrial labour to be the key. Communism, however, went further than these partial insights and represented 'the positive expression of private property as overcome'.[57] But even communism had its stages.

The first form – 'crude' communism – was merely the universalization of private property. 'On the one hand the domination of material property bulks so large that it wants to destroy everything which cannot be possessed by everyone as private property. It wants to abstract from talent, etc., by force. Immediate physical possession is for it the sole aim of life and existence.'[58] This conception of communism had its counterpart in the proposal to abolish marriage and substitute the community of women. For it was the relationship between the sexes that was 'the immediate, natural necessary relationship of human being to human being'.[59]

This communism – in that it negates man's personality everywhere – is only the logical expression of the private property which is this negation. Universal envy establishing itself as a power is only the disguised form in which greed re-establishes and satisfies itself in another way.... How little this overcoming of private property is an actual appropriation is shown precisely by the abstract negation of the entire world of culture

57. 'Paris Manuscripts', *Frühe Schriften*, p. 590; Easton and Guddat, p. 301.

58. 'Paris Manuscripts', *Frühe Schriften*, pp. 590 f.; Easton and Guddat, pp. 301 f.

59. 'Paris Manuscripts', *Frühe Schriften*, p. 592; Easton and Guddat, p. 303.

and civilization, the reversion to the unnatural simplicity of the poor and wantless man who has not gone beyond private property, has not yet even achieved it.[60]

Here the only community was a community of (alienated) labour and the only equality was one of wages paid out by the community as universal capitalist.

Marx seems here to be referring to two groups, the *Travailleurs Égalitaires* and the *Humanitaires*, mentioned by Engels in his article 'The Progress of Social Reform on the Continent', published in the Owenite paper *New Moral World* in November 1843. According to Engels, the former 'were just like the Babouvists of the great revolution, rather "rough hewn"; they proposed to turn the world into a community of workers and thus to abolish every refinement of culture, science and art as useless, dangerous and aristocratic luxury.'[61] The *Humanitaires* were 'particularly known for their attacks on marriage, the family and similar institutions'.[62] The *Travailleurs Égalitaires* and their newspaper, *L'Humanitaire*, came into being about 1840, after the dissolution of the *Société des Saisons* in 1839, following its abortive attempt to organize a *coup*. *L'Humanitaire* took its main inspiration from Silvain Maréchal, author of the Babouviste *Manifeste des Égaux*, and from Blanqui.[63]

The second form of communism that Marx wishes to brand as inadequate is of two sorts: the first he describes as 'still of political nature, democratic or despotic', and the second as achieving 'the overcoming of the state but still

60. 'Paris Manuscripts', *Frühe Schriften*, p. 591; Easton and Guddat, p. 302.

61. *MEGA* I, ii, 439.

62. ibid.

63. Cf. E. Dolléans, *Histoire du mouvement ouvrier* (Paris, 1957) I, 179. There is a lot of useful background information in Kägi, *Genesis des historischen Materialismus*, pp. 238 ff.

incomplete and influenced by private property, that is, by the alienation of man'.[64] Of both these forms Marx says

> Communism already knows itself as the reintegration or return of man to himself, as the overcoming of human self-alienation, but since it has not yet understood the positive essence of private property and just as little the human nature of needs, it still remains captive to and infected by private property. It has, indeed, grasped its concept but still not its essence.[65]

The democratic communism that Marx mentions here must be the utopian sort advocated by Étienne Cabet which was increasingly popular in Paris about this time; the despotic type probably alludes to the transitory dictatorship of the proletariat advocated by the followers of Babeuf. The second type of communism, involving the abolition of the state, was represented by Dézamy, author of the famous phrase about an accountant and a register being all that was necessary to ensure the perfect functioning of the future communist society.

Thirdly, Marx describes his own idea of communism – the culmination of previous inadequate conceptions:

> Communism as positive overcoming of private property, as human self-alienation, and thus as the actual appropriation of the human essence through and for man; therefore as the complete and conscious restoration of man to himself within the total wealth of previous development, the restoration of man as a social, that is, human being. This communism as completed naturalism is humanism, as completed humanism is naturalism. It is the genuine resolution of the antagonism between man and nature and between man and man; it is the true resolution of the conflict between existence and essence, objectification and

64. 'Paris Manuscripts', *Frühe Schriften*, p. 593; Easton and Guddat, p. 303.
65. 'Paris Manuscripts', *Frühe Schriften*, p. 593; Easton and Guddat, pp. 303 f.

self-affirmation, freedom and necessity, individual and species.
It is the riddle of history solved and knows itself as this
solution.[66]

This is the first time Marx declares himself in favour of
communism. The words socialism and communism were
used almost interchangeably about this time. The word
'socialism' first became current in England among the
Owenites in the 1820s; 'communism' was a more particular
term of recent French origin, applying to the doctrines of
men such as Cabet and Dézamy and involving especially
the abolition of private property. When did Marx become
a communist? He was familiar with communist ideas from
the latter half of 1842, for in the articles rejecting the
accusations of communism by the *Augsburger Allgemeine
Zeitung* he cites Leroux, Considérant and Proudhon, adding that he 'cannot even concede theoretical reality to
communistic ideas in their present form'.[67] The *Rheinische
Zeitung* in general was hostile to communism and Hess's
articles were the exception. Marx himself said that on the
suppression of the *Rheinische Zeitung* he 'withdrew from
the public stage into the study' in order to form an opinion
on 'French tendencies'.[68] In September 1843 Marx again
rejects communism as a 'dogmatic abstraction' and even
socialism was for him at that time 'only one side of the
reality of true human nature'.[69] It is true that Engels in an
article published in November 1843 refers to Marx and
others as 'philosophical communists',[70] but Engels was in

66. 'Paris Manuscripts', *Frühe Schriften*, pp. 593 f.; Easton and
Guddat, p. 304. For an extraordinarily perceptive modern continuation of the 'utopian' themes evident in Marx in such passages as
his, see the works by Ernest Bloch cited in the bibliography.

67. 'Communism and the *Augsburger Allgemeine Zeitung*', *MEGA*
, i (1) 263; Easton and Guddat, p. 134.

68. K. Marx–F. Engels, *Selected Works*, 1, 362.

69. 'Letter to Ruge', *MEGA* 1, i (1) 573; Easton and Guddat, p. 212.

70. *MEGA* 1, ii, 448.

England at the time and did not know Marx well. It seems clear that Marx was not a communist until the appearance of the *Deutsch-Französische Jahrbücher*. A *terminus ante quem* is established by the 'Paris Manuscripts' written during the summer of 1844, and by October 1844 Marx and Engels both took communism for granted in their correspondence. This fits well with Ruge's statement in his memoirs that Marx gave as his reason for breaking with him that he (Marx) was a communist. Ruge dated this conversion of Marx's very specifically: 'From September 1843 to March 1844 Marx made the transition to "crass socialism".'[71] Thus Marx became a communist in the first three months of 1844.

Having outlined his conception of communism, Marx goes on to enlarge on three of its particular aspects: its historical bases, its social character and its regard for the individual.

Dealing with the first aspect – the historical bases of communism – Marx draws a further distinction between his own communism and the other 'underdeveloped' sort. This latter (as examples of which he cites the utopian communism of Cabet and Villegardelle) tries to justify itself by appealing to certain historical forms of community that were opposed to private property. But this choice of isolated aspects or epochs of past history implied, for Marx, that the rest of history was *not* an argument for communism. In his own version, on the other hand, 'The entire movement of history is therefore both its actual genesis – the birth of its empirical existence – and also for its thinking awareness the conceived and conscious movement of its becoming.'[72] Thus the whole revolution-

71. Ruge, *Zwei Jahre in Paris*, I, 139 f. Cf. Ruge, *Briefwechsel*, ed Nerrlich, I, 341.

72. 'Paris Manuscripts', *Frühe Schriften*, p. 594; Easton and Guddat, p. 304.

ary movement 'finds both its empirical as well as theoretical basis in the development of private property – in the economy, to be exact'.[73] This was so because the alienation of human life was expressed in the existence of private property, and it was in the movement of private property, in production and consumption, that man had hitherto attempted to realize himself. 'Religion, family, state, law, morality, science, art, etc., are only particular forms of production and fall under its general law. The positive overcoming of private property as the appropriation of human life is thus the positive overcoming of all alienation and the return of man from religion, family, state, etc., to his human, that is, social existence.'[74] The basic alienation, Marx goes on, occurs in the economic sphere: religious alienation only occurred in the consciousness of man, whereas economic alienation occurred in his real life and thus its supersession involved the supersession of all alienations. Of course, the preaching of atheism might be important where religion was strong, but atheism was only a stage on the path to communism, and an abstract one at that; only communism proposed a doctrine of action that affected what was real.

Secondly, in emphasizing the social character of communism Marx begins by recapitulating the contents of a manuscript that has not survived, probably the continuation of the one on alienated labour. The relation of man to himself, to other men and to what he produced in an unalienated situation showed that it was the social character of labour that was basic. He says, in a passage similar to the third thesis on Feuerbach: 'As society itself produces man as man, so it is produced by him. Activity

73. 'Paris Manuscripts', *Frühe Schriften*, p. 594; Easton and Guddat, p. 304.

74. 'Paris Manuscripts', *Frühe Schriften*, pp. 594 f.; Easton and Guddat, p. 305.

and satisfaction, both in their content and mode of existence, are social, social activity and social satisfaction.'[75] Marx then extends the reciprocal relation of man and society to man and nature:

The human essence of nature primarily exists only for social man, because only here is nature a link with man, as his existence for others and their existence for him, as the life-element of human actuality – only here is nature the foundation of man's own human existence. Only here has the natural existence of man become his human existence and nature become human. Thus society is the completed, essential unity of man with nature, the true resurrection of nature, the fulfilled naturalism of man and humanism of nature.[76]

This passage, and other similar ones, show Marx very much under the influence of Hegel, to such an extent that he almost says that nature is *produced* by man.[77] Returning to the social aspect, Marx shows that the capacities peculiar to man are produced in social intercourse. Even when a man was working in isolation, he performed a social act simply in virtue of his being human. Even thinking – since it used language – was a social activity.

However – and this is Marx's third point – this emphasis on the social aspects of man's being did not destroy man's individuality: 'Though man is therefore a particular individual – and precisely his particularity makes him an individual, an actual individual communal being – he is equally the totality, the ideal totality, the subjective existence of society explicitly thought and experienced.'[78]

75. 'Paris Manuscripts', *Frühe Schriften*, p. 596; Easton and Guddat, p. 305.

76. 'Paris Manuscripts', *Frühe Schriften*, p. 596; Easton and Guddat, pp. 305 f.

77. See, for example, the interpretation of J.-Y. Calvez, *La Pensée de Karl Marx* (Paris, 1956) pp. 380 ff.

78. 'Paris Manuscripts', *Frühe Schriften*, p. 597; Easton and Guddat, p. 307.

Marx adds a (not very convincing) remark on death, which 'seems to be a harsh victory of the species over the particular individual and to contradict the species' unity, but the particular individual is only a particular generic being and as such mortal'.[79]

Marx devotes most of the rest of this section to drawing a picture of unalienated man, man whom he calls 'total' and 'allsided'. One should not, he says, have too narrow an idea about what the supersession of private property will achieve: just as the state of alienation totally vitiated all human faculties, so the supersession of this alienation would be a total liberation. It would not just be limited to the enjoyment or possession of material objects. All human faculties – Marx lists seeing, hearing, smelling, tasting, touching, thinking, observing, feeling, desiring, acting, loving – would, in their different ways, become means of appropriating reality. This was difficult to imagine for alienated man, since private property had made men so stupid that they could only imagine an object to be theirs when they actually used it and even then it was only employed as a means of sustaining life which was understood as consisting of labour and the creation of capital.

Referring to Hess's work on the subject, Marx declares that all physical and intellectual senses have been replaced by a single alienation – that of *having*. But this absolute poverty would give birth to the inner wealth of human beings:

The overcoming of private property means therefore the complete emancipation of all human senses and aptitudes, but it means this emancipation precisely because these senses and aptitudes have become human both subjectively and

79. 'Paris Manuscripts', *Frühe Schriften*, p. 598; Easton and Guddat, p. 307.

objectively. The eye has become a human eye, just as its object has become a social, human object derived from and for man. The senses have therefore become theoreticians immediately in their *praxis*. They try to relate themselves to their subject matter itself in an objective human relation to itself and to man, and vice versa. Need or satisfaction have thus lost their egoistic nature, and nature has lost its mere utility by use becoming human use.[80]

A man's contact with reality, Marx continued, was not merely an individual one: he appropriated objects with and through other men. The way the faculties of unalienated man appropriated their objects became totally different when the object became an object that corresponded to man's nature. Then man was no longer lost in it. Marx here divides his discussion of the relation of man to nature into an objective and a subjective side. Objectively, alienated man dealt with objects that were objectifications of himself. This link is so intimate that Marx says: 'All objects become for him the objectification of himself, become objects which confirm and realize his individuality as his objects, that is, he himself becomes the object.'[81] Subjectively, beauty of music or of form only had meaning for a faculty trained to appreciate it. This cultivation or creation of the faculties could only be achieved in certain surroundings. 'For not only the five senses but also the so-called spiritual and moral senses (will, love, etc.), in a word, human sense and the humanity of the senses come into being only through the existence of their object, through nature humanized. The development of the five senses is a labour of the whole previous

80. 'Paris Manuscripts', *Frühe Schriften*, p. 598; Easton and Guddat, p. 308.

81. 'Paris Manuscripts', *Frühe Schriften*, p. 600; Easton and Guddat, p. 309.

history of the world.'[82] For plainly a starving man appreciated food in a purely animal way; and a dealer in minerals saw only value, and not necessarily beauty, in his wares. For his faculties to become human faculties, man needed to be liberated from all external constraints.

In the past, cultural development had depended on the development of private property, with all the malformations that that implied; the transcendence of private property would thus give rise to a full and harmonious development of man's cultural potentialities. Abstract intellectual oppositions – that, for example, between spiritualism and materialism – would disappear when the real problems of life were tackled. 'It is apparent how the resolution of theoretical antitheses is possible only in a practical way, only through man's practical energy.'[83]

It is passages such as this that have led people to say that Marx's model of human activity is an artistic one and that he draws much of his picture of man from romantic sources and particularly from Schiller. The idea of man's alienated senses finding objects appropriate to them, the attempt to form a connection between freedom and aesthetic activity, the picture of the all-round man – all these occur in Schiller's *Briefe*. The following passages show what Schiller was describing:

... Enjoyment was separated from labour, the means from the end, exertion from recompense. Eternally fettered only to a single little fragment of the whole, man fashions himself only as a fragment; ever hearing only the monotonous whirl of the wheel which he turns, he never displays the full harmony of his being....[84] The aesthetic formative impulse establishes ... a

82. 'Paris Manuscripts', *Frühe Schriften*, p. 601; Easton and Guddat, p. 309.

83. 'Paris Manuscripts', *Frühe Schriften*, p. 602; Easton and Guddat, p. 310.

84. F. Schiller, *Über die ästhetische Erziehung des Menschen*, ed. W. Henckmann (Munich, 1967), p. 92.

joyous empire wherein it releases man from all the fetters of circumstance, and frees him, both physically and morally, from all that can be called constraint.[85]

It is also possible that there was a more contemporary and personal influence of the same nature, in that Marx spent a lot of his time in Paris in the company of Heine and Herwegh, two poets who did their best to embody the German romantic ideal. Heine Marx declared to be the only man that he was sorry to leave when expelled from Paris, and it was Marx's attachment to Herwegh that led to his quarrel with Ruge.

Marx goes on to sketch the importance of industry in the history of mankind. The passage anticipates his later, more detailed accounts of historical materialism. It was the history of industry, Marx maintained, that really revealed human capabilities and human psychology. Since human nature had been misunderstood in the past, history had been turned into the history of religion, politics and art. Industry, however, revealed man's essential faculties and was the basis for any science of man. In the past, natural science had only been viewed from a utilitarian angle. But its recent immense growth had enabled it, through industry, to transform the life of man. If industry were conceived of as the exterior expression of man's essential faculties, then natural science would be able to form the basis of human science. This science had to be based on sense-experience, as described by Feuerbach. But since this was *human* sense-experience, there would be a single, all-embracing science: 'Natural science will in time include the science of man as the science of man will include natural science: there will be one science.'[86] Thus

85. ibid., p. 185. Quoted in S. Lukes, 'Alienation and Anomie', in *Philosophy, Politics and Society*, 3rd series (Oxford, 1967).

86. 'Paris Manuscripts', *Frühe Schriften*, p. 604; Easton and Guddat, p. 312.

the reciprocal relationship that Marx had outlined before between man and nature is reflected here in his idea of a natural science of man.

Marx here adds an aside on the meaning of wealth and poverty for socialist man:

It is apparent how the rich man and wide human need appear in place of economic wealth and poverty. The rich man is simultaneously one who needs a totality of human manifestations of life and in whom his own realization exists as inner necessity, as need. Not only the wealth but also the poverty of man equally acquire – under the premise of socialism – a human and thus social meaning. It is the passive bond which lets man experience the greatest wealth, the other human being, as need.[87]

The last part of Marx's manuscript consists of a rather uncharacteristic digression on the question of whether the world was created or not. One of the key ideas in Marx's picture of man is that man is his own creator; any being that lived by the favour of another was a dependent being. Accordingly, Marx rejects the idea that the world was created: although the notion of creation was a difficult one to dispel, it had been practically refuted by the science of geogeny which taught that the world was generated spontaneously. Marx then rehearses Aristotle's argument about the individual owing his existence to his parents and they to their parents and so forth. To this he replies, relying on his conception of man as a species-being: 'You must also keep in mind the circular movement sensibly apparent in that process whereby man reproduces himself in procreation; thus man always remains the subject.'[88]

87. 'Paris Manuscripts', *Frühe Schriften*, p. 605; Easton and Guddat, p. 312.
88. 'Paris Manuscripts', *Frühe Schriften*, p. 606; Easton and Guddat, p. 313.

Marx's imaginary opponent then asks who created the first man and nature as a whole. Marx replies:

If you ask about the creation of nature and man, you thus abstract from nature and man. You assert them as non-existent and yet want me to prove them to you as existing. I say to you: give up your abstraction and you will also give up your question. Or if you want to maintain your abstraction, be consistent and if you think of man and nature as non-existent, think of yourself as non-existent as you too are nature and man. Do not think, do not question me, for as soon as you think and question, your abstraction from the existence of nature and man makes no sense. Or are you such an egoist that you assert everything as nothing and yet want yourself to exist.[89]

Marx's argument is plainly rather stilted and when his opponent replies that he does not want to assert the nothingness of nature but only to ask about its genesis, as he might ask an anatomist about the formation of bones, Marx breaks off the argument and continues in a much more characteristic vein: 'Since for socialist man, however, the entire so-called world history is only the creation of man through human labour and the development of nature for man, he has evident and incontrovertible proof of his self-creation, his own formation process.'[90] Thus for socialist man the question of an alien being beyond man and nature whose existence would imply their unreality had become impossible. For him the mutual interdependence of man and nature was what was essential and anything else seemed unreal. 'Atheism as a denial of this unreality no longer makes sense because it is a negation of God and through this negation asserts the existence of man. But socialism as such no longer

89. 'Paris Manuscripts', *Frühe Schriften*, pp. 606 f.; Easton and Guddat, pp. 313 f.

90. 'Paris Manuscripts', *Frühe Schriften*, p. 607; Easton and Guddat, p. 314.

needs such mediation. It begins with the sensuous perception, theoretically and practically, of man and nature as
essential beings.'[91] This perception, once established, no
longer required the overcoming of religion, just as man's
life, once rid of alienation, no longer needed the overcoming of private property, no longer needed communism.
Marx finishes with a very Hegelian remark on the tran-
sitoriness of the communist phase: 'The position of communism is the negation of the negation and hence, for
the next stage of historical development, the necessary
actual phase of man's emancipation and rehabilitation.
Communism is the necessary form and dynamic principle
of the immediate future but not as such the goal of human
development – the form of human society.'[92] Here communism seems to be viewed as merely a stage in the dialectical evolution, a stage that at a given moment would
have served its purpose and be superseded. The earlier
picture of 'true communism' as 'the solution to the riddle
of history'[93] was much more static and unhistorical.

4. HEGEL'S DIALECTIC

a. Preliminary

The section to which the editors of the *MEGA* gave the
title 'Critique of Hegelian Dialectic and Philosophy in
General' follows, in Marx's manuscript, directly on, and
forms part of his section on communism. This section on
divided numerically into five parts and the section on
Hegel's dialectic is preceded by a number six, as though it

91. 'Paris Manuscripts', *Frühe Schriften*, p. 607; Easton and
Guddat, p. 314.
92. 'Paris Manuscripts', *Frühe Schriften*, p. 608; Easton and
Guddat, p. 314.
93. 'Paris Manuscripts', *Frühe Schriften*, p. 594; Easton and
Guddat, p. 304.

formed a continuation of Marx's comments on communism. In the preface he does say: 'In contrast to the critical theologians of our time I have regarded the concluding chapter of the present work – the discussion of the Hegelian dialectic and philosophy in general – to be absolutely necessary because such a task has not yet been accomplished.'[94] But what we have here are only 'some comments' and unfinished comments at that, for Marx says he will deal with the Young Hegelians also but does not do so. The elaboration of themes that had arisen in the previous sections on communism – particularly the relationship between man and nature and the eventual irrelevance of atheism – show how closely this section is linked to previous ones. In a paragraph a few pages further on, Marx indicates how his discussion of Hegel is relevant to the preceding themes of the manuscript. The point is that 'Hegel's standpoint is that of modern political economy.'[95] However abstract and mental was Hegel's conception of labour, he saw that labour was the creator of value: the structure of philosophy accurately reflected the real economic alienation of man in his work process. Hegel had grasped the essence of man's labour in a way that was hidden from classical economists. Having attacked the classical economists for their neglect of this fact, Marx is now attacking Hegel for having 'mystified' his very real discoveries.

What Marx does in this section is to discuss the various attitudes of the Young Hegelians to Hegel, and to single out Feuerbach as the only constructive thinker; he then uses Hegel to show up the weaknesses in Feuerbach's approach and finally settles down to a long analysis of

94. 'Paris Manuscripts', *Frühe Schriften*, p. 508; Easton and Guddat, p. 285.

95. 'Paris Manuscripts', *Frühe Schriften*, p. 646; Easton and Guddat, p. 322.

Hegel's fundamental error, first in the *Phenomenology* in general and particularly in the last chapter. The style is often obscure, involved and extremely repetitive, as Marx is constantly working over and reformulating his attitude to Hegel.

b. The Young Hegelians

Marx thinks that, until very recently, the Young Hegelians had scarcely spared a thought for their methodology: 'Modern German criticism has been so much preoccupied with the past, so much restricted by the development of its subject matter, that it has had a completely uncritical attitude toward methods of criticism and has been completely oblivious to the seemingly formal but actually essential question: how do we now stand in relation to the Hegelian dialectic?'[96] Marx has in mind Strauss and particularly Bruno Bauer who, with most of the Berlin Young Hegelians, had retired from the political battle and were turning their criticism into something completely transcendental and uncommitted. Feuerbach, on the other hand, was the only one of Hegel's disciples who had been able to come to terms with Hegel's dialectic. 'Feuerbach is the only one who has a serious, critical relation to Hegel's dialectic, who has made genuine discoveries in this field, and who above all is the true conqueror of the old philosophy. The magnitude of Feuerbach's achievement and the unpretentious simplicity with which he presents it to the world stand in a strikingly opposite inverse ratio.'[97] Marx divides Feuerbach's great achievements into three:

96. 'Paris Manuscripts', *Frühe Schriften*, p. 637; Easton and Guddat, p. 315.
97. 'Paris Manuscripts', *Frühe Schriften*, p. 639; Easton and Guddat, p. 316.

(1) Proof that philosophy is nothing more than religion brought to and developed in reflection, and thus is equally to be condemned as another form and mode of the alienation of man's nature.

(2) The establishment of true materialism and real science by making the social relationship of 'man to man' the fundamental principle of his theory.

(3) Opposing to the negation of the negation, which claims to be the absolute positive, the self-subsistent positive positively grounded on itself.[98]

Further evidence of Marx's respect for Feuerbach is contained in a letter of his written in August 1844 and only published a few years ago. Enclosing a copy of his 'Introduction to a Critique of Hegel's Philosophy of Law', Marx says:

> I am glad to find an opportunity of assuring you of the great admiration and – allow me the word – love that I bear towards you. Your *Philosophy of the Future* and *Essence of Faith* are in any case, in spite of their limited size, of more weight than all the present-day German literature put together. In these writings you have given – whether intentionally I do not know – a philosophical basis to socialism, and the communists, too, have immediately understood these works in this sense. The unity of man with man, which is based on the real difference between men, the concept of a human species drawn down from the heaven of abstraction to the real earth, what can this be but the concept of society?[99]

Put briefly, what Feuerbach had succeeded in showing (according to Marx) was that Hegel had started from the abstract, infinite point of view of religion and theology, superseded this by the finite and particular attitude of

98. 'Paris Manuscripts', *Frühe Schriften*, p. 639; Easton and Guddat, pp. 316 f.

99. L. Feuerbach, *Briefwechsel*, ed. W. Schuffenhauer (Leipzig, 1963) pp. 183 f.

philosophy and then superseded this attitude by a restoration of the abstraction typical of theology. Philosophy, having superseded theology, then went back on its tracks and contradicted itself. Feuerbach thought the final stage – the negation of the negation – was a regression and Marx agreed, saying that it enabled Hegel to find 'only the abstract, logical, speculative expression of the movement of history, not the actual history of man as a given subject but only man's genesis, the history of his origin'.[100]

c. Hegel

Marx breaks off to have a look at Hegel's system. He begins by copying out the table of contents of the *Phenomenology*, 'the true birth-place and secret of his philosophy'.[101] He then summarizes the elements in Hegel's philosophy and accuses Hegel of a double mistake.[102] Firstly, though Hegel said that man suffered from economic and political alienation, it was only the thought of economics and politics in which Hegel was interested. The whole process ended in absolute knowledge, with the result that it was the philosopher who judged the world. Thus, according to Hegel:

It is not that the human being objectifies himself inhumanly in opposition to himself, but that he objectifies himself by distinction from and in opposition to abstract thought – this is the

100. 'Paris Manuscripts', *Frühe Schriften*, p. 640; Easton and Guddat, p. 317.

101. 'Paris Manuscripts', *Frühe Schriften*, p. 641; Easton and Guddat, p. 318.

102. For an analysis of the implications of this 'double mistake' for Marx's later writings, see J. O'Neill, 'The Concept of Estrangement in the Early and Later Writings of Karl Marx', *Philosophy and Phenomenological Research* (September 1964) pp. 65 ff.

essence of alienation as given and as to be transcended. The appropriation of man's essential capacities which have become things, even alien things, is thus primarily only an appropriation taking place in consciousness, in pure thought, that is, in abstraction.[103]

Marx's second objection is, in effect, the same as the first – that Hegel had made all the entities that in reality belonged objectively and sensuously to man into mental entities, since for him spirit alone was the genuine essence of man.

However, this criticism of Hegel is tempered by an analysis of Hegel's achievements that shows clearly how much, in spite of his stringent criticism, Marx owes to Hegel. For Marx considers that, although in the *Phenomenology* criticism was still liable to mystify and was not sufficiently self-aware, this criticism nevertheless went far beyond later developments; in other words, none of the disciples had as yet been able to outstrip their master. Indeed, Marx makes the astonishing claim for the *Phenomenology* that 'All the elements of criticism are implicit in it, already prepared and elaborated in a manner far surpassing the Hegelian standpoint. The sections on the "unhappy consciousness", the "honest consciousness", the struggle between the "noble and base consciousness", etc. etc., contain the critical elements – though still in an alienated form – of whole spheres such as religion, the the state, civil life, etc.'[104] This was because the *Phenomenology* had understood the alienation of man, had achieved insights into the process of man's development and had seen that the objects which appeared to order men's lives – their religion, their wealth – in fact belonged

103. 'Paris Manuscripts', *Frühe Schriften*, pp. 643 f.; Easton and Guddat, p. 320.

104. 'Paris Manuscripts', *Frühe Schriften*, p. 644; Easton and Guddat, pp. 320 f.

to man and were the product of essential human capacities. Marx sums up his attitude to Hegel as follows:

The great thing in Hegel's *Phenomenology* and its final result – the dialectic of negativity as the moving and productive principle – is simply that Hegel grasps the self-development of man as a process, objectification as loss of the object, as alienation and transcendence of this alienation; that he thus grasps the nature of work and comprehends objective man, authentic because actual, as the result of his work.[105]

Man could only become the species-being that he was by first treating his species-powers as objects separate from himself, and this meant that alienation was a necessary stage in mankind's evolution. Before finishing his general comments on the *Phenomenology*, however, Marx returns to what he considers Hegel's basic defect, saying that though Hegel does grasp labour as the self-confirming essence of man, yet 'the only labour Hegel knows and recognizes is abstract, mental labour.'[106]

Although Marx's language is, as often, involved and his arrangement somewhat haphazard, this is the passage where he gives his fullest and clearest account of his debt to, and disagreements with, Hegel. Hegel thought that reality was Spirit realizing itself. In this process Spirit produced a world that it thought at first was external; only later did it realize that this world was its own production. Spirit was not something separate from this productive activity; it only existed in and through this activity. At the beginning of this process Spirit was not aware that it was externalizing or alienating itself. Only gradually did Spirit realize that the world was not external

105. 'Paris Manuscripts', *Frühe Schriften*, p. 645; Easton and Guddat, p. 321.

106. 'Paris Manuscripts', *Frühe Schriften*, p. 646; Easton and Guddat, p. 322.

to it. It is the failure to realize this that constituted, for Hegel, alienation. This alienation would cease when men became fully self-conscious and understood their environment and their culture to be emanations of Spirit. Freedom consisted in this understanding, and freedom was the aim of history. What Marx did, roughly, was to reject the notion of Spirit and retain only finite individual beings: thus the Hegelian relationship to spirit and the world became the Marxian notion of the relationship of man to his social being. Marx says that Hegel only takes account of man's mental activities, that is, of his ideas, and that these, though important, are by themselves insufficient to explain social and cultural change.

In fact, this criticism of Hegel is not quite accurate. Hegel certainly took more factors into account than simply man's intellectual and cultural activities. Even in the *Phenomenology* Hegel deals with man as a political and biological animal. The sections on master and slave and on the need for and struggle for recognition are deeply political. Indeed, it is often asserted[107] that the passage in the *Phenomenology* that particularly impressed Marx was the one on master and slave,[108] however, it seems possible that the reverse is true and that Marx, when criticizing Hegel for being abstract and mental, did not pay sufficient attention to this section of the *Phenomenology*; certainly Marx (though he does specify other sections that appealed to him) never alludes to this one.

Marx then turns his attention exclusively to the last chapter of Hegel's *Phenomenology* – he had made an extended précis of it which still survives as the fourth of the manuscripts. His main point here is that, according

107 Cf., for example, Tucker, *Philosophy and Myth in Karl Marx*, p. 147.

108. For a lucid exposition of this passage, see Plamenatz, *Man and Society*, ii, 154 ff.

to Hegel, self-consciousness has only itself for object and so man can be equated with self-consciousness. It followed that it was objectivity which constituted alienation and that the overcoming of alienation involved the overcoming of objectivity, these two terms being for Hegel practically synonymous.[109] As Marx says some pages later, 'The appropriation of alienated, objective being or the transcendence of objectivity in the mode of alienation ... for Hegel means also or primarily the transcendence of objectivity since the objective character of the object for self-consciousness, not its determinateness, is the scandal of alienation.'[110] Marx sets out to summarize Hegel's view of the overcoming of alienation, prefacing it with the remark that whereas Hegel talked as though human nature were but *one* attribute of self-consciousness, in reality self-consciousness was an attribute of human nature. For Hegel, Marx continues, all alienation was alienation of self-consciousness. Thus actual alienation, alienation that had to do with natural objects, was only apparent – hence the word 'phenomenology'.

The rest of this section consists of a critical commentary on this idea of the overcoming of alienation and divides into two parts: in the first, Marx explains his conception of man as an objective, natural being; in the second, he criticizes in detail Hegel's idealism.

Firstly, then, in opposition to Hegel's conception of man as self-consciousness, Marx proclaims:

It is entirely to be expected that a living, natural being endowed with objective (i.e. material) capacities should have real natural objects corresponding to its nature and also that its

109. Further on this see J. Hyppolite, *Logique et existence* (Paris, 1953) last chapter.
110. 'Paris Manuscripts', *Frühe Schriften*, p. 653; Easton and Guddat, p. 327.

self-externalization should establish an actual objective world, but a world in the form of externality, one which does not belong to such a being's nature, an overpowering world. There is nothing incomprehensible or mysterious in this. The contrary, rather, would be mysterious.[111]

It was equally clear that, if man were reduced to self-consciousness then he could only establish outside himself abstract objects that were constructs of man's mind. These objects would have no independence *vis-à-vis* man's self-consciousness. Marx's view of human nature is very different: 'When actual, corporeal man with his feet firmly planted on the solid ground, inhaling and exhaling all of nature's energies, establishes his actual, objective essential capacities as alien objects through his externalization, the establishing is not the subject but the subjectivity of objective capacities whose action must therefore be objective.'[112] Marx calls his view 'naturalism' or 'humanism', and distinguishes this from both idealism and materialism and claims that it unites what is essential both to idealism and to materialism. 'We see here how a consistent naturalism or humanism is distinguished from both idealism and materialism as well, and at the same time is the unifying truth of both. We also see how only naturalism is able to comprehend the act of world history.'[113] Marx follows this with two concise paragraphs, very reminiscent of the previous section on private property and communism, on the meaning of naturalism and objectivity. Nature seems to mean to Marx what is opposed to man, what affords him scope for his activities

111. 'Paris Manuscripts', *Frühe Schriften*, p. 649; Easton and Guddat, p. 324.
112. 'Paris Manuscripts', *Frühe Schriften*, p. 649; Easton and Guddat, p. 325.
113. 'Paris Manuscripts', *Frühe Schriften*, p. 650; Easton and Guddat, p. 325.

and satisfies his needs. It is these needs and drives that make up man's nature. Marx calls his view 'naturalism' both because man is orientated towards nature and fulfils his needs in and through nature and also more fundamentally, because man is a part of nature. Thus man as an active natural being was endowed with certain natural capacities, powers and drives. But he was also a limited, dependent, suffering creature. The objects of his drives were independent of him, yet he needed them to satisfy himself and express his objective nature. Thus, 'A being which does not have its nature outside itself is not a natural one and has no part in the system of nature.'[114]

This leads on to a discussion of what it is to be objective: 'A being which has no object outside itself is not objective. A being which is not itself an object for a third being has no being for its object, that is, not related objectively, its being is not objective. An unobjective being is a nonentity.'[115] Marx went on to suppose a being that was neither an object itself nor had an object. Such a being would be the only existing being, and so nonobjective, a mere abstraction. Marx finishes: 'To be sentient is to suffer. As an objective sentient being man is therefore a suffering being, and since he feels his suffering, he is a passionate being. Passion is man's essential capacity energetically bent on its object.'[116] This contains echoes of the eighteenth-century French materialists,

114. 'Paris Manuscripts', *Frühe Schriften*, p. 651; Easton and Guddat, p. 326. On this passage, see also J. O'Neill, 'The Concept of Estrangement in the Early and Later Writings of Karl Marx', *Philosophy and Phenomenological Research* (September 1964) pp. 68 f.

115. 'Paris Manuscripts', *Frühe Schriften*, p. 651; Easton and Guddat, p. 326.

116. 'Paris Manuscripts', *Frühe Schriften*, pp. 651 f.; Easton and Guddat, p. 321.

Holbach and Helvétius, but the main source for Marx's ideas and language on nature and objectivity is Feuerbach's *Philosophy of the Future*.[117]

Marx now makes an unconvincing attempt (which he later crossed out, as he did the section on naturalism above) to distinguish man from other natural beings. He says that neither the objects man deals with nor his perceptions are immediately adequate to a thoroughly human being. What he seems to mean is that humanism is more than materialism because its objects are mediated through the species. This theme (and the idea of history as the self-conscious genesis of man) have been more fully dealt with by Marx in the section on communism proper.

After this digression on his own conception of human nature, Marx continues with his commentary on the last chapter of the *Phenomenology*. He summarizes a discussion in which, he says, 'All the illusions of speculation are assembled.'[118] Hegel's two main points here were, according to Marx, that consciousness knew the nullity of its object in that it knew that its objects were its own self-alienation and that there was no distinction between its object and itself; and that consciousness, in this knowledge, had transcended the alienation and was at one with itself. Marx's objections here are twofold: firstly, Hegel had equated alienation with objectivity; secondly, man seemed, having recognized the spiritual world as a sphere of alienation, to reaffirm it in its alienated form and consider it a facet of his authentic existence, that is, to feel himself at one with it.

117. A commentary that emphasizes the French materialists is Kägi, *Genesis des historischen Materialismus*, pp. 262 ff. For the debt to Feuerbach, see McLellan, *The Young Hegelians and Karl Marx*, pp. 101 ff.

118. 'Paris Manuscripts', *Frühe Schriften*, p. 654; Easton and Guddat, p. 328.

Thus, after transcending religion, for example, and recognizing it as a product of self-externalization, he yet finds confirmation of himself in religion as religion. Here is the root of Hegel's false positivism or of his merely apparent criticism which Feuerbach noted as the position, negation and re-establishment of religion or theology – but which has to be conceived in more general terms. Thus, reason is at one with itself in unreason as unreason. Having recognized that man leads an externalized life in law, politics, etc., man leads in this externalized life as such his truly human life.[119]

Thus for Marx the issue of Hegel's accommodation (that had been in his mind since he wrote his doctoral thesis) was quite clear: Hegel's false positivism was 'the lie of his principle'.[120] Marx differed fundamentally from Hegel on the meaning of the term *Aufhebung* (transcendence, suppression). He considered that Hegel's account was merely a speculative trap: 'With Hegel the negation of the negation is not the confirmation of my authentic nature even through the negation of its appearance. It is the confirmation of the apparent or self-alienated nature in its denial.'[121] But private property, morality, the family, civil society, the state, all remained in existence in spite of their having been 'transcended' in thought. This was because Hegel's transcendence was radically ambivalent, a transcendence in which 'denial and preservation' were bound together. There was the additional consequence that man was only truly human when he was engaging in philosophy and that, for example, the most authentically religious man was the philosopher of religion.

In his usual see-sawing manner, Marx now returns to

119. 'Paris Manuscripts', *Frühe Schriften*, pp. 654 ff.; Easton and Guddat, pp. 328 f.

120. 'Paris Manuscripts', *Frühe Schriften*, p. 655; Easton and Guddat, p. 329.

121. 'Paris Manuscripts', *Frühe Schriften*, p. 655; Easton and Guddat, p. 329.

his comments at the beginning of the section on Hegel's achievements and addresses himself to the 'positive' aspects of the Hegelian dialectic. What Hegel had arrived at was insight (albeit a still alienated one) into the process of alienation and its transcendence. Hegel's dialectic was a chart that made plain how atheism transcended God to produce theoretical humanism and how communism transcended private property to produce practical humanism. Both these limitations, religion and private property, seemed (though Marx's language is very obscure here) to be attempts to arrive at humanism, but attempts that had to be transcended to give rise to a self-creating, positive humanism. Marx reiterates his previous statements that communism was no return to primitive simplicity but involved a full development of all man's capacities. He repeats, too, his assertion that Hegel had grasped the true nature of human labour, but (for he could never stop criticizing him for long) immediately explores the consequence of Hegel's speculative inversion of this act of self-creation. These consequences were three (it is obvious that Marx is here merely reformulating what he has already written): this act of self-creation was merely formal; as a consequence the alleged transcendence of alienation only confirmed it in spite of Hegel's calling it a 'divine process'; thirdly, since the subject of the process – God or the Absolute Spirit – only emerged as a result, actual contemporary man was turned into mere predicate.

Marx does not get beyond elaborating on the first before the manuscript breaks off. He points out the contrast between 'the rich, living, sensuous, concrete activity of self-objectification',[122] afforded by his own view of human nature and the formalism of Hegel's abstract negation of the negation. Marx then becomes extremely abstract in

122. 'Paris Manuscripts', *Frühe Schriften*, pp. 659 f.; Easton and Guddat, p. 333.

his own right and alleges that the Absolute Idea must turn to its opposite, nature. For this he gives two reasons: either because it is still subject to the dialectic, or else because boredom drives it to something different. Marx adds two very involved paragraphs on Hegel's view of nature and then the manuscript breaks off.

This section of the 'Paris Manuscripts', involved and repetitive as it is, comprises Marx's definitive criticism of Hegel's dialectic. He referred to this work more than thirty years later, in 1873, in the preface to the second edition of *Capital,* which can serve as a summary of what he conceived to be the essence of this criticism:

My dialectical method is not only different from the Hegelian, but is its direct opposite. To Hegel, the life-process of the human brain, i.e. the process of thinking, which, under the name of 'The Idea', he even transforms into an independent subject, is the demiurgus of the real world, and the real world is only the external, phenomenal form of 'The Idea'. With me, on the contrary, the ideal is nothing else than the material world reflected by the human mind, and translated into forms of thought. The mystifying side of Hegelian dialectic I criticized nearly thirty years ago, at a time when it was still the fashion. . . . The mystification which dialectic suffers in Hegel's hands by no means prevents him from being the first to present its general form of working in a comprehensive and conscious manner. With him it is standing on its head. It must be turned right side up again, if you would discover the rational kernel within the mystical shell. In its mystified form dialectic became the fashion in Germany, because it seemed to transfigure and to glorify the existing state of things. In its rational form it is a scandal and abomination to bourgeoisdom and its doctrinaire professors, because it includes in its comprehension and affirmative recognition of the existing state of things at the same time also the recognition of the negation of that state, of its inevitable breaking up; because it regards every historically developed social form as in fluid movement, and therefore takes into account its transient nature not less than its momentary existence; because it lets nothing impose upon it, and is in its essence critical and revolutionary.[123]

There is a certain continuity evident in Marx's attitude to Hegel from the 'Doctoral Thesis' to the 'Paris Manuscripts'. In his thesis Marx rejected the idea that Hegel was guilty of 'accommodation' and demanded that apparent contradictions be resolved by appeal to Hegel's 'essential consciousness'.[124] In his 'Critique of Hegel's Philosophy of the State', Marx showed by reference to particular examples that Hegel's principles inevitably involved accommodation. But it was not until Marx transferred his attention from Hegel's *Philosophy of Law* to his *Phenomenology* that he was able to formulate a general criticism of Hegel's dialectic. Here it is clear that Marx, although still at home with Hegel's concepts and terminology, did not confine himself to internal criticism. At the same time, he still respected Hegel as a great thinker and considered his dialectic a valuable instrument for investigating the world. He also credited Hegel with having discovered, though in a mystifying form, the process of man's alienation and of its overcoming.

5. NEEDS, PRODUCTION, THE DIVISION OF
LABOUR AND MONEY

The concluding portions of the 'Paris Manuscripts' consist of twenty pages of reflections on the morality of private property and a short section on the meaning of money.

The discussion of capitalist morality does not add much to previous sections of the manuscripts and belongs in the

123. K. Marx, *Capital* (Moscow, 1954) I, 19 f.
124. 'Doctoral Thesis', *MEGA* I, i (1) 64; Easton and Guddat, p. 61.

framework of the first section on wages, rent and profit. Marx contrasts the socialist attitude to the wealth of human needs with the attitude brought about by private property which artificially created needs in order to bring men into dependence. As a result, poverty increased as men and their needs were at the mercy of the money market, and eventually men's living conditions became worse than those of animals. The theoretical counterpart of this state of affairs was political economy. It reduced the needs of the worker to the miserable necessities of life and preached utter asceticism:

> Thus, despite its worldly and pleasure-seeking appearance, it is a truly moral science and the most moral of all sciences. Its principal thesis is the renunciation of life and of human needs. The less you eat, drink, buy books, go to the theatre or to balls, or to the public house, and the less you think, love, theorize, sing, paint, fence, etc., the more you will be able to save and the greater will become your treasure which neither moth nor rust will corrupt – your capital. The less you are, the less you express your life, the more you have, the greater is your alienated life and the greater is the saving of your alienated being.[125]

The cynicism of Ricardo was quite in keeping with political economy, which it had its own private laws, for 'The nature of alienation implies that each sphere applies a different and contradictory norm, that morality does not apply the same norm as political economy, etc., because each of them is a particular alienation of man; each is concentrated upon a specific area of alienated activity and is itself alienated from the other.'[126]

Marx mentions briefly how classical economists wish to limit the population and think even people a luxury; and

125. 'Paris Manuscripts', *Frühe Schriften*, p. 612; Bottomore, p. 171.

126. 'Paris Manuscripts', *Frühe Schriften*, p. 614; Bottomore, p. 173.

how paradoxical it was that the greatest wealth was often extracted from the extremest poverty, for example, the rents of slum dwellings. He then makes some further remarks on communism. The equality proclaimed by some French communists was merely a political foundation and was no better than the German attempt to base communism on universal self-consciousness. The situation in England was a surer basis; 'The transcendence of alienation always proceeds from the form of alienation which is the dominant power; in Germany, self-consciousness; in France equality, because politics; in England, the real, material, self-sufficient, practical need.'[127] Marx then re-emphasizes that communism is not the final state of society and that it could only come about through 'genuine communist activity'.[128] He then makes some remarks on the meetings of communist workers in Paris that show that his picture of communist society was drawn in part from his observations there:

When communist artisans form associations, teaching and propaganda are their first aims. But their association itself creates a new need – the need for society – and what appeared to be a means has become an end. The most striking results of this practical development are to be seen when French socialist workers meet together. Smoking, eating and drinking are no longer simply means of bringing people together. Society, association, entertainment which also has society as its aim, is sufficient for them; the brotherhood of man is no empty phrase but a reality, and the nobility of man shines forth upon us from their toil-worn bodies.[129]

127. 'Paris Manuscripts', *Frühe Schriften*, p. 617; Bottomore, p. 176.
128. 'Paris Manuscripts', *Frühe Schriften*, p. 618; Bottomore, p. 176.
129. 'Paris Manuscripts', *Frühe Schriften*, p. 618; Bottomore, p. 176.

In the second half of this section, Marx returns to the dehumanizing effects of capital and discusses the declining rate of interest and the abolition of land rent. Most of the section is taken up with the question of the division of labour, with quotations from Smith, Mill and Say, but Marx comes to no substantive conclusion.

In the short section on money, Marx quotes extensively from Goethe's *Faust* and Shakespeare's *Timon of Athens* to show that money is the ruin of society. Since money could purchase anything, it could remedy all deficiencies: it was 'the bond of all bonds'.[130] Since money, as the existing and active concept of value, confounds and exchanges everything, it is 'the universal confusion and transposition of all things, the inverted world, the confusion and transposition of all natural and human qualities.'[131] In a truly human society where man was man then everything would have a definite, human value and only love could be exchanged for love, and so on. Here the manuscript breaks off.

Marx himself supplied no conclusion to the 'Paris Manuscripts' and it is impossible to draw one from such a disjointed work: economics, social criticism, philosophy, history, logic, dialectics and metaphysics are all present. Although each section is dominated by a different subject matter, there is a certain amount of mutual influence. Here for the first time what Engels described as three constituent elements in Marx's thought – German idealist philosophy, French socialism and English economics – appear together, if not yet united.

130. 'Paris Manuscripts', *Frühe Schriften*, p. 633; Bottomore, p. 191.

131. 'Paris Manuscripts', *Frühe Schriften*, p. 636; Bottomore, p. 193.

CHAPTER EIGHT

Conclusion

1. MARX'S EARLY WRITINGS IN HISTORICAL PERSPECTIVE

At the time when they were written, Marx's early writings did not make much impact. His contemporaries – Hess above all – certainly considered him a very gifted person: he was only twenty-four when appointed to the editorship of the *Rheinische Zeitung*. Nevertheless, Marx could not find a publisher for his *German Ideology* and even the popularly-written *Communist Manifesto* of 1848 had very little effect. In the 1840s and 1850s, both inside and outside socialist circles, Proudhon, and even Engels, were much better known than Marx.

This neglect of Marx's early writings by his contemporaries was quite normal considering the lack of interest in them displayed by Marx and Engels themselves. They seemed indifferent even to preserving their manuscripts: in the preface to his *Critique of Political Economy*, Marx said that he and Engels had abandoned the manuscript of the *German Ideology* (1846) 'to the gnawing criticism of the mice all the more willingly as we had achieved our main purpose – self-clarification'.[1] When in 1867 a German friend, Dr Kugelmann, an enthusiastic admirer of Marx, presented him with a copy of *The Holy Family* (1844), he wrote to Engels: 'He possesses a much better collection of our works than both of us put together. Here I also found the *Holy Family* again; he has presented it

1. K. Marx, 'Preface to a Critique of Political Economy', in Marx–Engels, *Selected Works*, I, 364.

to me and will send you a copy. I was pleasantly surprised
to find that we do not need to be ashamed of this work,
although the cult of Feuerbach produces a very humorous
effect upon one now.'[2] Engels, writing in 1888, dismissed
the *German Ideology* very curtly: 'Before sending these
lines to the press, I have once again ferreted out and
looked up the old manuscript of 1845-6. The section
dealing with Feuerbach is not completed. The finished
portion consists of an exposition of the materialistic conception of history which proves only how incomplete our
knowledge of economic history still was at that time.'[3]
Engels's attitude is very clearly shown in a conversation
that a Russian visitor, Alexis Voden, had with him in
1893. Voden, recalling in 1927 a conversation concerning
the early works of Marx and Engels, reported:

Our next conversation was on early works by Marx and
Engels. At first Engels was embarrassed when I expressed interest in these works. He mentioned too that Marx had written
poetry in his student years, but that it would hardly interest
anybody. Then he asked which of Marx's and his works interested Plekhanov and his fellow thinkers. And what was the
exact reason for that interest? Was not the fragment on Feuerbach, which Engels considered the most meaty of those 'old
works', sufficient?
I gave all Plekhanov's arguments in favour of publishing as
soon as possible the whole of Marx's philosophical legacy and
his and Engels's joint works. Engels said that he had heard that
more than once from certain Germans, the seriousness of whose
interest in those 'old works' he had no reason to doubt; but he
asked me for an honest answer to the question: which was
more important – for him, Engels – to spend the rest of his life
publishing old manuscripts from publicistic work of the
forties, or to set to work, when Book Three of *Capital* came

2. Marx–Engels, *Selected Correspondence*, p. 217.
3. F. Engels, 'Ludwig Feuerbach and the End of Classical German
Philosophy', Marx–Engels, *Selected Works*, II, 359.

out, on the publication of Marx's manuscripts on the history
of the theories on surplus value?...

I availed myself of what seemed to me the most favourable
moment to urge Engels to redeem from undeserved oblivion at
least the most essential of Marx's earlier works, Feuerbach
alone being insufficient. Engels said that in order to penetrate
into that 'old story' one needed, in fact, to have an interest in
Hegel himself, which was not the case with anybody then, or,
to be exact, 'neither with Kautsky nor with Bernstein'.[4]

As Engels's remarks here indicate, the Hegelian
approach of the early writings soon became out of date.
Well on into the 1860s Marx was not well known outside
a small circle, being thrown into the shade by Lassalle.
When he did become known, after the publication in
1867 of the first volume of *Capital*, it was as an economist
who had set out to prove scientifically the inevitable
decline of capitalism. Already in 1859 Engels wrote, in a
review of Marx's *Critique of Political Economy*: 'The
Germans have long ago proved their equality and in most
cases their superiority to the civilized nations in all fields
of knowledge. Only one single discipline counted no German name among its devotees. Now here it is: Karl
Marx.'[5] About the same time, the *Communist Manifesto*
began to have an effect. Isolated sayings from the early
writings, such as religion being the opium of the people,
began to be well known. Bernstein did publish a few
extracts from the *German Ideology*, but there was no real
interest in the early Marx and (until very recently) this
has remained so with orthodox Marxists.

One reason for this lack of interest is that not many of
Marx's early writings were available. The political essays

4. A. Voden, 'Talks with Engels', *Reminiscences of Marx and
Engels* (Moscow, no date) pp. 330 f.
5. Quoted in E. Thier, 'Etappen der Marxinterpretation', *Marxismusstudien* (1954), I, 15.

written mainly for the *Rheinische Zeitung* in 1842 were re-edited in Cologne in 1851; the *Holy Family* and the essays published in the *Deutsch-Französische Jahrbücher* were long out of print and forgotten; and Marx's doctoral thesis, the 'Critique of Hegel's Philosophy of the State', the 'Paris Manuscripts' and the *German Ideology* had never been published at all. After the turn of the century, however, Marx's early writings began to arouse the (peripheral) interest of historians and in particular of Mehring, the first biographer of Marx and historian of the German Social Democrat Party. In 1902 Mehring published some of the literary remains of Marx and Engels, including the doctoral thesis, the essays in the *Deutsch-Französische Jahrbücher* and the *Holy Family*. These were accompanied by introductions that contained a wealth of detail. However, Mehring's edition did not contain the 'Critique of Hegel's Philosophy of the State', the 'Paris Manuscripts', or the *German Ideology*. Perhaps as a consequence (the 'Critique of Hegel's Philosophy of the State' and the 'Paris Manuscripts' are the most Hegelian of Marx's early writings), no importance was attached to the influence of Hegel on Marx. In the same year, Bernstein published fragments of Marx's attack on Stirner in the *German Ideology*. But it was not until 1927 that a complete edition of Marx's early writings was produced. Published in Frankfurt and later in Berlin, it was edited by D. Rjazanov under the supervision of the Marx–Engels Institute in Moscow. Unfortunately, this superb edition was discontinued in 1932 for political reasons. It did, however, contain the 'Paris Manuscripts', the work which, above all others, seemed to show Marx in a new light.

Lack of availability was not the only reason for the delay of interest in the young Marx. There was also a political reason for the underemphasis of even such of Marx's early writings as were known. A revival of interest in the young Marx implied a revival of interest in the bourgeois philosophical tradition and principally in Hegel. But in the first two decades of this century, social democrats and communists were concerned to emphasize their distinctions from the bourgeoisie and to portray Marxism as a scientific and proletarian world-view in opposition to past and present bourgeois ideals. Thus they sharply contrasted the young and the old Marx to the detriment of the former. However, with the rise of the twin totalitarianisms of Fascism and Stalinism, oppositional elements with humanist aspirations were driven into alliance, and the time was ripe for emphasizing the continuity of Marx with the Western philosophical tradition in the face of new barbarisms.[6] It was thought important and necessary to stress the continuity between the bourgeois and proletarian revolutionary movements in order to prevent the German and Italian bourgeoisie from supporting the Fascists. Obviously, too, for non-Stalinist socialists, the early writings of the young Marx could serve as weapons against the growing authoritarianism and bureaucracy of official communism.

Intellectually, too, the climate of the 1920s favoured an interest in Marx's early writings. A vogue had developed for researching into the origins of the ideas of important thinkers: Dilthey had written on the early works of Schleiermacher and Hegel; in 1920 Mayer published the first volume of his definitive biography of Engels; above all, Hegel's early theological writings were published for the first time in 1907. This led to a renewal of interest in Hegel in general and his part in the formation of Marxism. By the end of the nineteenth century positivism and neo-Kantian liberalism had thrown Hegel into oblivion. The practically-minded revisionists, such as Bernstein, had no

6. Cf. I. Fetscher, 'The Young and the Old Marx', *Marx and the Western World* (Notre Dame, 1967).

time for Hegel, even had they been able to understand him. Kautsky and the orthodox Marxists arrived at the same result for very different reasons, those of doctrinal purity: they wished to be able to preach a scientific socialism free of any ethical or metaphysical elements. Lenin had certainly studied Hegel in his Swiss exile, but there was not much evidence of influence either in his theory or in his practice.

By the 1920s, however, interest in Hegel was renewed. Already in 1911 Plenge had published a book depicting the young Marx as a genuine pupil of Hegel. And in 1923 two interpretations of Marxism were published which emphasized the Hegelian element. Both anticipated the publication of the remainder of Marx's early writings and prepared the way for an understanding of their importance. These two books, both written in German, were Karl Korsch's *Marxism and Philosophy* and George Lukacs' *History and Class Consciousness*. Korsch took seriously Marx's doctrine of the unity of theory and practice, his phrases about the 'realization of philosophy', and his debt to Hegel. His book gave the impression that official Marxism was being criticized from the more open and critical position of the young Marx. Lukacs adopted the same line, sharply criticized the conception of a dialectic of nature and elaborated the idea of reification, a reformulation of Marx's 'alienation'. Lukacs' book was sub-titled *Studies in Marxist Dialectic*, and said in the introduction: 'It is impossible to discuss the problem of concrete and historical dialectics without closer study of the founder of this method, Hegel, and his relationship to Marx. The warning of Marx not to treat Hegel as a "dead dog" has remained a dead letter, even for many good Marxists.'[7] Most theoreticians of the Second International viewed historical materialism as an objective and scienti-

7. G. Lukacs, *Histoire et conscience de classe* (Paris, 1960) p. 12.

fic doctrine of the laws of social development, laws that
were similar to those enunciated by natural scientists.
Lukacs followed the young Marx in considering the
natural sciences to be conditioned by historical development and integral points of the social whole, and put at
the centre of his doctrine the idea of the proletariat's class
consciousness becoming practical. Both Korsch and Lukacs
were strongly criticized by the orthodox, principally by
the veteran Kautsky, and expelled from the party, but
their books continued to have influence.

In this climate, the publication of the 'Critique of
Hegel's Philosophy of the State' and the 'Paris Manuscripts', the two main accounts that Marx gave of his relationship to Hegel, made a swift impression, and interest
in the young Marx has since been intense, particularly in
Germany, France and Eastern Europe. In Germany
around 1930 the discussion was pre-eminently political,
with the dictatorship of the proletariat being regarded,
given the weakness of the parliamentary system, as the
only alternative to Fascism. The researchers of the Frankfurt school were interrupted by Hitler's rise to power, and
discussion ceased for twelve years. After 1945, since there
was no communist party in Germany, the discussion became academic: Marx was treated as one philosopher
among others and a favourite subject for doctoral theses.
In France, on the other hand, Marxism remained a subject of lively political debate. During the 1930s, Kojève's
brilliantly idiosyncratic view of Hegel through the early
Marx inspired the independent Left to constant battles
with Stalinist orthodoxy. After the war existentialist
thinkers like Sartre and Merleau-Ponty borrowed many
elements of Marx's early writings. There was a fairly constant stream of expulsions from the Communist Party for
'revisionism', the most important being that of Henri
Lefebvre who emphasized the themes of 'alienation' and

the 'all-round man' central to the 'Paris Manuscripts'.[8]
More recently, this debate has taken on renewed force:
Roger Garaudy, champion of an 'open' Marxism ready
for dialogue with other beliefs, propounds a humanist
version of Marx stemming essentially from the early
writings;[9] Louis Althusser denies that Marx can be called
a humanist, claiming that it is a term solely characteristic
of Marx's early writings and subsequently rejected.[10] The
impact of Marx's early work in the English-speaking world
has been much slower; the first translation of the 'Paris
Manuscripts' did not appear until 1961.

Thus, as far as the West was concerned, of Marx's two
major analyses of capitalist society the first, that of the
progressive pauperization of the proletariat and the necessity of its coming to a realization of its revolutionary role,
has been rendered less imminent. The creation of labour
unions and the growth of reformism demonstrates that, far
from aiding a proletarian revolution, the economic infrast-
ructure of society makes for the progressive integration of
the working classes into the social order. Nevertheless, the
second of Marx's major analyses, and the one most evident
in his early writings, that of alienation, has acquired an
importance far greater than he imagined. Marx's analysis
here aims at showing that in a commodity society the products of men's labour acquire a material power opposed to
the producers, and that this causes the relations between
persons to appear as relations between things. This is the
same conception that has been taken up and so strikingly
analysed particularly by such writers as Marcuse and
Lukacs under the name of 'reification'. The very wealth
and complexity of highly developed societies has, in this
respect, made Marx's analysis more significant than could

8. Cf. H. Lefebvre, *Le Matérialisme dialectique* (Paris, 1937).
9. Cf. R. Garaudy, *From Anathema to Dialogue* (London, 1967).
10. Cf. L. Althusser, *For Marx* (London, 1970).

have been anticipated in the nineteenth century. The contemporary use of such a concept as alienation is bewildering. It has recently been said of it: 'Its evident resonance for neo-Marxist thinkers, in both the West and the East, for existentialist philosophers and theologians, for psychiatrists and industrial psychologists, for *déracinés* and intellectuals and student rebels has meant that it has been widely extended and altered in the interests of a number of contemporary preoccupations.'[11] However, this very width of application has robbed the concept of much of its usefulness, and some of the most interesting recent discussions have been about the ability of the concepts contained in Marx's early writings to identify and explain certain factors in existing societies. The fruitful use to which Marx's concepts can be put when given a sufficiently empirical reference is shown by Blauner's research in Chicago on car-assembly workers, Friedmann's discussion of the *kibbutz* and current research into workers' control experiments in Yugoslavia.

In Eastern Europe, on the other hand, it is the gap between ideology and reality that has caused the spread of interest in Marx's early writings. Particularly in Czechoslovakia, Poland and Yugoslavia, the early writings of Marx have had an increasing influence on intellectuals. After Khrushchev's denunciation of Stalin in 1956, the humanist attitudes of the young Marx were used as a basis for opposition to remaining Stalinist elements in Eastern Europe, much as the New Testament was used by the Reformers to oppose the Catholic Church. In Czechoslovakia the 'human face of socialism' that the country's leaders were trying to achieve in 1968 prior to the Russian invasion, and particularly the '2,000 Words' manifesto, are

11. Lukes, 'Alienation and Anomie', in *Philosophy, Politics and Society* (Oxford, 1967).

very close to Marx's early works. In Poland the discussion began in 1959 with the publication of Kolakowski's article 'Karl Marx and the Classical Definition of Truth'. This article drew a sharp distinction between the theories of knowledge of the young Marx on the one hand and of Engels and Lenin on the other, and implied that Marx was not a dialectical materialist at all in Engels' and Lenin's sense. Kolakowski's views were taken up by Adam Schaff, a member of the Central Committee of the Communist Party, and expanded into an inquiry into the reasons for socialism's inability to do away with human alienation.[12] In Yugoslavia, studies of the young Marx have been much more widespread, and a lot of work has been done on the sources of Marx's thought. The main organs of the philosophers is the Zagreb journal *Praxis*.

2. THE YOUNG MARX AND MATURE MARXISM

It is important to ask whether the early writings of Marx should be valued solely for their own sake or whether, too, they shed light on the inspiration of Marx's thought as a whole. As the above quotations from Marx and Engels indicate, they themselves showed no concern for their early manuscripts.[13]

Nevertheless, though Marx and Engels later avoided the 'philosophical' language of their early years, and in the *Communist Manifesto* derided the German literati who 'beneath the French criticism of the economic function of

12. See the articles by Kolakowski and Schaff in *Revisionism*, ed. L. Labedz (London, 1962); G. Kline, 'Leszek Kolakowski and the Revision of Marxism', *European Philosophy Today* (Chicago, 1965).

13. The following few pages are a slightly altered version of the last section of my Introduction to *Karl Marx: The Early Texts* (Oxford, 1971).

money, wrote "Alienation of Humanity"',[14] they always recognized that 'the German working-class movement is the inheritor of classical German philosophy'.[15] His contemporaries may have been incapable of understanding Hegel, but Marx never lost his interest in him, and it is obvious that the problem of the continuity of Marx's thought is bound up with his continuing interest in Hegel. In 1858 he wrote to Engels:

I am getting some nice developments. For instance, I have thrown over the whole doctrine of profit as it has existed up to now. In the *method* of treatment, the fact that by mere accident I have again glanced through Hegel's *Logic* has been of great service to me—Freiligrath found some volumes of Hegel's which originally belonged to Bakunin and sent them to me as presents. If there should ever be time for such work again, I should greatly like to make accessible to the ordinary human intelligence, in two or three printer's sheets, what is *rational* in the method which Hegel discovered but at the same time enveloped in mysticism.[16]

In 1873, in the afterword to the second German edition of *Capital*, Marx made clear his position with regard to Hegel and specifically referred to his essay on Hegel's dialectic in his 'Paris Manuscripts'.[17] Engels, too, shared this view of Hegel's importance. In his essay on Feuerbach, he wrote: 'With Hegel philosophy comes to an end: on the one hand, because his system is its whole development in the most splendid fashion; and on the other hand, because even though unconsciously, he showed us the way out of

14. K. Marx–F. Engels, 'The Communist Manifesto', in *Selected Works*, 1, 58.

15. F. Engels, 'Ludwig Feuerbach and the End of Classical German Philosophy', in Marx–Engels, *Selected Works*, 11, 402.

16. K. Marx–F. Engels, *Selected Correspondence*, p. 102.

17. See the quotation above, pp. 202 f.

the labyrinth of systems to real positive knowledge of the world.'[18]

If, then, as these quotations suggest, there is some unity in Marx's thought, what does this unity consist in and what are the themes which are common both to the early and to the later writings? One possible answer is that attempts to read Marxism as a 'scientific' account of social development are mistaken, and that the central inspiration of Marx is really pseudo-religious and that the evidence for this is clearest in Marx's earliest writings.[19] Another view would claim that Marx's central thesis is an ethical one; that the early writings are evidence for the moral indignation that leads him to adhere to the cause of the proletariat; and that Hegel's influence was not over-riding.[20] The most usual answer, however, is that the problem of the unity of Marxist thought is closely bound up with the question of the relationship of Marx to Hegel; that Marx always remained in some sense a Hegelian; and that the early writings are important since they document the formation of Marx's attitude to Hegel's philosophy. Lenin himself lent some support to this view by writing in 1914: 'It is impossible to fully grasp Marx's *Capital* and especially the first chapter, if you have not studied or understood the *whole* of Hegel's *Logic*. Consequently, none of the Marxists for the past half century has understood Marx!'[21] The most usual document quoted to show Marx's 'Hegelianism' is the 'Paris Manuscripts'. Recently, however, it has been maintained that Marx's decisive encounter with Hegel was a year earlier in his 'Critique of Hegel's Philosophy of the State' and that Marx's basic

18. F. Engels, 'Ludwig Feuerbach and the End of Classical German Philosophy', in Marx–Engels, *Selected Works*, II, 365.
19. Cf. Tucker, *Philosophy and Myth in Karl Marx*.
20. Cf. Rubel, *Karl Marx. Essai de biographie intellectuelle*.
21. V. I. Lenin, quoted in *Socialist Humanism*, ed. Fromm, p. 68.

ideas on materialism, the disappearance of the state, and communism are to be found here.[22]

If there were a theme running through the whole of Marx's writings, the most obvious would be 'alienation', a concept that Marx adopted directly from Hegel, though its origins are much earlier. Those who claim to find a break between the 'young' and the 'old' Marx usually maintain that alienation is a concept that was central to Marx's early thought but which he abandoned later.[23] Sidney Hook, for example, wrote recently: 'It is easy to show that the notion of human alienation – except for the sociological meaning it has in *Capital* – is actually foreign to Marx's conception of man.'[24] And Daniel Bell has said that 'Whereas in the young Marx there was a double vision of the nature of alienation ... Marx's thoughts developed along one narrow road of economic conceptions of poverty and exploitation, while the other road, which might have lead to new humanistic concepts of work and labour, was left unexplored.'[25] These statements are, however, inaccurate. Not only the concept but also the term itself occurs on several occasions in *Capital*.[26] Marx writes for example: 'The character of independence and estrangement which the capitalist mode of production as a whole gives to the instruments of labour and to the product, as against the workman, is developed by means of machinery into a thorough antagonism.'[27] Yet it is not only a question

22. Cf. Avineri, *The Social and Political Thought of Karl Marx.*

23. Cf. L. Feuer, 'What is alienation? The Career of a Concept', *New Politics* (spring 1962).

24. Hook, *From Hegel to Marx*, p. 5.

25. D. Bell, 'The Debate on Alienation', in *Revisionism*, ed. Labedz, p. 210.

26. For a fuller treatment of this point, see: R. Dunayevskaya, *Marxism and Freedom*, New York, 1958, pp. 103 ff.; E. Fromm, *Marx's Concept of Man*, New York, 1961, pp. 50 ff. and pp. 69 ff.

27. K. Marx, *Capital*, I, 432.

of terminology; the content, too, of *Capital* is a continuation of Marx's early thoughts. The main theme of Volume I of *Capital*, surplus-value, rests on the equation of work and value that goes back to the conception of man as a being who creates himself and the conditions of his life – a conception outlined in the 'Paris Manuscripts'. It is man's nature – according to the Marx of the 'Paris Manuscripts' – to be constantly developing himself and the world about him in co-operation with other men. What Marx in *Capital* is describing is how this fundamental nature of man – to be the initiator and controller of historical process – has been transferred or alienated and how it belongs to the inhuman power of capital. The counterpart to alienated man, the unalienated or 'total' man of the 'Manuscripts', also appears in *Capital*. In the chapter of Volume I on 'Machinery and Modern Industry' Marx makes the same contrast between the effects of alienated and unalienated modes of production on the development of human potentiality. He writes:

Modern industry, indeed, compels society under penalty of death to replace the detail-worker of today, crippled by life-long repetition of one and the same trivial operation, and thus reduced to the mere fragment of a man, by the fully developed individual, fit for a variety of labours, ready to face any change of production, and to whom the different social functions he performs are but so many modes of giving free scope to his own natural and acquired powers.[28]

The fact that in *Capital* the conclusion is supported by a detailed analysis of the effect of advanced technology should not obscure the continuity.

The section of *Capital* that most recalls the early writings is the final section of Chapter I, entitled 'Fetishism of commodities'. The whole section is reminiscent of the

28. K. Marx, *Capital*, 1, 488.

section on alienated labour in the 'Paris Manuscripts' and the notes on James Mill that Marx composed in 1844. Marx writes: 'A commodity is therefore a mysterious thing, simply because in it the social character of men's labour appears to them as objective character stamped upon that labour; because the relation of the producers to the sum total of their own labour is presented to them as a social relation, existing not between themselves, but between the products of their labour.'[29] He goes on, as so often in his earlier writings, to draw a parallel with religion: 'In order, therefore, to find an analogy, we must have recourse to the mist-enveloped regions of the religious world. In that world the productions of the human brain appear as independent beings endowed with life, and entering into relation both with one another and the human race. So it is in the world of human commodities with the products of men's hands.'[30]

It should be remembered, of course, that *Capital* is only an unfinished fragment of the task that Marx set himself. He complained frequently to Engels of the time he was forced to spend studying economics. In the preface to the 'Paris Manuscripts' he had outlined the programme of his life's work:

I will therefore present one after another a critique of law, of morality, politics, etc., in different independent brochures and then finally in a separate work try to show the connection of the whole and the relationship of the parts to each other and end with a criticism of the elaboration of the material by speculative philosophy. Therefore in the present work the connection of the political economy with the state, law, morality, civil life, etc. is only dealt with in so far as political economy itself professes to deal with these subjects.[31]

29. K. Marx, *Capital*, 1, 72.
30. ibid.
31. K. Marx, *Frühe Schriften*, 1, 506; Easton and Guddat, p. 284.

In fact, Marx never got beyond his first 'brochure' on political economy.

The continuity in Marx's thought has been demonstrated beyond all doubt by the publication, under the title *Grundrisse der Kritik der Politischen Ökonomie* ('Elements of the Critique of Political Economy'), of the 1,000-page draft that served Marx as a basis both for his *Critique of Political Economy* (1859) and of *Capital* (1857). The *Grundrisse* were published for the first time in Moscow in 1939. The time and place of their publication prevented their attracting attention and it was not until 1953 that there was an accessible edition. The *Grundrisse*, of which the *Critique of Political Economy* and *Capital* are only partial elaborations, is the centrepiece of Marx's work.[32] It is the basic work which permitted the generalizations in the famous 'Preface of the Critique of Political Economy', a preface not matched by the work that follows it. Marx himself describes the *Grundrisse* in a letter to Lassalle as 'the result of fifteen years' research, that is to say the best years of my life'. The *Grundrisse* consists of an introduction in two parts, the first dealing with money and the second, much larger, dealing with capital, in the form of production, circulation and profit. Since it was only written for personal clarification, some parts of the *Grundrisse* are very difficult to follow, being written in note form and extremely elliptical. But in spite of its somewhat fragmentary character, the Hegelian categories in which Marx forms his thought are obvious. Questions that were prominent in Marx's 1844 writings – such as the alienation of the individual in capitalist society, the relationship between man and nature, the impact of machinery on labour, the nature of a truly communist society – are taken up again and filled out with a wealth of detail. Something of the tone of the *Grundrisse* is given by the following passage:

32. Cf. my Introduction to *Marx's Grundrisse* (London, 1971).

Universally developed individuals, whose social relationships are subject, as their own communal relationships, to their own collective control, are the product not of nature but of history. The extent and universality of the development of capacities which make possible this sort of individuality, presupposes precisely production on the basis of exchange values. The universal nature of this production creates an alienation of the individual from himself and others, but also for the first time the general and universal nature of his relationships and capacities.

Or again:

Labour power has not only produced alien wealth and its own poverty, but also the relationship of this intrinsic wealth to itself as poverty, through the consumption of which wealth puts new life into itself and again makes itself fruitful. This all arose from the exchange in which labour power exchanged its living power for a quantity of objectified labour, except that this objectified labour – these conditions of its existence which exist outside it, and the independent external nature of these material conditions – appears as its own product. These conditions appear as though set up by labour power itself, both as its own objectification, and as the objectification of its own power which has an existence independent of it and, even more, rules over it, rules over it by its own doing.[33]

The *Grundrisse*, then, are as Hegelian as the 'Paris Manuscripts' and their publication makes it impossible to maintain that only Marx's early writings are of philosophical interest, and that in the later Marx specialist economic interests have obscured the earlier humanist vision. The early writings contain all the subsequent themes of Marx's thought and show them in the making. Marx's work lends support to Aristotle's saying that to understand a thing one must study its origins.

33. *Marx's Grundrisse*, ed. D. McLellan (London, 1971), pp. 70 f. and 99. For other passages of a similar nature see pp. 61 f., 108 ff., 133 ff.

Chronological Table

1818	May:	Birth of Marx	
1830		Marx begins at Trier High School	
1831		Death of Hegel	
1835	Summer:	D. F. Strauss, *Das Leben Jesu* (*The Life of Jesus*)	August: School-leaving essays
	October:	Marx enters University of Bonn	
1836	Autumn:	Secret engagement to Jenny von Westphalen	
	October:	Marx transfers to Berlin	
1837		Marx joins Doctors' Club	Early poetry
	November:	'Cologne affair'	Letter to his father
1838	January:	Founding of *Hallische Jahrbücher*	
	May:	Death of Heinrich Marx	
1839			Marx begins doctoral thesis
1840	June:	Frederick William IV succeeds to the throne of Prussia	
1841	February:	Feuerbach publishes *The Essence of Christianity*	April: Marx submits doctoral thesis
	June:	Marx leaves Berlin for Bonn	

1842	January:	Founding of *Rheinische Zeitung* Marx moves to Trier	
	March:	Death of Baron von Westphalen	
	April:	Marx moves to Bonn	April: 'The Philosophical Manifesto of the Historical School of Law'
1842			May: 'Debates on the Freedom of the Press'
			July: 'The Leading Article of the *Kölnische Zeitung*'
	October:	Marx becomes editor of the *Rheinische Zeitung*	'Communism and the *Augsburger Allgemeine Zeitung*'
			October: 'Debate on the Law on Thefts of Timber'
	November:	Lorenz von Stein publishes *Socialism and Communism in Contemporary France*	'On a Proposed Divorce Law'
1843	March:	Suppression of *Rheinische Zeitung* Marx moves to Kreuznach Feuerbach publishes his *Preliminary Theses*	March – August: 'Critique of Hegel's Philosophy of the State

June:	Marriage of Marx	March, May, Sept.: 'Letters to Ruge'
October:	Marx moves to Paris	October: 'On the Jewish Question'
1844		January: 'Introduction to a Critique of Hegel's Philosophy of Law'
February:	Publication of *Deutsch-Französische Jahrbücher*	
April:	Marx breaks with Ruge	August: 'Critical Notes on "The King of Prussia and Social Reform"'
		Summer: 'Paris Manuscripts'
1845 February:	Marx expelled from Paris	

Select Bibliography

TEXTS

1. *German*

K. Marx – F. Engels, *Historisch-kritische Gesamtausgabe*, ed
    D. Razjanov and V. Adoratskji (Berlin, 1927 ff.) (=*MEGA*
K. Marx – F. Engels, *Werke* (Berlin, 1956 ff.) (=*MEW*).
K. Marx, *Frühe Schriften*, ed. H.-J. Lieber and P. Furth (Stut
    gart, 1962).
K. Marx, *Die Frühschriften*, ed. S. Landshut (Berlin, 1953).
K. Marx, *Texte zu Methode und Praxis*, ed. G. Hillman
    (Hamburg, 1966).
K. Marx – F. Engels, *Studienausgabe*, ed. I. Fetscher (Fran
    furt, 1966).

2. *English*

K. Marx, *Early Writings*, ed. T. B. Bottomore (London, 196
K. Marx, *Writings of the Young Marx on Philosophy an
    Society*, ed. L. Easton and K. Guddat (New York, 1967).
K. Marx, *The Early Texts*, ed. D. McLellan (Oxford, 1971).

3. *French*

K. Marx, *Œuvres complètes*, ed. J. Molitor (Paris, 1935).
K. Marx, *Manuscrits de 1844*, ed. E. Bottigelli (Paris, 1962).
K. Marx, *Œuvres*, ed. M. Rubel (Paris, 1962 ff).

COMMENTARIES

1. *Books in English*

H. P. Adams, *Karl Marx in his Earlier Writings* (London, 194
    2nd edn London, 1965).

L. Althusser, *For Marx* (London, 1970).

S. Avineri, *The Social and Political Thought of Karl Marx* (Cambridge, 1968).

I. Berlin, *Karl Marx*, 3rd edn (Oxford, 1963).

A. Cornu, *The Origins of Marxian Socialism* (Springfield, 1957).

B. Delfgaauw, *The Young Marx* (London, 1967).

P. Demetz, *Marx, Engels and the Poets* (Chicago, 1965).

L. Dupré, *The Philosophical Foundations of Marxism* (New York, 1966).

E. Fromm (ed.), *Socialist Humanism* (London, 1967).

E. Fromm, *Marx's Concept of Man* (New York, 1961).

R. Garaudy, *Karl Marx: The Evolution of his Thought* (London, 1967).

S. Hook, *From Hegel to Marx*, 2nd edn (Michigan, 1962).

J. Hyppolite, *Studies on Marx and Hegel* (London, 1969).

Z. Jordan, *The Evolution of Dialectical Materialism* (London, 1967).

E. Kamenka, *The Ethical Foundations of Marxism* (London, 1962).

G. Lichtheim, *Marxism* (London, 1961).

N. Lobkowicz, *Theory and Practice: The History of a Marxist Concept* (Notre Dame, 1967).

K. Löwith, *From Hegel to Nietzsche* (London, 1965).

J. Maguire, *Marx's Paris Writings* (Dublin, 1972).

D. McLellan, *The Young Hegelians and Karl Marx* (London, 1969).

D. McLellan, *The Thought of Karl Marx* (London, 1971).

H. Marcuse, *Reason and Revolution* (New York, 1941).

F. Mehring, *Karl Marx* (London, 1936).

B. Nicolaievsky and O. Maenchen-Helfen, *Karl Marx* (London, 1936).

B. Ollman, *Alienation: Marx's Critique of Man in Capitalist Society* (Cambridge, 1971).

N. Rotenstreich, *Basic Principles of Marx's Philosophy* (Indianapolis and New York, 1965).

J. Talmon, *The Origins of Totalitarian Democracy* (London, 1952).

R. Tucker, *Philosophy and Myth in Karl Marx* (Cambridge, 1961).

R. Tucker, *The Marxian Revolutionary Idea* (London, 1970).

V. Venable, *Human Nature: The Marxian View* (London, 1946).

2. *Articles in English*

S. Avineri, 'Marx and Jewish Emancipation', *Journal of the History of Ideas*, xxv (1964).

S. Avineri, 'The Hegelian Origins of Marx's Political Thought', *Review of Metaphysics* (Sept. 1967).

D. Bell, 'Two Roads from Marx: The Themes of Alienation and Exploitation and Workers' Control in Socialist Thought', in *The End of Ideology* (Glencoe, 1960).

D. Bell, 'The Debate on Alienation', in *Revisionism*, ed. L. Labedz (London, 1962).

R. Bowles, 'The Marxian Adaptation of the Ideology of Fourier', *South Atlantic Quarterly*, LIV, ii (1955).

D. Braybrooke, 'Diagnosis and Remedy in Marx's Doctrine of Alienation', *Social Research* (autumn 1958).

G. Cohen, 'Bourgeois and Proletarians', *Journal of the History of Ideas* (Jan. 1968).

F. Conklin, 'Some Aspects of the Marxian Philosophy of God', *The New Scholasticism*, xxviii (1954).

L. Easton, 'Alienation and History in the Early Marx', *Philosophy and Phenomenological Research* (Dec. 1961).

M. Evans, 'Marx Studies', *Political Studies* (autumn 1970).

I. Fetscher, 'The Young and the Old Marx', in *Marx and the Western World*, ed. N. Lobkowicz (Notre Dame, 1967).

L. Halle, 'Marx's Religious Drama', *Encounter* (Oct. 1965).

M. Harrington, 'Marx versus Marx'. *New Politics* (autumn 1961).

A. L. Harris, 'Utopian Elements in Marx's Thought', *Ethics*, LX (Jan. 1950).

D. Hodges, 'The Young Marx: A Reappraisal', *Philosophy and Phenomenological Research* (Dec. 1966).

W. Johnston, 'Marx's Verse of 1836–37', *Journal of the History of Ideas* (Apr. 1967).

E. Kamenka, 'The Primitive Ethic of Karl Marx', *Australasian Journal of Philosophy*, xxxv, ii (1957).

N. Lobkowicz, 'Marx's Attitude towards Religion', in *Marx and the Western World*, ed. N. Lobkowicz (Notre Dame, 1967).

K. Löwith, 'Self-alienation in the Early Writings of Marx'. *Social Research* (1954).

S. Lukes, 'Alienation and Anomie', in *Philosophy, Politics and Society*, 3rd series, ed. P. Laslett and W. G. Runciman (Oxford, 1967).

D. McLellan, 'Marx's View of the Unalienated Society', *Review of Politics* (Oct. 1969).

S. Moore, 'Marx and the State of Nature', *Journal of the History of Philosophy* (1967).

E. Olssen, 'Marx and the Resurrection', *Journal of the History of Ideas* (1968).

J. O'Malley, 'History and Man's "Nature" in Marx', *Review of Politics* (Oct. 1966).

J. O'Neill, 'Alienation, Class Struggle and Marxian Anti-politics', *Review of Metaphysics* (1964).

J. O'Neill, 'The Concept of Estrangement in the Early and Later Writings of Karl Marx', *Philosophy and Phenomenological Research* (Sept. 1964).

H. Parsons, 'The Prophetic Mission of Karl Marx', *Journal of Religion* (Jan. 1964).

R. Pranger, 'Marx and Political Theory', *Review of Politics* (Apr. 1968).

M. Rader, 'Marx's Interpretation of Art and Aesthetic Value', *British Journal of Aesthetics* (1967).

A. Ryan, 'A New Look at Professor Tucker's Marx', *Political Studies* (1967).

A. Schaff, review of Fromm and Tucker, *History and Theory*, II (1962).

T. Sowell, 'Marx and the Freedom of the Individual', *Ethics* (Oct. 1962).

3. *Books in French*

L. Althusser, *Pour Marx* (Maspero, Paris, 1966).

K. Axelos, *Marx, penseur de la technique* (Éditions de Minuit, Paris, 1961).

E. Bottigelli, *Genèse du socialisme scientifique* (Éditions Sociales, Paris, 1967).

J. Y. Calvez, *La Pensée de Karl Marx* (Seuil, Paris, 1956).

A. Cornu, *Karl Marx. Sa vie et son œuvre* (Alcan, Paris, 1934).

A. Cornu, *Karl Marx et Friedrich Engels. Leur vie et œuvre*, 3 vols (Presses Universitaires de France, Paris, 1955–62).

G. Cottier, *L'Athéisme du jeune Marx* (Urin, Paris, 1959).

G. Cottier, *Du romantisme au marxisme* (Alsatia, Paris, 1961).

H. Desroches, *Marxisme et religions* (P.U.F., Paris, 1962).

H. Desroches, *Socialisme et sociologie religieuse* (Paris, 1965).

R. Garaudy, *Karl Marx* (Seghers, Paris, 1964).

F. Grégoire, *Aux sources de la pensée de Marx: Hegel, Feuerbach* (Louvain and Paris, 1947).

H. Lefebvre, *Le Matérialisme dialectique* (P.U.F., Paris, 1937).

H. Lefebvre, *Marx: sa vie, son œuvre* (P.U.F., Paris, 1964).

H. de Lubac, *Le Drame de l'humanisme athée* (Spes, Paris, 1943).

E. Mandel, *La Formation de la Pensée économique de Karl Marx* (Maspero, Paris, 1967).

P. Naville, *Le Nouveau Léviathan* (Paris, 1957).

R. Ollivier, *Marx et Engèls, poètes* (Mercure de France, Paris, 1935).

M. Rubel, Introduction to K. Marx, *Œuvres*, Vol. 2 (Paris, 1968).

L. Somerhausen, *L'Humanisme agissant de Karl Marx* (Paris, 1946).

C. Wackenheim, *La Faillite de la religion d'après Karl Marx* (Paris, 1963).

E. Weil, *Hegel et l'État* (Paris, 1950).

4. *Articles in French*

H. C. Desroches, 'Socialisme et sociologie du christianisme', *Cahiers Internationaux de Sociologie* (1956).

R. Duchac, 'Bourgeoisie et prolétariat à travers l'œuvre de Marx', *Cahiers Internationaux de Sociologie* (1961).

M. Dufrenne, 'Histoire et historicité : un aspect de la sociologie du jeune Marx', *Cahiers Internationaux de Sociologie* 1948).

E. Grollier, 'Classes et rapports de classes dans des premières œuvres de Marx', *Cahiers Internationaux de Sociologie* (1954).

G. Gurvitch, 'La Sociologie du Jeune Marx', *Cahiers Internationaux de Sociologie* (1948).

J. Hyppolite, 'Marxisme et Philosophie', *Revue Socialiste*, v, reprinted in: *Études sur Hegel et Marx*, 2nd edn (Paris, 1965).

J. Hyppolite, 'De la structure philosophique du "Capital" et quelques présupposées philosophiques de l'œuvre de Marx', *Bulletin de la société française de Philosophie*, XLII (Oct. 1948) (reprinted as above).

J. Hyppolite, 'La Conception hégélienne de l'État et sa critique par Karl Marx', *Cahiers Internationaux de Sociologie* (1947) (reprinted as above).

H. Jaegar, 'Savigny et Marx', *Archives de la Philosophie du Droit* (1967).

M. Rubel, 'Les Cahiers d'études de Karl Marx (1840–1853)', *International Review of Social History* (1957).

M. Rubel, 'Science, éthique et idéologie', *Cahiers Internationaux de Sociologie* (1966).

R. van der Gucht, 'Aventures du marxisme', *Frères du Monde*, XLV (1967).

5. *Books in German*

J. Barion, *Hegel und die marxistische Staatslehre* (Bonn, 1963).

H. Barth, *Wahrheit und Ideologie* (Zürich, 1945).

K. Bekker, *Marx' philosophische Entwicklung – Sein Verhältnis zu Hegel* (Zürich, 1940).

E. Bloch, *Das Prinzip Hoffnung*, 2 vols (Berlin, 1954 f.).

W. Blumenberg, *Karl Marx* (Hamburg, 1962).

K. Bockmuehl, *Leiblichkeit und Gesellschaft* (Göttingen, 1961).

K. H. Breuer, *Der Junge Marx – Sein Weg zum Kommunismus* (Cologne, 1954).

G. Dicke, *Der Identitätsgedanke bei Feuerbach und Marx* (Cologne-Opladen, 1960).

M. Friedrich, *Philosophie und Ökonomie beim jungen Marx* (Berlin, 1960).

G. Hillmann, *Karl Marx: Texte zu Methode und Praxis*, 3 vols (Hamburg, 1966).

G. Hillman, *Marx und Hegel* (Frankfurt, 1966).

J. Hommes, *Der technische Eros* (Freiburg, 1955).

P. Kägi, *Genesis des historischen Materialismus* (Vienna, 1965).

H. Klages, *Technischer Humanismus: Philosophie und Soziologie der Arbeit bei Marx* (Stuttgart, 1964).

H. König, *Die Rheinische Zeitung von 1842/3 in ihrer Einstellung zur Kulturpolitik des Preussischen Staates* (Münster, 1927).

A. Kuenzli, *Marx – Eine Psychographie* (Vienna, 1966).

S. Landshut, *Karl Marx: Die Frühschriften – Einleitung* (Stuttgart, 1953).

K. Löwith, *Von Hegel zu Nietzsche*, 2nd edn (Stuttgart, 1950).

A. Massiczek, *Der menschliche Mensch* (Vienna, 1968).

G. Mende, *Karl Marx' Entwicklung vom revolutionären Demokraten zum Kommunisten*, 3rd edn (Berlin, 1960).

S. Miller and B. Sawadzki, *Karl Marx in Berlin* (Berlin, 1956).

H. Monz, *Karl Marx und Trier* (Trier, 1964).

T. Oiserman, *Die Entstehung der marxistischen Philosophie* (Berlin, 1965).

J. Plenge, *Marx und Hegel* (Tübingen, 1911).

M. Reding, *Der politische Atheismus* (Vienna, 1957).

R. Sannwald, *Marx und die Antike* (Basel, 1957).

A. Schaff, *Marxismus und das menschliche Individuum* (Vienna, 1965).

H. Schiel, *Die Umwelt des jungen Marx* (Trier, 1964).

A. Schmidt, *Der Begriff der Natur in der Lehre von Marx* (Frankfurt am Main, 1962).

W. Schuffenhauer, *Feuerbach und der junge Marx* (Berlin, 1965).

W. Sens, *Karl Marx. Seine irreligiöse Entwicklung und antichristliche Einstellung* (Halle, 1935).

H. Stuke, *Philosophie der Tat* (Stuttgart, 1963).

E. Thier, *Das Menschenbild des jungen Marx* (Göttingen, 1957).

W. Victor, *Marx und Heine*, 3rd edn (Berlin, 1953).

6. *Articles in German*

D. Baumgarten, 'Über den "verloren geglaubten" Anhang zu Karl Marx' Doktordissertation' in *Gegenwartsprobleme der Soziologie, Alfred Vierkandt zum 80. Geburtstag*, ed. Eisermann (Potsdam, 1949).

E. Bloch, 'Der Student Marx', *Sinn und Form*, III iv (1951).

F. Borkenau, *Karl Marx – Auswahl und Einleitung* (Fischer Bücherei, Frankfurt am Main, 1956).

F. Delekat, 'Vom Wesen des Geldes', *Marxismusstudien*, I (1954).

I. Fetscher, 'Von der Philosophie des Proletariats zur proletarischen Weltanschauung', *Marxismusstudien*, II (1957).

I. Fetscher, 'Das Verhältnis des Marxismus zu Hegel', *Marxismusstudien*, III (1960).

J. Gebhardt, 'Karl Marx und Bruno Bauer', *Politische Ordnung und menschliche Existenz. Festgabe für Eric Voegelin* (Munich, 1962).

H. Gollwitzer, 'Die marxistische Religionskritik und christlicher Glaube', *Marxismusstudien*, IV (1962).

C. Gruenberg, 'Urkundliches aus den Universitätsjahren von Karl Marx', *Archiv für die Geschichte des Sozialismus und der Arbeiterbewegung*, XII (1926).

C. Gruenberg, 'Marx als Abiturient – Urkundliche Mitteilungen mit Einleitung', *Archiv für die Geschichte des Sozialismus und der Arbeiterbewegung*, (1925) XI, 6.

R. Heiss, 'Hegel und Marx', *Symposion, Jahrbuch für Philosophie*, I (1948).

H. Hirsch, 'Marx und das religiöse Opium', *Geist und Tat, V*, viii (1950).

H. Hirsch, 'Marxiana Judaica', *Cahiers de l'ISEA*, Series S (1963).

H. Hirsch, 'Marxens Milieu', *Cahiers de l'ISEA*, Series S (1965).

G. Huntemann, 'Der Gedanke der Selbstentfremdung bei Karl Marx und in den Utopien von E. Cabet bis G. Orwell', *Zeitschrift für Religions- und Geistesgeschichte*, VI (1954).

A. Kober, 'Karl Marx' Vater und das napoleonische Ausnahmegesetz gegen die Juden, 1808', *Jahrbuch des kölnischen Geschichtsvereins*, XIV (1932).

L. Landgrebe, 'Hegel und Marx', *Marxismusstudien*, I (1954).

L. Landgrebe, 'Das Problem der Dialektik', *Marxismusstudien*, III (1960).

E. Lenz, 'Karl Marx über die epikureische Philosophie', in *Archiv für die Geschichte des Sozialismus und der Arbeiterbewegung*, XIII (1918).

P. Ludz, 'Zur Situation der Marx–Forschung in West-Europa', *Kölner Zeitschrift für Soziologie und Sozialphilosophie*, X (1954).

W. Maihofer, 'Recht und Staat im Denken des jungen Marx', in *Karl Marx 1818–1968* (no editor) (Mainz 1968).

H. Marcuse, 'Neue Quelle zur Grundlegung des historischen Materialismus', *Die Gesellschaft*, IX (1932).

E. Metzke, 'Mensch und Geschichte im ursprünglichen Ansatz des Marx'schen Denkens', *Marxismusstudien*, II(1957).

H. Monz, 'Die soziale Lage der elterlichen Familie von Karl Marx', in *Karl Marx 1818–1968* (no editor) (Mainz, 1968).

T. Ramm, 'Die künftige Gesellschaftsordnung nach der Theorie von Marx und Engels', *Marxismusstudien*, II (1957).

A. Rich, 'Die kryptoreligiösen Motive in den Frühschriften von Karl Marx', *Theologische Zeitschrift*, VII (1951).

G. Rohrmoser, 'Stillstand der Dialektik', *Marxismusstudien*, V (1968).

H.-M. Sass, 'Freuerbach statt Marx', *International Review of Social History* (1967).

H. Schlawin, 'Grundzüge der Philosophie des jungen Marx', *Studia Philosophica*, XVII (1957).

H. Stein, 'Karl Marx und der Rheinische Pauperismus', *Jahrbuch des kölnischen Geschichtsvereins*, XIV (1932).

E. Thier, 'Etappen der Marxinterpretation', *Marxismus-studien*, 1 (1954).

7. *Books in Italian*

M. dal Pra, *La dialettica in Marx* (Bari, 1965).
G. Pischel, *Marx Giovane* (Milan, 1948).
M. Rossi, *Marx e la dialettica hegeliana* (Rome, 1962).
A. Sabetti, *Sulla fondazione del materialismo storico* (Florence, 1962).

Index

More About Penguins
and Pelicans

Penguinews, which appears every month, contains details
of all the new books issued by Penguins as they are
published. From time to time it is supplemented by
Penguins in Print, which is a complete list of all available
books published by Penguins. (There are well over three
thousand of these.)

A specimen copy of *Penguinews* will be sent to you free on
request, and you can become a subscriber for the price of
the postage. For a year's issues (including the complete
lists) please send 30p if you live in the United Kingdom, or
60p if you live elsewhere. Just write to Dept EP, Penguin
Books Ltd, Harmondsworth, Middlesex, enclosing a
cheque or postal order, and your name will be added to
the mailing list.

Note: *Penguinews* and *Penguins in Print* are not
available in the U.S.A. or Canada

Theory and Practice of Communism

R. N. Carew Hunt

'This is the best short account of Marxism and its Russian consequences written from a highly critical standpoint that has come my way' – Edward Crankshaw in the *Observer*

R. N. Carew Hunt has come to be recognized as one of the greatest western authorities on communism. This concise and critical study of Marxism and its interpretation in practice has quickly gained the standing of a classic. The author clearly demonstrates that modern Marxism is a synthesis, in which the basic creed of Karl Marx and Engels has been tailored by Lenin and Stalin to fit the twentieth century. In its analysis of the relationship and the contrasts between Marx's predictions and the policies of the communist governments of today the book provides an excellent outline of the institutions and events which have helped to shape the map of the contemporary world – the Communist League, the First and Second Internationals, the Russian Revolution, and developments both inside and outside Russia between the time of Lenin and Khrushchev.